Business Statistics

FOR

DUMMIES®

A Wiley Brand

by Alan Anderson, PhD

FOR

DUMMIES®

A Wiley Brand

Business Statistics For Dummies®

Published by John Wiley & Sons, Inc., 111 River Street, Hoboken, NJ 07030-5774, www.wiley.com

Copyright © 2014 by John Wiley & Sons, Inc., Hoboken, New Jersey

Published simultaneously in Canada

For general information on our other products and services, please contact our Customer Care Department within the U.S. at 877-762-2974, outside the U.S. at 317-572-3993, or fax 317-572-4002.

For technical support, please visit www.wiley.com/techsupport.

Wiley publishes in a variety of print and electronic formats and by print-on-demand. Some material included with standard print versions of this book may not be included in e-books or in print-on-demand. If this book refers to media such as a CD or DVD that is not included in the version you purchased, you may download this material at http://booksupport.wiley.com. For more information about Wiley products, visit www.wiley.com.

Library of Congress Control Number: 2013944875

ISBN 978-1-118-63069-3 (pbk); ISBN 978-1-118-78458-7 (ePub); ISBN 978-1-118-78449-5 (PDF)

Manufactured in the United States of America

10 9 8 7 6 5 4 3 2 1

Contents at a Glance

Table of Contents

Introduction

*H*ave you always been scared to death of statistics? You and just about everyone else! The equations are extremely intimidating, and the terminology sounds so . . . boring.

Why, then, is statistics so important? All business disciplines can be analyzed with statistical principles. Statistics make it possible to analyze real world problems with actual data, so that we can understand if our marketing strategy is really working, or how much a company should charge for its products, or any of a million other practical questions.

Without a formal framework for analyzing these types of situations, it would be impossible to have any confidence in our results. This is where the science of statistics comes in. Far from being an overbearing collection of equations, it is a logical framework for analyzing practical business problems with real-world data.

This book is designed to show you how to apply statistics to practical situations in a step-by-step manner, so that by the time you're done, you'll know as much about statistics as people with far more education in this area!

About This Book

All business degrees require at least some statistics courses, and there's a good reason for that! All business disciplines are empirical by nature, meaning that they need to analyze actual data to be successful. The purpose of this book is to:

- Give you the principles on which statistical analysis is based
- Provide you with many worked-out examples of these principles so that you can master them
- Improve your understanding of the circumstances in which each statistical technique should be used

As a *For Dummies* title, this book is organized into modules; you can skip around and learn about various statistical techniques in the order that suits you. In cases where the contents of a chapter are based on previous readings, you are guided back to the original material. Along the way, there are many helpful tips and reminders so that you get the most out of each chapter. I explain each equation in great detail, and all key terms are explained in depth. You will also find a summary of key formulas at the back of the book along with important statistical tables.

This book can't make you an expert in statistics, but provides you with a way of improving your knowledge very quickly so that you can use statistics in practical settings right away.

Foolish Assumptions

I am willing to make the following assumptions about you as the reader of this book:

✔ You need to use the techniques in this book in a practical setting and have little or no previous experience with statistics.

OR

✔ You're a student who feels overwhelmed by a traditional statistics course and feels the need for more background. You can benefit from seeing more examples of the material; statistics is a science that can be learned through practice!

OR

✔ You're simply interested in improving your knowledge of this field.

In all of these cases, you're extremely well motivated and can put as much effort into learning statistics as you need. Congratulations! Your reward for reading this book will be a greater understanding of business statistics.

Icons Used in This Book

The following icons are designed to help you use this book quickly and easily. Be sure to keep an eye out for them.

The Remember icon points to information that's especially important to remember for exam purposes.

The Tip icon presents information like a memory acronym or some other aid to understanding or remembering material.

When you see this icon, pay special attention. The information that follows may be somewhat difficult, confusing, or harmful.

The Technical Stuff icon is used to indicate detailed information; for some people, it might not be necessary to read or understand.

Beyond the Book

In addition to the informative, clever, and (if I may say so) well-written material you're reading right now, this product also comes with some access-anywhere goodies on the web. No matter how well you know statistics by the end of this book, a little extra information is always helpful. Check out the free Cheat Sheet at `www.dummies.com/cheatsheet/business statistics` to learn more about describing populations and samples, random variables, probability distributions, hypothesis testing, and more.

Where to Go from Here

When you've become more adept at statistical analysis, you may want to learn the capabilities of a spreadsheet program such as Excel. You may also want to tackle a full-blown statistical package, such as SPSS or SAS. These will eliminate a great deal of the computational burden, freeing you to concentrate on the analysis of the results.

You may also be interested in obtaining further education in this area. For example, you may want to pursue a graduate degree, such as an MBA (master of business administration.) This is an extremely important credential that will open a large number of doors in the business world. You'll need your statistical skills in order to earn this degree, since it is heavily used throughout the curriculum.

If you're not ready for graduate school, you may simply want to explore some college-level statistics courses at your local university. The most important thing is to continue using your statistical skills, as you'll only become adept at using them through constant practice.

Part I
Getting Started with Business Statistics

getting started with

business
statistics

In this part...

✔ Use histograms to provide a visual of the distribution of elements in a data set. A histogram can show which values occur most frequently, the smallest and largest values, how spread out these values are.

✔ Create graphs that reflect non-numerical data, such as colors, flavors, brand names, and so on. Graphs are used where numerical measures are difficult or impossible to compute.

✔ Identify the center of a data set by using the mean (the average), median (the middle), and mode (the most commonly occurring value). These are known as the measures of central tendencies.

✔ Use formulas for computing covariance and correlation for both samples and populations; a scatter plot is used to show the relationship (if there is one) between two variables.

Chapter 1

The Art and Science of Business Statistics

- -

In This Chapter

▶ Looking at the key properties of data

▶ Understanding probability's role in business

▶ Sampling distributions

▶ Drawing conclusions based on results

- -

This chapter provides a brief introduction to the concepts that are covered throughout the book. I introduce several important techniques that allow you to measure and analyze the statistical properties of real-world variables, such as stock prices, interest rates, corporate profits, and so on.

Statistical analysis is widely used in all business disciplines. For example, marketing researchers analyze consumer spending patterns in order to properly plan new advertising campaigns. Organizations use management consulting to determine how efficiently resources are being used. Manufacturers use quality control methods to ensure the consistency of the products they are producing. These types of business applications and many others are heavily based on statistical analysis.

Financial institutions use statistics for a wide variety of applications. For example, a pension fund may use statistics to identify the types of securities that it should hold in its investment portfolio. A hedge fund may use statistics to identify profitable trading opportunities. An investment bank may forecast the future state of the economy in order to determine which new assets it should hold in its own portfolio.

Whereas statistics is a quantitative discipline, the ultimate objective of statistical analysis is to explain real-world events. This means that in addition to the rigorous application of statistical methods, there is always a great deal of room for judgment. As a result, you can think of statistical analysis as both a science and an art; the art comes from choosing the appropriate statistical technique for a given situation and correctly interpreting the results.

Representing the Key Properties of Data

The word *data* refers to a collection of *quantitative* (numerical) or *qualitative* (non-numerical) values. Quantitative data may consist of prices, profits, sales, or any variable that can be measured on a numerical scale. Qualitative data may consist of colors, brand names, geographic locations, and so on. Most of the data encountered in business applications are quantitative.

The word *data* is actually the plural of *datum;* datum refers to a single value, while data refers to a collection of values.

You can analyze data with graphical techniques or numerical measures. I explore both options in the following sections.

Analyzing data with graphs

Graphs are a visual representation of a data set, making it easy to see patterns and other details. Deciding which type of graph to use depends on the type of data you're trying to analyze. Here are some of the more common types of graphs used in business statistics:

- **Histograms:** A histogram shows the distribution of data among different intervals or categories, using a series of vertical bars.

- **Line graphs:** A line graph shows how a variable changes over time.

- **Pie charts:** A pie chart shows how data is distributed between different categories, illustrated as a series of slices taken from a pie.

- **Scatter plots (scatter diagrams):** A scatter plot shows the relationship between two variables as a series of points. The pattern of the points indicates how closely related the two variables are.

Histograms

You can use a histogram with either quantitative or qualitative data. It's designed to show how a variable is distributed among different categories. For example, suppose that a marketing firm surveys 100 consumers to determine their favorite color. The responses are

Red:	23
Blue:	44
Yellow:	12
Green:	21

The results can be illustrated with a histogram, with each color in a single category. The heights of the bars indicate the number of responses for each color, making it easy to see which colors are the most popular (see Figure 1-1).

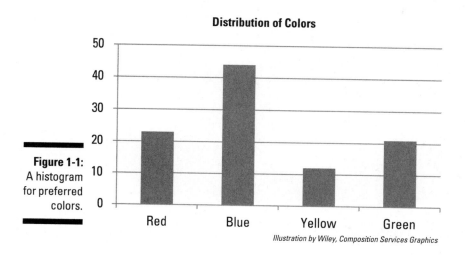

Distribution of Colors

Figure 1-1:
A histogram for preferred colors.

Based on the histogram, you can see at a glance that blue is the most popular choice, while yellow is the least popular choice.

Line graphs

You can use a line graph with quantitative data. It shows the values of a variable over a given interval of time. For example, Figure 1-2 shows the daily price of gold between April 14, 2013 and June 2, 2013:

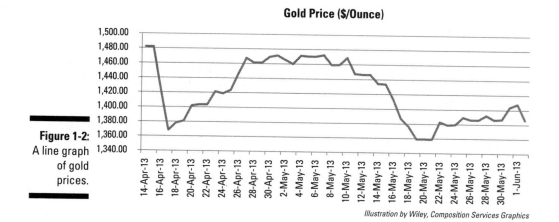

Gold Price ($/Ounce)

Figure 1-2:
A line graph of gold prices.

With a line graph, it's easy to see trends or patterns in a data set. In this example, the price of gold rose steadily throughout late April into mid-May before falling back in late May and then recovering somewhat at the end of the month. These types of graphs may be used by investors to identify which assets are likely to rise in the future based on their past performance.

Pie charts

Use a pie chart with quantitative or qualitative data to show the distribution of the data among different categories. For example, suppose that a chain of coffee shops wants to analyze its sales by coffee style. The styles that the chain sells are French Roast, Breakfast Blend, Brazilian Rainforest, Jamaica Blue Mountain, and Espresso. Figure 1-3 shows the proportion of sales for each style.

Distribution of Sales by Style

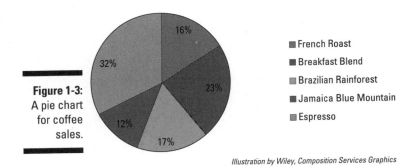

Figure 1-3: A pie chart for coffee sales.

- French Roast
- Breakfast Blend
- Brazilian Rainforest
- Jamaica Blue Mountain
- Espresso

Illustration by Wiley, Composition Services Graphics

The chart shows that Espresso is the chain's best-selling style, while Jamaica Blue Mountain accounts for the smallest percentage of the chain's sales.

Scatter plots

A scatter plot is designed to show the relationship between two quantitative variables. For example, Figure 1-4 shows the relationship between a corporation's sales and profits over the past 20 years.

Each point on the scatter plot represents profit and sales for a single year. The pattern of the points shows that higher levels of sales tend to be matched by higher levels of profits, and vice versa. This is called a positive *trend* in the data.

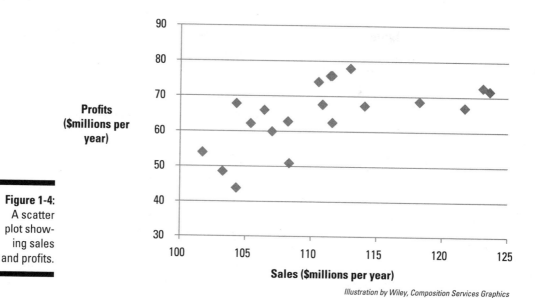

Figure 1-4:
A scatter plot showing sales and profits.

Defining properties and relationships with numerical measures

A *numerical measure* is a value that describes a key property of a data set. For example, to determine whether the residents of one city tend to be older than the residents in another city, you can compute and compare the average or *mean* age of the residents of each city.

Some of the most important properties of interest in a data set are the *center* of the data and the *spread* among the observations. I describe these properties in the following sections.

Finding the center of the data

To identify the center of a data set, you use measures that are known as *measures of central tendency;* the most important of these are the mean, median, and mode.

The *mean* represents the average value in a data set, while the *median* represents the midpoint. The median is a value that separates the data into two equal halves; half of the elements in the data set are *less than* the median, and the remaining half are *greater than* the median. The *mode* is the most commonly occurring value in the data set.

The mean is the most widely used measure of central tendency, but it can give deceptive results if the data contain any unusually large or small values, known as *outliers*. In this case, the median provides a more representative measure of the center of the data. For example, median household income is usually reported by government agencies instead of mean household income. This is because mean household income is inflated by the presence of a small number of extremely wealthy households. As a result, median household income is thought to be a better measure of how standards of living are changing over time.

The mode can be used for either quantitative or qualitative data. For example, it could be used to determine the most common number of years of education among the employees of a firm. It could also be used to determine the most popular flavor sold by a soft drink manufacturer.

Measuring the spread of the data

Measures of dispersion identify how spread out a data set is, relative to the center. This provides a way of determining if the members of a data set tend to be very close to each other or if they tend to be widely scattered. Some of the most important measures of dispersion are

- Variance
- Standard deviation
- Percentiles
- Quartiles
- Interquartile range (IQR)

The *variance* is a measure of the average squared difference between the elements of a data set and the mean. The larger the variance, the more "spread out" the data is. Variance is often used as a measure of risk in business applications; for example, it can be used to show how much uncertainty there is over the returns on a stock.

The *standard deviation* is the square root of the variance, and is more commonly used than the variance (since the variance is expressed in squared units). For example, the variance of a series of gas prices is measured in squared dollars, which is difficult to interpret. The corresponding standard deviation is measured in dollars, which is much more intuitively clear.

Percentiles divide a data set into 100 equal parts, each consisting of 1 percent of the total. For example, if a student's score on a standardized exam is in the 80th percentile, then the student outscored 80 percent of the other students who took the exam. A *quartile* is a special type of percentile; it divides a data set into four equal parts, each consisting of 25 percent of the total. The first quartile is the 25th percentile of a data set, the second quartile is the 50th percentile, and the third quartile is the 75th percentile. The *interquartile range* identifies the middle 50 percent of the observations in a data set; it equals the difference between the third and the first quartiles.

Determining the relationship between two variables

For some applications, you need to understand the relationship between two variables. For example, if an investor wants to understand the risk of a portfolio of stocks, it's essential to properly measure how closely the returns on the stocks track each other. You can determine the relationship between two variables with two measures of *association:* covariance and correlation.

Covariance is used to measure the tendency for two variables to rise above their means or fall below their means at the same time. For example, suppose that a bioengineering company finds that increasing research and development expenditures typically leads to an increase in the development of new patents. In this case, R&D spending and new patents would have a positive covariance. If the same company finds that rising labor costs typically reduce corporate profits, then labor costs and profits would have a negative covariance. If the company finds that profits are not related to the average daily temperature, then these two variables will have a covariance that is very close to zero.

Correlation is a closely related measure. It's defined as a value between –1 and 1, so interpreting the correlation is easier than the covariance. For example, a correlation of 0.9 between two variables would indicate a very strong positive relationship, whereas a correlation of 0.2 would indicate a fairly weak but positive relationship. A correlation of –0.8 would indicate a very strong negative relationship; a correlation of –0.3 would indicate a weak negative relationship. A correlation of 0 would show that two variables are *independent* (that is, unrelated).

Probability: The Foundation of All Statistical Analysis

Probability theory provides a mathematical framework for measuring uncertainty. This area is important for business applications since all results from the field of statistics are ultimately based on probability theory. Understanding probability theory provides fundamental insights into all the statistical methods used in this book.

Probability is heavily based on the notion of *sets*. A set is a collection of objects. These objects may be numbers, colors, flavors, and so on. This chapter focuses on sets of numbers that may represent prices, rates of return, and so forth. Several mathematical operations may be applied to sets — union, intersection, and complement, for example.

The union of two sets is a new set that contains all the elements in the original two sets. The intersection of two sets is a set that contains only the elements contained in *both* of the two original sets (if any.) The complement of a set is a set containing elements that are *not* in the original set. For example, the complement of the set of black cards in a standard deck is the set containing all red cards.

Probability theory is based on a model of how random outcomes are generated, known as a *random experiment*. Outcomes are generated in such a way that all *possible* outcomes are known in advance, but the *actual* outcome isn't known.

The following rules help you determine the probability of specific outcomes occurring:

✔ The addition rule

✔ The multiplication rule

✔ The complement rule

You use the addition rule to determine the probability of a union of two sets. The multiplication rule is used to determine the probability of an intersection of two sets. The complement rule is used to identify the probability that the outcome of a random experiment will *not* be an element in a specified set.

Random variables

A *random variable* assigns numerical values to the outcomes of a random experiment. For example, when you flip a coin twice, you're performing a random experiment, since:

✔ All possible outcomes are known in advance

✔ The actual outcome isn't known in advance

The experiment consists of two *trials*. On each trial, the outcome must be a "head" or a "tail."

Assume that a random variable X is defined as the number of "heads" that turn up during the course of this experiment. X assigns values to the outcomes of this experiment as follows:

Outcome	X
{TT}	0
{HT, TH}	1
{HH}	2

T represents a tail on a single flip

H represents a head on a single flip

TT represents two consecutive tails

HT represents a head followed by a tail

TH represents a tail followed by a head

HH represents two consecutive heads

X assigns a value of 0 to the outcome TT because no heads turned up. X assigns a value of 1 to both HT and TH because one head turned up in each case. Similarly, X assigns a value of 2 to HH because two heads turned up.

Probability distributions

A *probability distribution* is a formula or a table used to assign probabilities to each possible value of a random variable X. A probability distribution may be *discrete,* which means that X can assume one of a finite (countable) number of values, or *continuous,* in which case X can assume one of an infinite (uncountable) number of different values.

For the coin-flipping experiment from the previous section, the probability distribution of X could be a simple table that shows the probability of each possible value of X, written as $P(X)$:

X	P(X)
0	0.25
1	0.50
2	0.25

The probability that $X = 0$ (that no heads turn up) equals 0.25 because this experiment has four equally likely outcomes: HH, HT, TH, and TT and in only one of those cases will there be no heads. You compute the other probabilities in a similar manner.

Discrete probability distributions

Several specialized discrete probability distributions are useful for specific applications. For business applications, three frequently used discrete distributions are:

✔ Binomial

✔ Geometric

✔ Poisson

You use the *binomial distribution* to compute probabilities for a process where only one of two possible outcomes may occur on each trial. The *geometric distribution* is related to the binomial distribution; you use the geometric distribution to determine the probability that a specified number of trials will take place before the first success occurs. You can use the *Poisson distribution* to measure the probability that a given number of events will occur during a given time frame.

Continuous probability distributions

Many continuous distributions may be used for business applications; two of the most widely used are:

✔ Uniform

✔ Normal

The *uniform distribution* is useful because it represents variables that are evenly distributed over a given interval. For example, if the length of time until the next defective part arrives on an assembly line is equally likely to be any value between one and ten minutes, then you may use the uniform distribution to compute probabilities for the time until the next defective part arrives.

The *normal distribution* is useful for a wide array of applications in many disciplines. In business applications, variables such as stock returns are often assumed to follow the normal distribution. The normal distribution is characterized by a *bell-shaped curve,* and areas under this curve represent probabilities. The bell-shaped curve is shown in Figure 1-5.

The Normal Distribution

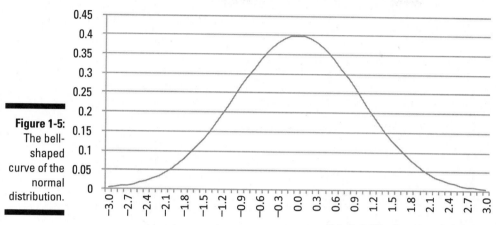

Illustration by Wiley, Composition Services Graphics

Figure 1-5:
The bell-shaped curve of the normal distribution.

The normal distribution has many convenient statistical properties that make it a popular choice for statistical modeling. One of these properties is known as *symmetry,* the idea that the probabilities of values below the mean are matched by the probabilities of values that are equally far above the mean.

Using Sampling Techniques and Sampling Distributions

Sampling is a branch of statistics in which the properties of a *population* are estimated from *samples.* A population is a collection of data that someone has an interest in studying. A sample is a selection of data randomly chosen from a population.

For example, if a university is interested in analyzing the distribution of grade point averages (GPAs) among its MBA students, the population of interest would be the GPAs of every MBA student at the university; a sample would consist of the GPAs of a set of randomly chosen MBA students.

Several approaches can be used for choosing samples; a sample is a *subset* of the underlying population.

A *statistic* is a summary measure of a sample, while a *parameter* is a summary measure of a population. The properties of a statistic can be determined with a *sampling distribution* — a special type of probability distribution that describes the properties of a statistic.

The *central limit theorem* (CLT) gives the conditions under which the mean of a sample follows the normal distribution:

- The underlying population is normally distributed.
- The sample size is "large" (at least 30).

A detailed discussion of the central limit theorem can be found at `http://en.wikipedia.org/wiki/Central_limit_theorem`.

Statistical Inference: Drawing Conclusions from Data

Statistical inference refers to the process of drawing conclusions about a population from randomly chosen samples. In the following sections, I discuss two techniques used for statistical inference: confidence intervals and hypothesis testing.

Confidence intervals

A *confidence interval* is a range of values that's expected to contain the value of a population parameter with a specified level of confidence (such as 90 percent, 95 percent, 99 percent, and so on). For example, you can construct a confidence interval for the population mean by following these steps:

1. **Estimate the value of the population mean by calculating the mean of a randomly chosen sample (known as the sample mean).**

2. **Calculate the lower limit of the confidence interval by subtracting a *margin of error* from the sample mean.**

3. **Calculate the upper limit of the confidence interval by adding the same margin of error to the sample mean.**

The margin of error depends on the size of the sample used to construct the confidence interval, whether the population standard deviation is known, and the level of confidence chosen.

The resulting interval is known as a confidence interval. A confidence interval is constructed with a specified level of probability. For example, suppose you draw a sample of stocks from a portfolio, and you construct a 95 percent confidence interval for the mean return of the stocks in the entire portfolio:

(lower limit, upper limit) = (0.02, 0.08)

The returns on the entire portfolio are the population of interest. The mean return in each sample drawn is an *estimate* of the population mean. The sample mean will be slightly different each time a new sample is drawn, as will the confidence interval. If this process is repeated 100 times, 95 of the resulting confidence intervals will contain the true population mean.

Hypothesis testing

Hypothesis testing is a procedure for using sample data to draw conclusions about the characteristics of the underlying population.

The procedure begins with a statement, known as the *null hypothesis*. The null hypothesis is assumed to be true unless strong evidence against it is found. An *alternative hypothesis* — the result accepted if the null hypothesis is rejected — is also stated.

You construct a *test statistic,* and you compare it with a *critical value* (or values) to determine whether the null hypothesis should be rejected. The specific test statistic and critical value(s) depend on which population parameter is being tested, the size of the sample being used, and other factors.

If the test statistic is too extreme (for example, it's too large compared with the critical value[s]) the null hypothesis is rejected in favor of the alternative hypothesis; otherwise, the null hypothesis is *not* rejected.

If the null hypothesis isn't rejected, this doesn't necessarily mean that it's true; it simply means that there is not enough evidence to justify rejecting it.

Hypothesis testing is a general procedure and can be used to draw conclusions about many features of a population, such as its mean, variance, standard deviation, and so on.

Simple regression analysis

Regression analysis uses sample data to estimate the strength and direction of the relationship between two or more variables. *Simple regression analysis* estimates the relationship between a dependent variable (Y) and a single independent variable (X).

For example, suppose you're interested in analyzing the relationship between the annual returns of the Standard & Poor's (S&P) 500 Index and the annual returns of Apple stock. You can assume that the returns of Apple stock are related to the returns to the S&P 500 because the index is a reflection of the overall strength of the economy. Therefore, the returns of Apple stock are the dependent variable (Y) and the returns of the S&P 500 are the independent variable (X). You can use regression analysis to measure the numerical relationship between the S&P 500 and Apple stock.

Simple regression analysis is based on the assumption that a linear relationship occurs between X and Y. A linear relationship takes this form:

$$\hat{Y}_i = \hat{\beta}_0 + \hat{\beta}_1 X_i$$

Y is the dependent variable, X is the independent variable, m is the slope, and b is the intercept.

The slope tells you how much Y changes due to a specific change in X; the intercept tells you what the value of Y would be if X had a value of zero.

The goal of regression analysis is to find a line that best fits or explains the data. The population regression line is written as follows:

$$Y_i = \beta_0 + \beta_1 X_i + \varepsilon_i$$

In this equation, Y_i is the dependent variable, X_i is the independent variable, β_0 is the intercept, β_1 is the slope, and ε_i is an error term.

A *sample* regression line, estimated from the data, is written as follows:

$$\hat{Y}_i$$

Here, $\hat{\beta}_0$ is the estimated value of Y, $\hat{\beta}_1$ is the estimated value of β_0, and X_i is the estimated value of β_1 and is the independent variable.

The sample regression line shows the estimated relationship between Y and X; you can use this relationship to determine how much Y changes due to a given change in X. You can also use it to *forecast* future values of Y based on assumed values of X.

After estimating the sample regression line, the results are subjected to a series of tests to determine whether the equation is valid. If the equation isn't valid, you reject the results and try a new model.

Multiple regression analysis

With *multiple regression analysis,* you estimate the relationship between a dependent variable (Y) and *two or more* independent variables (X_1, X_2, and so on).

For example, suppose that Y represents annual salaries (in thousands of dollars) at a corporation. A researcher has reason to believe that the salaries at this corporation depend mainly on the number of years of job experience and the number of years of graduate education for each employee. The researcher may test this idea by running a regression in which salary is the dependent variable (Y) and job experience and graduate education are the independent variables (X_1 and X_2, respectively.) The population regression equation in this case would be written as

$$Y_i = \beta_0 + \beta_1 X_{1i} + \beta_2 X_{2i} + \varepsilon_i$$

The sample regression line would be

$$\hat{Y}_i = \hat{\beta}_0 + \hat{\beta}_1 X_{1i} + \hat{\beta}_2 X_{2i}$$

Using multiple regression analysis introduces several additional complications compared with simple regression analysis, but you can use it for a much wider range of applications than simple regression analysis.

Forecasting techniques

You can forecast the future values of a variable, using one of several types of models. One approach to forecasting is *time series* models. A time series is a set of data that consists of the values of a single variable observed at different points in time. For example, the daily price of Microsoft stock taken from the past ten years is a time series.

Time series forecasting involves using past values of a variable to forecast future values.

Some forecasting techniques include:

- ✔ Trend models
- ✔ Moving average models
- ✔ Exponential moving average models

A *trend model* is used to estimate the value of a variable as it evolves over time. For example, suppose annual data is used to estimate a trend model that explains the behavior of gasoline prices over time. The price is currently $3.50 per gallon, and you determine that on average, gasoline prices rise by $0.10 per year. A simple trend model that expresses this information would be written as:

$$Y_t = 3.50 + 0.10t + \varepsilon_t$$

In this equation, Y_t represents the estimated gas price at time t, where t represents a specific year. ($t = 0$ represents the present time.) The term 3.50 indicates the current price of gasoline; $0.10t$ indicates that the price of gasoline rises by $0.10 per year. The term ε_t is known as an "error term"; this reflects random fluctuations in the price of gasoline over time.

A *moving average model* shows that the value of a variable evolves over time based on its most recent values. For example, if the price of gasoline over the past three years was:

2010 $3.25

2011 $3.32

2012 $3.42

A three-period moving average model would produce an estimated value of ($3.25 + $3.32 + $3.42) / 3 = $3.33 for 2013.

An *exponential weighted average model* is closely related to a moving average model. The difference is that with an exponential weighted average, older observations aren't given the same "weight" as newer observations. The calculation of an exponential weighted average is more complex, but may give more realistic results.

The appropriate choice of model depends on the properties of the particular time series being used.

Chapter 2

Pictures Tell the Story: Graphical Representations of Data

In This Chapter

▶ Describing the properties of data with a frequency distribution

▶ Illustrating frequency distributions with histograms

▶ Tracking trends with line graphs, pie charts, and scatter diagrams

Much of statistical analysis is based on numerical techniques, such as confidence intervals, hypothesis testing, regression analysis, and so on. (These topics are covered in Chapters 11, 12, and 15, respectively.)

In many cases, these techniques are based on assumptions about the data being used. One way to determine if the data conform to these assumptions is to analyze a graph of the data, as a graph can provide many insights into the properties of a data set. For example, a graph may be used to show:

✔ How frequently a value occurs in a data set

✔ The average value of the elements in a data set

✔ Whether the elements in a data set are increasing or decreasing over time

✔ Whether the elements in two different data sets are related to each other

Graphs are particularly useful for non-numerical data, such as colors, flavors, brand names, and more, where numerical measures are difficult or impossible to compute.

This chapter explains how to organize data in a convenient form so you can easily analyze it. I introduce charts and graphs — from histograms to line graphs to pie charts and scatter plots — that can help you visualize the most important properties of a data set.

Analyzing the Distribution of Data by Class or Category

To graph *quantitative* (numerical) data, you start by organizing the data into *classes* (also known as *intervals*). For example, suppose the government is conducting a study that measures the salary ranges for employees in the software industry in the United States. Here's one possible set of classes:

$0 to $24,999 per year

$25,000 to $49,999 per year

$50,000 to $74,999 per year

$75,000 to $99,999 per year

$100,000 and more per year

By counting the number of employees that fall into each class, you can easily see how salaries are distributed in the software industry. If you make the data into a graph, you can then easily compare this information with salaries in other industries.

Qualitative (non-numerical) data may be organized into *categories*. For example, suppose that a marketing firm is studying the spending habits of consumers and wants to determine the most popular colors for a new line of watches. In this case, the colors are relevant categories.

What type of graph you use for analyzing a set of data depends on the type of data (quantitative or qualitative) and the type of analysis you are performing. The following sections introduce several important types of graphs.

I also introduce the concept of a *frequency distribution*. This is a list of classes and the number of elements that belong to each class (known as *frequencies*). I cover the steps required to construct a frequency distribution, and I show two related types of distribution: relative frequency distribution and cumulative frequency distribution.

This section covers several widely used types of graphs, including histograms, pie charts, line graphs, and scatter plots. Histograms represent frequency distributions as a series of bars. Pie charts show what proportion of the elements of a data set belongs to various categories. A line graph shows how the value of a variable changes over time. Scatter plots are used to show the *relationship* between two variables.

Frequency distributions for quantitative data

Quantitative data consists of numerical values, such as prices, weights, distances, and so on.

To graphically analyze quantitative data, you first have to organize them into a *frequency distribution* — a table that shows the number of observations that fall into each class within the data set.

For example, suppose that the following values represent the price of gasoline (dollars per gallon) at 20 randomly selected gas stations:

$4.42	$4.34
$4.17	$3.73
$3.92	$3.56
$4.49	$3.65
$3.91	$3.58
$4.46	$4.12
$4.27	$4.21
$3.92	$3.85
$3.57	$4.10
$4.10	$3.63

Now suppose you organize the data into four classes, as follows:

$3.50 to $3.74

$3.75 to $3.99

$4.00 to $4.24

$4.25 to $4.49

Table 2-1 shows the frequency distribution for these.

Table 2-1 Frequency Distribution of Prices for 20 Gas Stations	
Gas Prices ($/Gallon)	**Number of Gas Stations**
$3.50–$3.74	6
$3.75–$3.99	4
$4.00–$4.24	5
$4.25–$4.49	5

Table 2-1 shows that the distribution of gas prices among these classes is very nearly equal. Seeing how the prices are distributed with a frequency distribution is much easier than inspecting the raw (original) data, which in this case is a list of 20 gas prices.

When you're constructing a frequency distribution, one of the most important considerations is the *width* of the classes. The class width equals the difference between the largest value that may be included in the class and the smallest. In Table 2-1, the class widths are $0.25. Usually, the class widths will be equal.

Deciding how many classes to use depends on how much data you have and how detailed you need the results to be. For example, if the class width is too large, it can disguise the distribution of values within each class. If the class width is too small, then several classes may contain no elements or very few elements, which makes analyzing the results more cumbersome.

As a rule of thumb, the optimal number of classes in a frequency distribution is between 5 and 15.

Figuring the class width

In the gas station example, each class has a width of $0.25. In general, you can determine the class width by subtracting the smallest value from the largest value and dividing by the total number of desired classes:

$$\text{Class width} = \frac{\text{Largest value in raw data} - \text{Smallest value in raw data}}{\text{Number of classes}}$$

Referring to the raw data (the list of 20 gas prices), you see that the largest price in the sample is $4.49 and the smallest is $3.56. To construct a frequency distribution with four classes, the width of each interval should be

$$\text{Class width} = \frac{\$4.49 - \$3.56}{4} = \frac{\$0.93}{4} = \$0.2325$$

So the class width is equal to approximately $0.25. Although the class width could be kept at $0.2325, using a width of $0.25 is intuitively easier to follow (since prices can't be expressed in quarters of a cent).

When you construct a frequency distribution, remember these key points:

✔ The classes must not overlap. For example, if the frequency distribution refers to gasoline prices, it would be incorrect to have a class for $1.00 to $2.00 and another class for $2.00 to $3.00, because both contain $2.00. It would be unclear which class contains prices of $2.00.

✔ The classes must cover all elements in the data set being analyzed.

✔ Ideally, the classes should have equal widths; otherwise, analyzing the results is much more difficult.

✔ Class widths should ideally be "round" numbers, such as $0.50, $1.00, $10.00, and so on, compared with numbers such as $0.43, $1.87, and $2.15. These numbers are more difficult to grasp intuitively. For the gas station example, the widths are $0.25, and this is preferable to $0.2325, because $0.2325 isn't a round number.

Observing relative frequency distributions

A frequency distribution shows the number of elements in a data set that belong to each class. In a relative frequency distribution, the value assigned to each class is the *proportion* of the total data set that belongs in the class. For example, suppose that a frequency distribution is based on a sample of 200 supermarkets. It turns out that 50 of these supermarkets charge a price between $8.00 and $8.99 for a pound of coffee. In a relative frequency distribution, the number assigned to this class would be 0.25 (50/200). In other words, that's 25 percent of the total.

Here's a handy formula for calculating the relative frequency of a class:

$$\frac{\text{class frequency}}{n}$$

Class frequency refers to the number of observations in each class; *n* represents the total number of observations in the entire data set. For the supermarket example in this section, the total number of observations is 200.

The relative frequency may be expressed as a proportion (fraction) of the total or as a percentage of the total. See Table 2-2, which gives both types of relative frequency based on the gas station data in Table 2-1.

Table 2-2	Relative Frequencies for Gas Station Prices		
Gas Prices ($/Gallon)	Number of Gas Stations	Relative Frequency (fraction)	Relative Frequency (percent)
$3.50–$3.74	6	6/20 = 0.30	30%
$3.75–$3.99	4	4/20 = 0.20	20%
$4.00–$4.24	5	5/20 = 0.25	25%
$4.25–$4.49	5	5/20 = 0.25	25%

With a sample size of 20 gas stations, the relative frequency of each class equals the actual number of gas stations divided by 20. The result is then expressed as either a fraction or a percentage. For example, you calculate the relative frequency of prices between $3.50 and $3.74 as 6/20 to get 0.30 (30 percent). Similarly, the relative frequency of prices between $3.75 and $3.99 equals 4/20 = 0.20 = 20 percent.

One of the advantages of using a relative frequency distribution is that you can compare data sets that don't necessarily contain an equal number of observations. For example, suppose that a researcher is interested in comparing the distribution of gas prices in New York and Connecticut. Because New York has a much larger population, it also has many more gas stations. The researcher decides to choose 1 percent of the gas stations in New York and 1 percent of the gas stations in Connecticut for the sample. This turns out to be 800 in New York and 200 in Connecticut. The researcher puts together a frequency distribution as shown in Table 2-3.

Table 2-3	Frequency Distribution of Gas Prices in New York and Connecticut	
Price	New York Gas Stations	Connecticut Gas Stations
$3.00–$3.49	210	48
$3.50–$3.99	420	96
$4.00–$4.49	170	56

Based on this frequency distribution, it's awkward to compare the distribution of prices in the two states. By converting this data into a relative frequency distribution, the comparison is greatly simplified, as seen in Table 2-4.

Table 2-4	Relative Frequency Distribution of Gas Prices in New York and Connecticut			
Price	New York Gas Stations	Relative Frequency	Connecticut Gas Stations	Relative Frequency
$3.00–$3.49	210	210/800 = 0.2625	48	48/200 = 0.2400
$3.50–$3.99	420	420/800 = 0.5250	96	96/200 = 0.4800
$4.00–$4.49	170	170/800 = 0.2125	56	56/200 = 0.2800

The results show that the distribution of gas prices in the two states is nearly identical. Roughly 25 percent of the gas stations in each state charge a price between $3.00 and $3.49; about 50 percent charge a price between $3.50 and $3.99; and about 25 percent charge a price between $4.00 and $4.49.

Frequency distribution for qualitative values

In this section, I use a qualitative data set to illustrate frequency distributions.

Suppose that a data set consists of *qualitative* (non-numerical) values. In this example, consumers were asked to identify their favorite color on a survey. The 20 responses are listed here.

blue	blue	blue	black
black	black	black	black
white	blue	white	blue
red	red	red	red
silver	silver	black	white

In this case, the categories are colors. The frequency distribution of these data is:

Color	Number of Reponses
Black	6
Blue	5
Red	4
Silver	2
White	3

Table 2-5 shows the relative frequency distribution.

Table 2-5	Relative Frequency Distribution of Favorite Colors		
Color	*Number of Responses*	*Relative Frequency (fraction)*	*Relative Frequency (percent)*
Black	6	6/20 = 0.30	30%
Blue	5	5/20 = 0.25	25%
Red	4	4/20 = 0.20	20%
Silver	2	2/20 = 0.10	10%
White	3	3/20 = 0.15	15%

You can easily see from the table that the most popular choice is black, and the least popular is silver.

Cumulative frequency distributions

Cumulative frequency refers to the total frequency of a given class and all prior classes.

For example, Table 2-6 lists the cumulative frequencies for the gas station data from the earlier section "Frequency distributions for quantitative data."

Table 2-6	Cumulative Frequency of Prices at 20 Gas Stations		
Gas Prices ($/Gallon)	*Number of Gas Stations*	*Cumulative Frequency*	*Cumulative Frequency (percent)*
$3.50–$3.74	6	6	30%
$3.75–$3.99	4	6 + 4 = 10	50%
$4.00–$4.24	5	6 + 4 + 5 = 15	75%
$4.25–$4.49	5	6 + 4 + 5 + 5 = 20	100%

To figure out the cumulative frequency of the $3.75 to $3.99 class, you add its class frequency (4) to the frequency of the previous class ($3.50 to $3.74, which is 6), so 6+4 = 10. This result shows you that ten gas stations' prices are between $3.50 and $3.99. Because 20 gas stations were used in the sample, the percentage of all gas stations with prices between $3.50 and $3.99 is 10/20 or 50 percent of the total.

Histograms: Getting a Picture of Frequency Distributions

You can illustrate a frequency distribution, a relative frequency distribution, or a cumulative frequency with a special type of graph known as a *histogram*. (See the previous section, "Analyzing the Distribution of Data by Class or Category.") With histograms, you list classes or categories on the horizontal axis and frequencies on the vertical axis. A bar represents each class or category.

A histogram's job is to provide a visual of the distribution of elements in a data set. The histogram can show which values in a data set occur most frequently, the smallest and largest values in the data set, how "spread out" these values are, and so on.

Figure 2-1 shows a histogram of the frequency distribution for the gas station prices from the previous section.

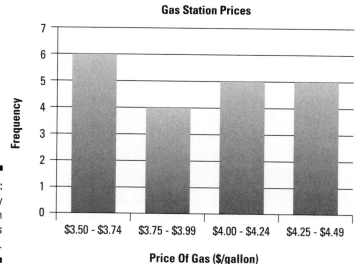

Figure 2-1:
Frequency
distribution
of gas
prices.

Figure 2-2 shows the relative frequency distribution.

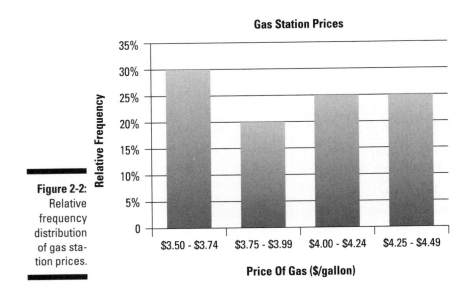

Figure 2-3 shows the cumulative frequency distribution.

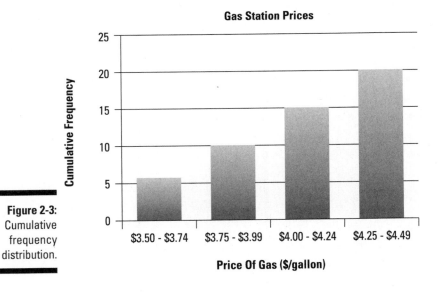

As another example, two restaurants, Pegasus and Orion, each asked 40 customers to estimate how much time they waited to receive their entrees. Figure 2-4 shows the results for the Pegasus survey, and Figure 2-5 shows the results for the Orion survey.

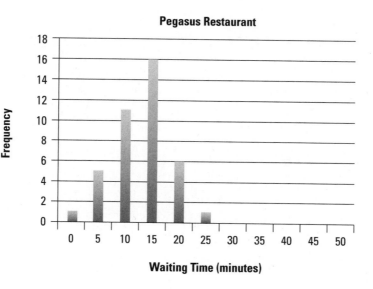

Figure 2-4:
Histogram
of waiting
times at the
Pegasus
restaurant.

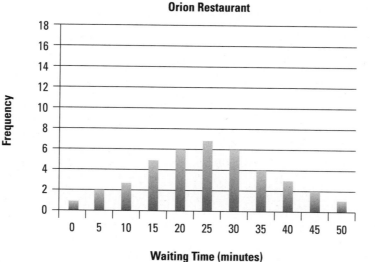

Figure 2-5:
Histogram
of waiting
times at the
Orion
restaurant.

As you can see, the most common waiting time at Pegasus was 15 to 20 minutes, and at Orion, 25 to 30 minutes. The histograms also show that the waiting times are more spread out at Orion — in other words, the actual waiting time is more uncertain at Orion than at Pegasus.

Checking Out Other Useful Graphs

In addition to histograms, several other types of graphs can illustrate the properties of a data set. This section introduces you to some of the more common types of graphs you're likely to encounter and use.

Line graphs: Showing the values of a data series

A *line graph* is useful for showing how the value of a variable changes over time. With a line graph, the vertical axis represents the value of the variable, and the horizontal axis represents time. Each point on the graph represents the value of the variable at a single point in time, and a line connects the points. This line shows any trends in the data, such as whether the variable increases or decreases over time.

The following shows the price of gold (dollars per ounce) during the first six months of 2012:

Month	*Gold Price ($/Ounce)*
January 2012	$1,652.42
February 2012	$1,723.33
March 2012	$1,676.30
April 2012	$1,646.77
May 2012	$1,567.08
June 2012	$1,602.27

The line chart in Figure 2-6 illustrates how the price of gold changed during this time period, based on the data shown in the table.

Gold Price ($/Ounce)

Using a line chart to detect patterns in the data is much easier than looking at the original data.

Pie charts: Showing the composition of a data set

A *pie chart* is a circle graph that's divided into slices to represent the distribution of values in a data set. The area of each slice is proportional to the number of values in a given class or category.

For example, suppose a bank has 100 branches throughout the country; the following is the geographical distribution of these branches:

Branch Location	*Number of Branches*
Northeast	44
Northwest	32
Southeast	15
Southwest	9

The pie chart in Figure 2-7 illustrates these results.

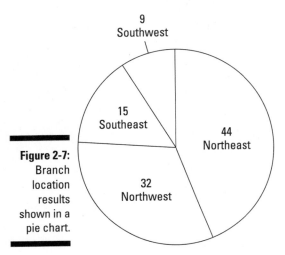

Branch Locations

Figure 2-7:
Branch
location
results
shown in a
pie chart.

The area of each slice in the pie chart indicates the proportional number of branches in each region. With this chart, you can easily see that the majority of the branches are in the northeast, with the fewest in the southwest.

Scatter plots: Showing the relationship between two variables

A *scatter plot* (also known as a *scatter diagram*) shows the relationship between two quantitative (numerical) variables. These variables may be positively related, negatively related, or unrelated:

- ✔ **Positively related variables** indicate that

    When one variable increases, the other variable tends to increase.

    When one variable decreases, the other variable tends to decrease.

- ✔ **Negatively related variables** indicate that

    When one variable increases or decreases, the other variable tends to do the opposite.

> ✔ **Unrelated variables** indicate that
>
> No relationship is seen between the changes in the two variables.

The scatter diagram in Figure 2-8 shows the relationship between the monthly returns to Microsoft stock and the Standard & Poor's (S&P) 500 Index from 2008 to 2012:

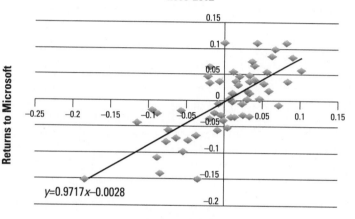

Figure 2-8: Scatter diagram showing relationship of monthly returns.

Each point on the graph represents the return to Microsoft stock and the return to the S&P 500 Index during a single month. The general direction of these points is from the lower-left corner of the graph to the upper-right corner, indicating that the two variables have a positive relationship.

The graph contains a *trend line,* which is a straight line designed to come as close as possible to all the points in the diagram. If two variables are positively related, the trend line has a positive slope; similarly, if two variables are negatively related, the trend line has a negative slope. If two variables are unrelated to each other, the trend line has a zero slope (that is, the trend line will be *flat*).

In the case of Microsoft and the S&P 500 Index, the equation of the trend line is

$$y = -0.0028 + 0.917x$$

Even more types of graphs

In addition to the graphs covered in this chapter — histograms, line graphs, pie charts, and scatter plots — there are many other types of graphs that you can use to analyze statistical data. Many of these have interesting names, such as stemplots, box-and-whisker diagrams, and ogives. These types may be used as alternatives to numerical methods to identify the distribution of elements within a data set, the relationship between the mean and the median of a data set, and several other factors.

In this equation, –0.0028 is the *intercept* (where the trend line crosses the vertical axis) and the *slope* is 0.917 (how much y changes due to a change in x).

Because the slope of the trend line is positive (0.917), the relationship between the returns to Microsoft stock and the S&P 500 Index is positive. The value of the slope also shows that each 1 percent increase in the returns to the S&P 500 Index increases the return to Microsoft by 0.917 percent, and that each 1 percent decrease in the returns to the S&P 500 Index decreases the return to Microsoft by 0.917 percent.

Chapter 3

Finding a Happy Medium: Identifying the Center of a Data Set

In This Chapter

▶ Computing the mean, median, and mode of a data set

▶ Noting the specific characteristics of the mean, median, and mode

The center of a data set (sample or population) provides useful information in many business applications. For example, it may be extremely important for a marketing firm to determine the average age of the customers who buy a specific product. Understanding the average household income of a company's customers would also be extremely useful in determining which types of new products to introduce. The portfolio manager at a pension fund is extremely interested in knowing the average rate of return of various stocks that he may be thinking about buying.

This chapter focuses on the techniques you use to find the center of a data set. There are several different ways to define the center: the average value, the middle value, the most frequently occurring value, and so on. Three of the most important measures of the center, formally known as measures of central tendency, are the mean, median, and mode.

The mean is the most commonly used measure of the center; it has the advantage of being easy to compute and interpret. In statistics, the word *mean* is used interchangeably with *average*.

The median and mode are mainly used in situations where the mean is likely to give misleading results. This can happen if the data set contains any extremely large or small values, known as *outliers*.

An *outlier* is a value that's significantly different from the other elements in a data set. Outliers may have a dramatic impact on the accuracy of your calculations.

The *median* is the middle value of a data set (just like a median divides a highway into two equal halves). The *mode* is the most frequently occurring value in a data set. Each of these measures has its own unique set of advantages and disadvantages.

Looking at Methods for Finding the Mean

You can calculate the mean of a data set in several ways; the appropriate choice depends on the type of data and the application. This section explains how to find the three most common types of mean.

Arithmetic mean

The *arithmetic mean* is what most people think of when they hear the word *mean*. This type of mean is the easiest to calculate; it's the sum of the elements in a data set divided by the number of elements.

You use different formulas for computing the arithmetic mean for a *population* and a *sample*. A population is a collection of data that you're interested in studying; a sample is a selection chosen from a population. For example, if a government is interested in the distribution of household incomes, the population of interest would be the incomes of every household. A sample would be a set of incomes for households randomly chosen from the population.

Calculating the sample arithmetic mean

The formula for finding the sample arithmetic mean is

$$\bar{X} = \frac{\sum_{i=1}^{n} X_i}{n}$$

The key terms in this formula are:

- $\bar{X}$ (pronounced "X bar") = the sample mean
- n = the number of elements in the sample
- i = an *index*, which assigns a number to each sample element, ranging from 1 to n
- X_i = a single element in the sample
- Σ = the uppercase Greek letter sigma, known as the *summation operator*, which indicates that a sum is being computed

The summation operator is shorthand notation for adding a set of numbers. For example, if a data set contains five elements, the summation operator tells you to perform the following calculations:

$$\sum_{i=1}^{5} X_i = X_1 + X_2 + X_3 + X_4 + X_5$$

Each of the Xs in this formula is *indexed* by a number ranging from 1 to n, where n is the size of the data set. In this example, n is 5.

Suppose an investor wants to compute the arithmetic mean return of the stock of Omega Airlines, Inc. He or she takes a sample of annual returns — the period from 2008 to 2012.

Year	Omega Airlines Annual Return (percent)
2008	2
2009	−1
2010	3
2011	5
2012	1

To find the arithmetic mean, follow these steps:

1. **Assign an index to each return in the sample.**

   $X_1 = 2, X_2 = -1, X_3 = 3, X_4 = 5, X_5 = 1$

   Here, X_1 represents the return in 2008; X_2 is the return in 2009, and so on.

2. **Compute the sum of the returns:**

   $$\sum_{i=1}^{5} X_i = X_1 + X_2 + X_3 + X_4 + X_5 = 2 - 1 + 3 + 5 + 1 = 10$$

3. **Divide the sum of the returns by the number of returns in the sample:**

   $$\bar{X} = \frac{\sum_{i=1}^{5} X_i}{5} = \frac{10}{5} = 2$$

This result shows that the average return of this stock is 2 percent per year.

Calculating the population arithmetic mean

When you calculate the arithmetic mean of a population, the calculation is the same as for arithmetic mean of a sample, but the notation is slightly different. Here's the formula for computing the arithmetic mean of a population:

$$\mu = \frac{\sum_{i=1}^{n} X_i}{n}$$

The new term in this formula is μ, the lowercase Greek letter mu, which replaces $\bar{X}$ from the sample arithmetic mean formula in the previous section. The μ represents the mean of a population.

In statistics, it's common to use Greek letters to represent population measures and Latin letters (that is, the alphabet that you use every day) to represent sample measures.

Geometric mean

The main difference between the arithmetic and geometric means is that the arithmetic mean is based on *sums,* while the geometric mean is based on *products*.

For the Omega Airlines example in the previous section, the arithmetic mean doesn't reflect the fact that the size of an investment in this stock grows over time and so it underestimates the true rate of return during the five-year sample period. This underestimation is one of the major drawbacks of the arithmetic mean. Based on the arithmetic mean return of 2 percent per year, the investor would have earned a cumulative return of 10 percent: 2 + 2 + 2 + 2 + 2 = 10 percent from 2008 to 2012.

In fact, the cumulative return was approximately 10.3 percent. To illustrate this return, assume that an investor started with $100,000 at the beginning of 2008. Table 3-1 shows the value of this investment from 2008 to 2012.

Table 3-1	Computing the Return to Omega Airlines Stock		
Year	Omega Airlines Annual Return (percent)	Starting Balance	Ending Balance
2008	2	$100,000.00	$100,000.00(1.02) = $102,000.00
2009	−1	$102,000.00	$102,000.00(0.99) = $100,980.00

Year	Omega Airlines Annual Return (percent)	Starting Balance	Ending Balance
2010	3	$100,980.00	$100,980.00(1.03) = $104,009.40
2011	5	$104,009.40	$104,009.40(1.05) = $109,209.87
2012	1	$109,209.87	$109,209.87(1.01) = $110,301.97

In each year, the starting balance is multiplied by the *gross return* (one plus the rate of return) during the year to get the ending balance. Each year's starting balance equals the previous year's ending balance.

The ending balance in 2012 equals $110,301.97. The cumulative rate of return during this period is the ratio of the ending balance to the starting balance minus one:

$$\text{Cumulative rate of return} = \left(\frac{\text{Ending balance}}{\text{Starting balance}} \right) - 1$$

$$= \left(\frac{110,301.97}{100,000.00} \right) - 1$$

$$= 1.1030197 - 1$$

$$= 0.1030197$$

$$= 10.30197 \text{ percent}$$

The cumulative return over period 2008–2012 is 10.30197 percent, more than the 10 percent implied by the arithmetic mean. In this case, the geometric mean provides a more accurate result than the arithmetic mean because the geometric mean takes into account the increasing size of the investment, while the arithmetic mean doesn't.

Because the geometric mean is based on products, for a sample or a population, you multiply the gross returns for each year to get the cumulative five-year return:

$$\left(1 + r_{2008}\right)\left(1 + r_{2009}\right)\left(1 + r_{2010}\right)\left(1 + r_{2011}\right)\left(1 + r_{2012}\right)$$

$$= \left(1.02\right)\left(0.99\right)\left(1.03\right)\left(1.05\right)\left(1.01\right) = 1.1030197$$

The returns are multiplied in order to indicate that *each year's return* is applied to the cumulative value of the investment, not the original value.

Because this sample has five returns, the next step is to raise the final result 1.1030197 to the *one-fifth* power:

$$(1.1030197)^{(1/5)} = 1.0198039$$

Raising a number to the one-fifth power is also known as taking the *fifth root* of the number. This corresponds to dividing by five when computing the arithmetic mean.

You can determine any exponent on a calculator with the exponentiation key; for most calculators, this key appears as Y^X or X^Y.

Subtracting 1 from the example's result gives you $1.0198039 - 1 = 0.0198039 = 1.98039$ percent per year. If the investor earns this return each year for five years, the five-year return will be computed as follows. First, the annual return plus one is multiplied by itself five times.

$$(1.0198039)(1.0198039)(1.0198039)(1.0198039)(1.0198039)$$

Subtracting one gives the cumulative five year return:

$$= (1.0198039)^5 - 1$$

$$= 0.1030199$$

$$= 10.30199 \text{ percent}$$

(Note that there are slight differences in the results due to rounding.)

You use this process for calculating either the geometric mean of a sample or the geometric mean of a population.

Weighted mean

Sometimes a data set contains a large number of repeated values. In these situations, you can simplify the process of computing the mean by using *weights* — the frequencies of a value in a sample or a population. You can compute both the arithmetic mean and geometric mean as weighted averages.

Calculating the weighted arithmetic mean

The formula for computing a weighted arithmetic mean for a sample or a population is

$$\frac{\sum_{i=1}^{n} w_i X_i}{\sum_{i=1}^{n} w_i}$$

Here, w_i represents the *weight* associated with element X_i; this weight equals the number of times that the element appears in the data set.

The *numerator* (the top half of the formula) tells you to multiply each element in the data set by its weight and then add the results together, as shown here:

$$\sum_{i=1}^{n} w_i X_i = w_1 X_1 + w_2 X_2 + w_3 X_3 + \ldots + w_n X_n$$

The *denominator* (the bottom half of the formula) tells you to add the weights together:

$$\sum_{i=1}^{n} w_i = w_1 + w_2 + w_3 + \ldots + w_n$$

You find the weighted arithmetic mean by dividing the numerator by the denominator.

As an example, suppose that a marketing firm conducts a survey of 1,000 households to determine the average number of TVs each household owns. The data show a large number of households with two or three TVs and a smaller number with one or four. Every household in the sample has at least one TV and no household has more than four. Here's the sample data for the survey:

Number of TVs per Household	Number of Households
1	73
2	378
3	459
4	90

Because many of the values in this data set are repeated multiple times, you can easily compute the sample mean as a weighted mean. Doing so is quicker than summing each value in the data set and dividing by the sample size.

Follow these steps to calculate the weighted arithmetic mean:

1. **Assign a weight to each value in the data set:**

   $X_1 = 1, w_1 = 73$

   $X_2 = 2, w_2 = 378$

   $X_3 = 3, w_3 = 459$

   $X_4 = 4, w_4 = 90$

2. **Compute the numerator of the weighted mean formula.**

   Multiply each sample by its weight and then add the products together:

   $$\sum_{i=1}^{4} w_i X_i = w_1 X_1 + w_2 X_2 + w_3 X_3 + w_4 X_4$$

   $$= (1)(73) + (2)(378) + (3)(459) + (4)(90)$$

   $$= 2,566$$

3. **Compute the denominator of the weighted mean formula by adding the weights together:**

   $$\sum_{i=1}^{4} w_i = w_1 + w_2 + w_3 + w_4$$

   $$= 73 + 378 + 459 + 90$$

   $$= 1,000$$

4. **Divide the numerator by the denominator:**

   $$\frac{\sum_{i=1}^{4} w_i X_i}{\sum_{i=1}^{4} w_i} = \frac{2,566}{1,000} = 2.566$$

The mean number of TVs per household in this sample is 2.566.

Calculating the weighted geometric mean

You can calculate the weighted geometric mean in the same way for both samples and populations. The formula is:

$$\left(\prod_{i=1}^{n} X_i^{w_i} \right)^{1/\sum_{i=1}^{n} w_i}$$

Here's the breakdown of this equation:

- ✔ Π = the uppercase Greek letter pi used to indicate that a product is being computed
- ✔ X_i = a single element in the sample or population
- ✔ w_i = the weight of element X_i
- ✔ $\sum_{i=1}^{n} w_i$ = the sum of the weights w_1, w_2, ..., w_n

You apply an *exponent* to each element in the data set that equals the weight of the element. You then multiply these values together and raise to a power equal to one divided by the sum of the weights.

TIP

An exponent is the superscript in an expression such as 3^4; in this case, the *base* is 3 and the *exponent* is 4. This is shorthand for multiplying 3 by itself four times: $3 \times 3 \times 3 \times 3 = 81$. Note that in many formulas and Microsoft Excel, the asterisk (*) represents multiplication. In Excel the carat (^) represents exponentiation.

As an example, a marketing firm conducts a survey of 20 households to determine the average number of cellphones each household owns. Here's the sample data from this survey:

Number of Cell Phones Per Household	Number of Households
1	2
2	5
3	6
4	4
5	3

To figure out the weighted geometric mean, follow these steps:

1. **Compute the value of each X_i with an exponent equal to its weight w_i:**

   $X_1^{w_1} = 1^2 = 1$

   $X_2^{w_2} = 2^5 = 32$

   $X_3^{w_3} = 3^6 = 729$

   $X_4^{w_4} = 4^4 = 256$

   $X_5^{w_5} = 5^3 = 125$

2. **Multiply these results together:**

   $$\left(\prod_{i=1}^{5} X_i^{w_i} \right) = X_1^{w_1} X_2^{w_2} X_3^{w_3} X_4^{w_4} X_5^{w_5}$$

   $$= (1)(32)(729)(256)(125) = 746,496,000$$

3. **Divide 1 by the sum of the weights:**

   $$\frac{1}{\sum_{i=1}^{5} w_i} = \frac{1}{2+5+6+4+3} = \frac{1}{20}$$

4. **Combine these results to find the weighted geometric mean:**

$$\left(\prod_{i=1}^{5} X_i^{w_i} \right)^{1/\sum_{i=1}^{5} w_i} = 746,496,000^{(1/20)} = 2.77748$$

So on average, each household has approximately 2.78 cellphones.

Getting to the Middle of Things: The Median of a Data Set

The *median* is a value that divides a sample or a population in half. In other words:

- ✔ Half of the elements in the data set are *below* the median.
- ✔ Half of the elements in the data set are *above* the median.

For example, the sample of returns of Omega Airlines stock from 2008 to 2012 is shown here:

Year	Omega Airlines Annual Return (percent)
2008	2
2009	−1
2010	3
2011	5
2012	1

You can compute the median of this sample, using the following steps:

1. **Sort the elements from the smallest to the largest.**

   Original data:

   2, −1, 3, 5, 1

   Sorted data:

   −1, 1, 2, 3, 5

2. **Identify the *middle* observation.**

   Because the sample contains five elements, the median is the third largest element (ensuring that two elements are below the median and two are above). The resulting value of the median is 2.

   −1, 1, **2**, 3, 5

Note: If the sample contains an even number of elements, then no element exists in the middle of the data. Instead, you calculate the median as the *average* of the middle two elements.

Here's another example. This list is a sample of the returns onto Epsilon Railways stock from 2007 to 2012:

Year	Epsilon Railways Annual Return (percent)
2007	0
2008	2
2009	3
2010	6
2011	1
2012	4

1. **Sort the elements from smallest to largest.**

   Original data:

   0, 2, 3, 6, 1, 4

   Sorted data:

   0, 1, 2, 3, 4, 6

2. **Identify the middle observation.**

   In this example, there are six sample elements. Because 6 is an even number, you compute the median as the average of the third and fourth elements:

   0, 1, *2, 3*, 4, 6

   (2 + 3)/2 = 2.5

   Note that three sample elements are below 2.5, and three elements are above 2.5.

The procedure for computing the median of a sample is the same as for computing the median of a population.

Comparing the Mean and Median

In some data sets, the mean and median may equal each other. When this occurs, the data set is said to be *symmetrical about the mean,* meaning that values below the mean balance the values above the mean. A data set may also be *negatively skewed,* indicating the presence of extreme values below the mean. Likewise, a data set may be *positively skewed,* indicating the presence of extreme values above the mean.

If a data set is skewed, the mean and median won't equal each other; instead, the relationship between them will determine the direction of the skew. I explore the relationship of the mean and median as well as the advantages and disadvantages of each measure in the following sections.

Determining the relationship between mean and median

The relationship between the mean and median of a data set determines whether the data set is symmetrical about the mean, negatively skewed, or positively skewed.

Symmetrical

A data set is symmetrical if the mean equals the median. Mathematically, this is expressed as

mean = median

The histogram in Figure 3-1 shows the frequency distribution for the daily returns of a stock with the following mean and median:

mean = 0.00 percent

median = 0.00 percent

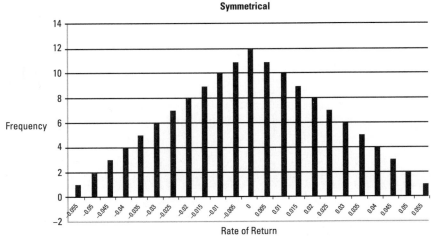

Figure 3-1: Symmetrical sample data.

Illustration by Wiley, Composition Services Graphics

The histogram shows that the left and right *tails* balance each other so that positive and negative values that are equal distances from the center are equally likely. (The left tail represents the smallest observations and the right tail represents the largest observations in the data set.) The left-hand side of this distribution is a mirror image of the right-hand side, showing that this distribution is symmetrical about the mean.

Negatively skewed

A data set is negatively skewed if the mean is less than the median. Mathematically, you can express this relationship as

mean < median

The histogram in Figure 3-2 shows the frequency distribution for the daily returns to a stock with the following mean and median:

mean = –0.95 percent

median = –0.75 percent

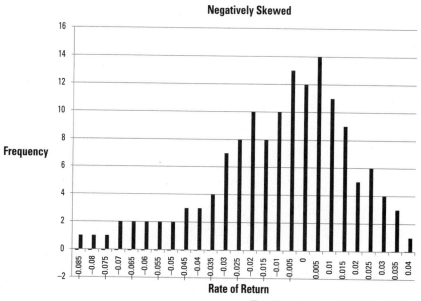

Figure 3-2:
Negatively
skewed
sample
data.

Illustration by Wiley, Composition Services Graphics

The histogram shows a long *left tail,* which results from extreme negative values in the data set.

Positively skewed

A data set is positively skewed if the mean is greater than the median. Mathematically, this relationship looks like this:

mean > median

The histogram in Figure 3-3 shows the frequency distribution for the daily returns on a stock with the following mean and median:

mean = 1.55 percent

median = 0.70 percent

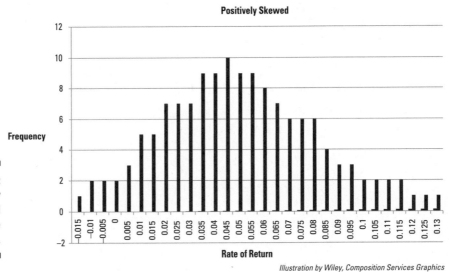

Positively Skewed

Frequency

Rate of Return

Illustration by Wiley, Composition Services Graphics

Figure 3-3:
Positively
skewed
sample
data.

The graph shows a *long right tail*, which results from extreme positive values in the data set.

Acknowledging the relative advantages and disadvantages of the mean and median

The mean is the most commonly used measure of the center of a data set. Under some conditions, though, the median (or even the mode) may be more representative of the center of the data set.

If a data set is symmetrical, the mean and the median are equal, so both are equally useful measures. When a data set is skewed, the median is likely to be a more representative measure of the center of the data than the mean because the median isn't as affected by extreme outcomes as much as the mean.

Discovering the Mode: The Most Frequently Repeated Element

The *mode* is the most frequently occurring value in a sample or a population. For example, suppose a bank chooses a sample of 20 of its branches in New York City, and for each branch, the number of ATMs in the lobby is recorded as follows:

Three branches have two ATMs.

Six branches have three ATMs.

Eight branches have four ATMs.

Three branches have five ATMs.

Because most branches have four ATMs, 4 is the mode in this sample.

One of the most unusual features of the mode is that it isn't necessarily unique; a data set can have two or more modes. It's also possible that a data set has no mode — that is, no values are repeated.

For example, suppose that the same bank chooses a sample of 20 of its branches in Connecticut. For each branch, the number of ATMs in the lobby is recorded. The results are given as follows:

Three branches have two ATMs.

Eight branches have three ATMs.

Eight branches have four ATMs.

One branch has five ATMs.

In this sample, more branches have three or four ATMs than any other number. Because the number of branches with three ATMs equals the number of banks with four ATMs, the mode of this sample is *both* 3 and 4.

The mode is most useful when a data set contains qualitative data (that is, non-numerical data). This type of data can include colors, flavors, brand names, and so on. With qualitative data, calculating a mean or a median is impossible, but you can still find the mode. With quantitative (numerical) data, the mean and the median are typically more useful than the mode.

As an example, suppose that a marketing firm conducts a survey to determine which color consumers would likely choose for a new car. The survey responses are as follows:

blue	red	blue
blue	red	blue
black	blue	black
blue	blue	black
blue	black	blue
white	silver	blue

Because this data is qualitative, calculating the mean or the median is impossible. But you can determine the mode by tabulating the frequency of the 15 responses. Because blue appears in the survey eight times, black, four times, white, red, and silver, one each, the mode is blue. Consumers in this survey prefer blue to other colors.

The distribution of colors is shown in Figure 3-4. In this example, the histogram shows colors on the horizontal axis and the corresponding frequencies on the vertical axis:

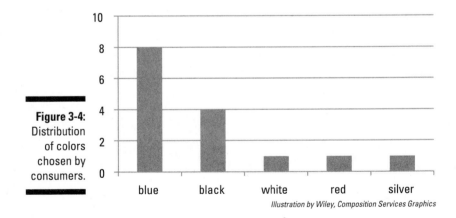

Figure 3-4: Distribution of colors chosen by consumers.

Illustration by Wiley, Composition Services Graphics

Because blue occurs most frequently in this sample, it's the sample's mode.

Chapter 4

Searching High and Low: Measuring Variation in a Data Set

In This Chapter

▶ Computing variance and standard deviation

▶ Finding the relative position of data: percentiles and quartiles

▶ Measuring relative variation: the coefficient of variation

*O*ne of the most important properties of a data set (a sample or population) is how "spread out" the data are from the center. (Techniques for measuring the center of a data set are covered in Chapter 3.) You can use several numerical measures, known as *measures of dispersion,* to calculate the spread of a data set.

This chapter covers the techniques used to compute the variance and standard deviation of a sample and a population. (Samples and populations are defined in Chapter 1.) Techniques for determining the relative position of an element within a sample or a population are also explained in detail; these include percentiles and quartiles. Finally, the coefficient of variation is introduced as a measure of *relative variation*; this enables a direct comparison of the properties of two samples or two populations.

Thanks to standard deviation and the mean (covered in Chapter 3), you can calculate relative variation, which has many handy applications.

Determining Variance and Standard Deviation

Variance and *standard deviation* are the two most widely used measures of dispersion in statistics. They're both based on the average squared distance between the elements of a data set and the mean.

Standard deviation and variance are usually better than some other measures of dispersion, such as the range. The range is the difference between the largest and smallest elements in a data set. Interesting, but not that great. The range suffers from the drawback that it's only based on two values, so it doesn't measure the spread among the remaining values.

The variance indicates the size of the average *squared* difference between the elements of a data set and the mean of the data set. And here's what you need to know: A large variance shows a substantial amount of spread among the elements of a data set.

Variance is often used as a measure of uncertainty or risk in business applications. For example, an investor may use variance to determine the degree of risk associated with owning a share of stock. If returns of the stock fluctuate significantly over time, it's a risky investment. Variance provides a method for assigning a numerical value to this fluctuation. The greater the stock's variance, the riskier it is.

Standard deviation is the *square root* of the variance. It's more commonly used than variance as a measure of risk because the variance is expressed in *squared units*. For example, the variance of stock returns is expressed as *percent squared*, which is difficult to visualize. On the other hand, the standard deviation of stock returns is measured as a percentage, which is much easier to interpret.

Finding the sample variance

Use the following formula to figure out the variance of a sample:

$$s^2 = \frac{\sum_{i=1}^{n}\left(X_i - \bar{X}\right)^2}{n-1}$$

Here's what each term means:

- ✔ s^2 = the sample variance
- ✔ $\bar{X}$ (pronounced "X bar"); this is the sample mean (the average value of the sample elements)
- ✔ n = the number of elements in the sample
- ✔ i = an *index,* assigning a number to each sample element ranging from 1 to n
- ✔ X_i = a single element in the sample
- ✔ Σ = the uppercase Greek letter sigma, which indicates a sum is being computed

The *numerator* (the top half) of the sample variance formula is:

$$\sum_{i=1}^{n}\left(X_i - \bar{X}\right)^2 = \left(X_1 - \bar{X}\right)^2 + \left(X_2 - \bar{X}\right)^2 + \ldots + \left(X_n - \bar{X}\right)^2$$

This expression tells you to perform the following three calculations:

1. For each sample element, subtract the sample mean.
2. Square the result.
3. Compute the sum of these squares.

The *denominator* (the bottom half) of the sample variance formula is $n - 1$ (the sample size minus 1). Then, you find the sample variance by dividing the numerator by the denominator.

Finding the sample standard deviation

The sample standard deviation is the *square root* of the sample variance:

$$s = \sqrt{\frac{\sum_{i=1}^{n}\left(X_i - \bar{X}\right)^2}{n - 1}}$$

Here's an example: Say you choose sample of coffee prices from 20 stores in 2 supermarket chains: Encore Markets and Pacifica Markets. Figure 4-1a shows the distribution of prices at Encore Markets, and Figure 4-1b shows the distribution of prices at Pacifica Markets. The price of coffee per pound is shown on the horizontal (X) axis, while the number of stores that charge a given price are shown on the vertical (Y) axis.

These graphs show that the prices are much more spread out at Pacifica's stores than at Encore's. In other words, Pacifica has greater *dispersion* among its prices. The range of possible prices at Pacifica's stores is much greater (at least one store charges $20 per pound!), while at Encore, no store charges more than $14. The stores at both chains charge at least $8 per pound. The dispersion among coffee prices is measured by the standard deviation, which is $3.6631 at Pacifica's stores and $2.1637 at Encore's stores. These numbers confirm what Table 4-1 shows: There's more spread among Pacifica's prices than Encore's prices.

Tables 4-1 and 4-2 show the prices at 20 stores in each of the two chains.

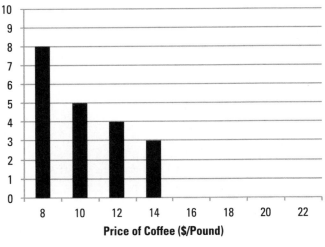

Encore Markets

Pacifica Markets

Figure 4-1 (a and b): Distribution of coffee prices at Encore Markets and Pacifica Markets.

Table 4-1	Sample Coffee Prices at Encore Markets		
8	10	11	8
8	9	8	8
13	8	9	14
12	8	12	14
10	12	8	9

Table 4-2	Sample Coffee Prices at Pacifica Markets		
15	17	9	7
13	7	7	9
9	8	7	7
9	13	7	11
19	11	7	7

The first step is to compute the sample mean coffee price. In this example, the sample mean for Encore is computed as follows:

$$\bar{X} = \frac{\sum_{i=1}^{n} X_i}{n}$$

The numerator is the sum of the coffee prices in the sample, which is 199. The denominator is the sample size, which is 20. The ratio of these two values is the sample mean, $9.95.

To compute the sample variance, subtract the sample mean from each sample coffee price, and square the results. The sum of these terms is the numerator of the sample variance formula. This is shown in the Table 4-3.

Table 4-3	Calculations for the Sample Variance at Encore Markets		
$(8 - 9.95)^2 =$ 3.8025	$(10 - 9.95)^2 =$ 0.0025	$(11 - 9.95)^2 =$ 1.1025	$(8 - 9.95)^2 =$ 3.8025
$(8 - 9.95)^2 =$ 3.8025	$(9 - 9.95)^2 =$ 0.9025	$(8 - 9.95)^2 =$ 3.8025	$(8 - 9.95)^2 =$ 3.8025
$(13 - 9.95)^2 =$ 9.3025	$(8 - 9.95)^2 =$ 3.8025	$(9 - 9.95)^2 =$ 0.9025	$(14 - 9.95)^2 =$ 16.4025
$(12 - 9.95)^2 =$ 4.2025	$(8 - 9.95)^2 =$ 3.8025	$(12 - 9.95)^2 =$ 4.2025	$(14 - 9.95)^2 =$ 16.4025
$(10 - 9.95)^2 =$ 0.0025	$(12 - 9.95)^2 =$ 4.2025	$(8 - 9.95)^2 =$ 3.8025	$(9 - 9.95)^2 =$ 0.9025

The sum of these terms is 88.95. The sample variance is, therefore:

$$s^2 = \frac{\sum_{i=1}^{n}\left(X_i - \bar{X}\right)^2}{n-1} = \frac{88.95}{19} = 4.6816$$

Now, at last! Take the square root. The sample standard deviation is:

$$s = \sqrt{\frac{\sum_{i=1}^{n}\left(X_i - \bar{X}\right)^2}{n-1}} = \sqrt{4.6816} = 2.1637$$

Compute the sample variance and sample standard deviation for Pacifica Markets the same way. Table 4-4 shows the calculations for the numerator of the sample variance formula.

Table 4-4	Calculations for the Sample Variance at Pacifica Markets		
$(15 - 9.95)^2 =$ 25.5025	$(17 - 9.95)^2 =$ 49.7025	$(9 - 9.95)^2 =$ 0.9025	$(7 - 9.95)^2 =$ 8.7025
$(13 - 9.95)^2 =$ 9.3025	$(7 - 9.95)^2 =$ 8.7025	$(7 - 9.95)^2 =$ 8.7025	$(9 - 9.95)^2 =$ 0.9025
$(9 - 9.95)^2 =$ 0.9025	$(8 - 9.95)^2 =$ 3.8025	$(7 - 9.95)^2 =$ 8.7025	$(7 - 9.95)^2 =$ 8.7025
$(9 - 9.95)^2 =$ 0.9025	$(13 - 9.95)^2 =$ 9.3025	$(7 - 9.95)^2 =$ 8.7025	$(11 - 9.95)^2 =$ 1.1025
$(19 - 9.95)^2 =$ 81.9025	$(11 - 9.95)^2 =$ 1.1025	$(7 - 9.95)^2 =$ 8.7025	$(7 - 9.95)^2 =$ 8.7025

The sum of these terms is 254.95. The sample variance is, therefore:

$$s^2 = \frac{\sum_{i=1}^{n}\left(X_i - \bar{X}\right)^2}{n-1} = \frac{254.95}{19} = 13.4184$$

The sample standard deviation is:

$$s = \sqrt{\frac{\sum_{i=1}^{n}\left(X_i - \bar{X}\right)^2}{n-1}} = \sqrt{13.4184} = 3.6631$$

These numbers confirm what Figure 4-1a and Figure 4-1b show: There's more spread among Pacifica's prices than Encore's prices. $2.1637 compared to $3.6631.

Although you can use graphs to inspect the dispersion of different samples or populations, comparing standard deviations is usually easier, and you don't have to examine the entire data set.

The standard deviation is a more useful measure of dispersion than variance. Again, variance is expressed in *squared* units (percent squared, dollars squared, and so on) because it's taken from the sum of *squared* differences between the elements in a data set and the mean of the data set. That's not as handy as standard deviation.

For example, Table 4-5 compares the variance and standard deviation of the Encore and Pacifica stores.

Table 4-5   Variance and Standard Deviation of Sample Stores

	Encore	*Pacifica*
Standard deviation ($/pound)	2.1637	3.6631
Variance ($²/pound)	4.6816	13.4184

Table 4-5 shows that the variance of coffee prices at Encore is $4.6816 *squared* per pound, while the variance of coffee prices at Pacifica is $13.4184 *squared* per pound. *Dollars squared* is a difficult concept to interpret — prices are never expressed in terms of dollars squared! So people most often use the standard deviation rather than the variance to show dispersion.

Calculating population variance and standard deviation

Unlike the mean, median, and mode, the variance and the standard deviation are calculated slightly differently for *samples* and *populations*. The following section shows the appropriate formulas for computing the variance and standard deviation of a population.

Finding the population variance

When you're calculating the variance for a population, use the following formula:

$$\sigma^2 = \frac{\sum_{i=1}^{n}(X_i - \mu)^2}{n}$$

The parameters are:

- σ^2 = population variance (σ is the lowercase Greek letter sigma)
- μ = the population mean (μ is the Greek letter mu)

Σ is the uppercase Greek letter sigma, which represents summation σ is the lowercase sigma, which represents the population standard deviation.

The *numerator* (the top half) of the population variance formula is:

$$\sum_{i=1}^{n}(X_i - \mu)^2 = (X_1 - \mu)^2 + (X_2 - \mu)^2 + \dots + (X_n - \mu)^2$$

Use this formula and do the following calculations:

1. **For each population element, subtract the population mean.**

2. **Square the result.**

3. **Compute the sum of the squares.**

The *denominator* (the bottom half) of the population variance formula is *n* (the population size.) You find the population variance by dividing the numerator of the population variance formula by the denominator.

Finding the population standard deviation

After you figure out the population variance, you can get the population standard deviation by taking the square root of the population:

$$\sigma = \sqrt{\frac{\sum_{i=1}^{n}(X_i - \mu)^2}{n}}$$

For example, suppose an investor wants to analyze the dispersion of Alpha, Inc.'s, sales from one year to the next. Table 4-6 shows the sample of annual profits the investor takes (measured in millions of dollars per year) from 2007 to 2012.

Table 4-6	Alpha, Inc. Sales 2007–2012
Year	*Sales ($ million)*
2007	18
2008	22
2009	31
2010	29
2011	42
2012	50

You find the population variance by following these steps:

1. **Find the population mean.**

   The formula for calculating the sample mean is

   $$\mu = \frac{\sum_{i=1}^{n} X_i}{n}$$

   Plug in the numbers from Table 4-6:

   $$\mu = \frac{\sum_{i=1}^{n} X_i}{n} = \frac{18 + 22 + 31 + 29 + 42 + 50}{6} = 32$$

   The average annual profit during this period was $32 million.

2. **Work through the numerator of the sample variance formula.**

   $$\sum_{i=1}^{n} (X_i - \mu)^2$$

   The calculations are shown in Table 4-7.

Table 4-7   Calculations of Population Variance for Alpha, Inc.

Year	Alpha, Inc. Sales ($ million)	$(X_i - \mu)$	$(X_i - \mu)^2$
2007	18	$18 - 32 = -14$	$(-14)^2 = 196$
2008	22	$22 - 32 = -10$	$(-10)^2 = 100$
2009	31	$31 - 32 = -1$	$(-1)^2 = 1$
2010	29	$29 - 32 = -3$	$(-3)^2 = 9$
2011	42	$42 - 32 = 10$	$(10)^2 = 100$
2012	50	$50 - 32 = 18$	$(18)^2 = 324$
		Sum	730

In the third column $((X_i - \mu))$, subtract the mean return from the actual return for each year. In the fourth column $((X_i - \mu)^2)$, square the result from the third column. The sum of the fourth column is the numerator of the sample variance formula; this equals 730.

3. **Solve the denominator of the population variance formula.**

   The denominator is 6. Because six elements are in this population, $n = 6$.

4. **Substitute these values into the population variance formula.**

$$\sigma^2 = \frac{\sum_{i=1}^{n}(X_i - \mu)^2}{n} = \frac{730}{6} = 121.667$$

The population variance of Alpha's sales is $121.667 dollars squared.

Finding the population standard deviation

After you figure out the population variance, you get the population standard deviation by taking the square root of the population variance:

$$\sigma = \sqrt{\frac{\sum_{i=1}^{n}(X_i - \mu)^2}{n}} = \sqrt{121.667} = 11.030$$

The population standard deviation of Alpha's sales is $11.030 million.

Finding the Relative Position of Data

Identifying the location or position of a value in a data set can be immensely useful, whether you're talking about business profitability, population statistics, or scores on school tests. You use three related measures known as *percentiles*, *quartiles*, and the *interquartile range*.

A percentile is a value that divides a sample or population into two groups, with a specified percentage in each group. For example, on a standardized exam, the 10th percentile is the score such that:

10 percent of the scores are below it

90 percent of the scores are above it

Quartiles are closely related to percentiles; they subdivide a sample or a population into four equal parts. The interquartile range identifies the middle 50 percent.

Percentiles: Dividing everything into hundredths

Percentiles split up a data set into 100 equal parts, each consisting of 1 percent of the values in the data set.

For example, suppose a corporation is analyzing the annual sales of its franchise owners. Those franchises whose sales belong to the 90th percentile will get an award. Being in the 90th percentile means that:

90 percent of the franchises have sales below this value

10 percent of the franchises have sales above this value

As a result, 10 percent of the franchises will receive the award. When you hear someone say that he or she is in the "top 10 percent," you can take that to mean that they are in the 90th percentile.

Percentiles provide a *relative ranking* for an element of a data set. For example, suppose that the corporation's New York franchise has sales of $1 million during the year. Judging whether this franchise is successful without knowing how this value compares with the other franchises is difficult. If it turns out that $1 million places the New York franchise in the 10th percentile, then 90 percent of the other franchises outperformed it this year. On the other hand, if $1 million places the New York franchise in the 80th percentile, then only 20 percent of the other franchises outperformed it this year.

The 50th percentile of a data set is the median because half of the values are below the median, and half are above.

Suppose the Federal Reserve Bank of New York conducts a survey of the assets of the savings banks in its district. A sample of ten banks is chosen; the results (in hundreds of millions of dollars) are:

2, 3, 5, 7, 6, 4, 8, 9, 1, 2

To compute percentiles, first sort the elements from the smallest value to the largest. In this example, the sorted values are:

1, 2, 2, 3, 4, 5, 6, 7, 8, 9

There are several possible approaches to computing percentiles. One of them is to apply the following formula to compute an *index*. This index represents the location of the appropriate percentile.

$$\frac{P}{100}n + 0.5$$

Here, P is the percentile of interest (30th, 40th, and so on), and n is the size of the sample or population. You round the number to the nearest integer (whole number). The percentile equals the corresponding value in the data set.

When rounding a number with a fractional part, if the fractional part is 0.5 or greater, round *up* to the next higher integer; otherwise, round *down* to the next lower integer. For example, you round 3.4 *down* to 3, and 3.5 *up* to 4.

For example, in order to find the 30th percentile of a set of ten, the index is

$$\frac{P}{100}n + 0.5 = \frac{30}{100}(10) + 0.5 = 3.5$$

Round 3.5 up to 4 to see that the fourth smallest value, the number 3 in this example, is the 30th percentile.

1, 2, 2, **3**, 4, 5, 6, 7, 8, 9

Similarly, you find the 70th percentile of a set of ten as follows:

$$\frac{P}{100}n + 0.5 = \frac{70}{100}(10) + 0.5 = 7.5$$

Don't forget to round 7.5 up to 8, which shows that the eighth smallest value, or the number 7 in this example, is the 70th percentile.

1, 2, 2, 3, 4, 5, 6, **7**, 8, 9

Microsoft Excel uses a somewhat different approach to computing percentiles. If you use the PERCENTILE function, you will get 2.7 for the 30th percentile and 6.3 for the 70th percentile.

Quartiles: Dividing everything into fourths

Quartiles split up a data set into four equal parts, each consisting of 25 percent of the sorted values in the data set. Quartiles are related to percentiles like so:

First quartile (Q_1) = 25th percentile

Second quartile (Q_2) = 50th percentile

Third quartile (Q_3) = 75th percentile

Because the second quartile is the 50th percentile, it's also the *median* of a data set. The fourth quartile usually isn't used because its value is greater than every element in a data set, so what's the point?

One commonly used approach for calculating quartiles follows these two steps:

1. **Split the data into a lower half and an upper half (leaving out the median).**

2. **Compute the median of the lower half and the upper half.**

   After you've split the data into lower and upper halves, you figure out the quartiles as follows:

Q_1 = the median of the lower half

Q_2 = the median of the entire data set

Q_3 = the median of the upper half

The following data represent a sample of eight stock returns for Gamma Industries:

5, 7, 6, 3, 0, –2, 4, 3

The sorted values are:

–2, 0, 3, 3, 4, 5, 6, 7

In this example, you have eight elements. Because 8 is an even number, the median is the average of the fourth and fifth elements: –2, 0, 3, **3, 4**, 5, 6, 7

$(3 + 4)/2 = 3.5$. Therefore, the second quartile (Q_2) is 3.5.

The values below the median constitute the lower half of the sorted sample

–2, 0, 3, 3

The values above the median constitute the upper half of the sorted sample

4, 5, 6, 7

Both the lower and upper halves have four sample elements. Because four is an even number, the median is the average of the second and third elements.

For the lower half, the median is: $(0 + 3)/2 = 1.5$. This is the *average* value of the two middle elements. Therefore, the first quartile (Q_1) is 1.5.

For the upper half, the median is $(5 + 6)/2 = 5.5$. Therefore, the third quartile (Q_3) is 5.5.

As with percentiles, Microsoft Excel uses a different approach to computing quartiles; if you use the QUARTILE function, you will get 3.5 for Q_2, but you will also get

2.25 for Q_1 (instead of 1.5)

5.25 for Q_3 (instead of 5.5)

Interquartile range: Identifying the middle 50 percent

The *interquartile range* (IQR) is the difference between the third quartile and the first quartile: $IQR = Q_3 - Q_1$. The IQR represents the middle 50 percent of the data set. For the Gamma Industries example, the IQR is $Q_3 - Q_1 = 5.5 - 1.5 = 4$.

An advantage of the IQR is that it isn't greatly affected by *outliers* — values within a data set that are significantly different than the other elements in the data set. In fact, the IQR can help identify outliers within a data set.

You can find the outliers in a data set in several ways. One of the simpler approaches is to create a *lower bound* and an *upper bound*. What this means is that if any elements are below the lower bound or above the upper bound, they're outliers. You set these bounds based on quartiles and the interquartile range:

lower bound: $Q_1 - 1.5(IQR)$

upper bound: $Q_3 + 1.5(IQR)$

Based on the Gamma Industries data, the lower bound = $1.5 - 1.5(4) = -4.5$, and the upper bound = $5.5 + 1.5(4) = 11.5$.

Because no value in this sample is below -4.5 or above 11.5, the sample has no outliers.

Measuring Relative Variation

Relative variation refers to the spread of a sample or a population as a proportion of the mean. Relative variation is useful because it can be expressed as a percentage, and is independent of the units in which the sample or population data are measured.

For example, you can use a measure of relative variation to compare the uncertainty or variation associated with the temperature in two different countries, even if one country uses Fahrenheit temperatures and the other uses Celsius temperatures. As another example, a measure of relative variation can be useful for comparing the returns earned by two portfolio managers. It wouldn't make any sense to compare the mean returns achieved by two different managers without explicitly considering the levels of risk that they have incurred. A measure of relative variation provides a number that considers both the risk and the return of a portfolio, so that it can be determined which portfolio is riskier relative to the return.

You can use several different types of measures of relative variation. One of the most popular is known as the coefficient of variation.

Coefficient of variation: The spread of a data set relative to the mean

The *coefficient of variation* (CV) indicates how "spread out" the members of a sample or population are relative to the mean. The coefficient of variation is measured as a percentage, so it's independent of the units in which the mean and standard deviation are measured. This enables the relative variation of different samples or populations to be compared directly to each other.

For example, the coefficient of variation can express the risk of an investment portfolio *per unit of return*. This means you can compare the performance of different portfolios to see which one offers the least amount of risk per unit of return.

Here's the formula for finding the coefficient of variation for either samples or populations:

$$CV = \left(\frac{\text{standard deviation}}{\text{mean}}\right) * 100$$

Suppose a corporation requires the services of a consulting firm to improve its accounting systems. The corporation has determined that the two best choices are Superior Accounting, Inc., and Data Services Corp. The corporation has done some research about the pricing practices of these two firms. The average price charged per hour, along with the standard deviation, are shown in Table 4-8:

Table 4-8	Comparative Prices Charged by Superior Accounting and Data Services	
	Superior Accounting	*Data Services*
Mean price ($/hour)	$200	$175
Standard deviation ($/hour)	$80	$75

Based on this data, the coefficient of variation for the prices charged by each firm are

Superior Accounting: $CV = \frac{\$80}{\$200} * 100 = 40.00$ percent

Data Services: $CV = \frac{\$75}{\$175} * 100 = 42.86$ percent

These results show that although the prices charged by Superior Accounting have a larger standard deviation than Data Services, the relative variation of Data Services is greater (42.86 percent compared with 40.00 percent.) This indicates that the relative uncertainty associated with Data Services' prices is greater than for Superior Accounting's prices.

Comparing the relative risks of two portfolios

Suppose a portfolio manager is responsible for an insurance company's equity portfolio and bond portfolio. He wants to know which portfolio is riskier in absolute and relative terms. He takes a sample of returns from the past ten years and computes the mean and standard deviation. See Table 4-9 for the results:

Table 4-9   Comparative Performance of Bond and Equity Portfolios

	Bond Portfolio	Equity Portfolio
Mean return	8%	20%
Standard deviation of returns	16%	30%

These results show that the equity portfolio offers a higher average (mean) return than the bond portfolio and that the equity portfolio is *riskier* in absolute terms than the bond portfolio.

Because the two portfolios offer different returns and different levels of risk, it's impossible to compare them directly without using a measure of *relative risk,* which shows how risky a portfolio is relative to its return. So you need to find the coefficient of variation for the two portfolios, using the CV formula:

$$\text{Bond: } CV = \frac{16 \text{ percent}}{8 \text{ percent}} * 100 = 200 \text{ percent}$$

$$\text{Equity: } CV = \frac{30 \text{ percent}}{20 \text{ percent}} * 100 = 150 \text{ percent}$$

The bond portfolio offers a level of risk that's 200 percent of the average return, while the equity portfolio offers a level of risk that's 150 percent of the average return. So while the equity portfolio is riskier in *absolute* terms (due to the higher standard deviation) the bond portfolio is riskier in *relative* terms (due to the higher coefficient of variation).

Chapter 5

Measuring How Data Sets Are Related to Each Other

In This Chapter

▶ Working with measures of association: covariance and correlation

▶ Determining the correlation coefficient

A *measure of association* is a numerical value that reflects the tendency of two variables to move in the same direction or in opposite directions. For example, it makes sense that corporate profits and sales would both tend to increase when the economy is strong, and decrease when the economy is weak. A measure of association is used to assign a numerical value to the strength and direction of this type of relationship.

Measures of association can help answer questions, such as, "If interest rates fall, do stock prices tend to rise?" or "If oil prices rise, does the unemployment rate tend to rise?" or "Does an increase in advertising expenditures lead to greater revenues?"

The two most widely used measures of association are known as *covariance* and *correlation*.

In this chapter, you see formulas for computing covariance and correlation for both samples and populations. The relationship between two variables is illustrated with a type of graph known as a *scatter plot,* which is useful for seeing the relationship that exists (if any) between two variables. (I cover several types of graphs such as the scatter plot in Chapter 2.) This chapter concludes by illustrating how the risks of a portfolio of stocks may be diversified if the stocks have low or negative correlations between them.

Understanding Covariance and Correlation

Two of the most widely used measures of association are known as *covariance* and *correlation*. These are closely related to each other. You can think of correlation as a modified version of covariance. Correlation is easier to interpret because its value is always between –1 and 1. For example, a correlation of 0.9 indicates a very strong relationship in which two variables nearly always move in the same direction; a correlation of –0.1 shows a very weak relationship in which there is a slight tendency for two variables to move in opposite directions. With covariance, there is no minimum or maximum value, so the values are more difficult to interpret. For example, a covariance of 50 may show a strong or weak relationship; this depends on the units in which covariance is measured.

Correlation is a measure of the strength and direction of two *linearly related* variables. Two variables are said to be linearly related if they can be expressed with the following equation:

$$Y = mX + b$$

X and Y are variables; m and b are constants. For example, suppose that the relationship between two variables is:

$$Y = 3X + 4$$

3 is the *coefficient* of X; this indicates that an increase of X by 1 causes Y to increase by 3. Equivalently, a decrease of X by 1 causes Y to decrease by 3. The 4 in this equation indicates that Y equals 4 when X equals 0.

Covariance and correlation show that variables can have a positive relationship, a negative relationship, or no relationship at all. With covariance and correlation, there are three cases that may arise:

- ✔ **If two variables increase or decrease at the same time, the covariance and correlation between them is *positive*.** For example, the covariance and correlation between the stock prices of two oil companies is positive because many of the same factors affect the stock prices in the same way.

- ✔ **If two variables move in opposite directions, the covariance and correlation between them is *negative*.** For example, the covariance and correlation between interest rates and new home sales is negative because rising interest rates increase the cost of purchasing a new home, which in turn reduces new home sales. The opposite occurs with falling interest rates.

- ✔ **If two variables are unrelated to each other, the covariance and correlation between them is *zero* (or very close to zero).** For example, the covariance and correlation between gold prices and new car sales is zero because the two have nothing to do with each other.

In the following sections, I introduce formulas for computing sample covariance, sample correlation, population covariance, and population correlation. These measures are illustrated with several examples.

Sample covariance and correlation

Sample covariance measures the strength and the direction of the relationship between the elements of two samples. (Recall from Chapter 1 that a sample is a randomly chosen selection of elements from an underlying population.)

The sample covariance between X and Y is

$$s_{XY} = \frac{\sum_{i=1}^{n}\left(X_i - \bar{X}\right)\left(Y_i - \bar{Y}\right)}{n-1}$$

Here's what each element in this equation means:

- s_{XY} = the sample covariance between variables X and Y (the two subscripts indicate that this is the sample covariance, not the sample standard deviation).
- $\bar{X}$ ("X bar") = the sample mean for X.
- $\bar{Y}$ ("Y bar") = the sample mean for Y.
- n = the number of elements in both samples.
- i = an *index* that assigns a number to each sample element, ranging from 1 to n.
- X_i = a single element in the sample for X.
- Y_i = a single element in the sample for Y.
- Σ = the uppercase Greek letter sigma that indicates that a sum is being computed.

The sample covariance may have any positive or negative value.

You calculate the *sample correlation* (also known as the sample *correlation coefficient*) between X and Y directly from the sample covariance with the following formula:

$$r_{XY} = \frac{s_{XY}}{s_X s_Y}$$

The key terms in this formula are

- r_{XY} = sample correlation between X and Y
- s_{XY} = sample covariance between X and Y
- s_X = sample standard deviation of X
- s_Y = sample standard deviation of Y

The formula used to compute the sample correlation coefficient ensures that its value ranges between –1 and 1.

For example, suppose you take a sample of stock returns from the Excelsior Corporation and the Adirondack Corporation from the years 2008 to 2012, as shown here:

Year	Excelsior Corp. Annual Return (percent) (X)	Adirondack Corp. Annual Return (percent) (Y)
2008	1	3
2009	–2	2
2010	3	4
2011	0	6
2012	3	0

What are the covariance and correlation between the stock returns? To figure that out, you first have to find the mean of each sample. (The sample mean is discussed in Chapter 3.) In this example, X represents the returns to Excelsior and Y represents the returns to Adirondack.

✔ The sample mean of X is

$$\bar{X} = \frac{\sum\limits_{i=1}^{n} X_i}{n}$$
$$= \frac{(1-2+3+0+3)}{5}$$
$$= \frac{5}{5} = 1$$

You obtain the sample mean by summing all the elements of the sample and then dividing by the sample size. In this case, the sample elements sum to 5 and the sample size is 5. Dividing these numbers gives a sample mean of 1.

✔ The sample mean of Y is

$$\bar{Y} = \frac{\sum\limits_{i=1}^{n} Y_i}{n}$$
$$= \frac{(3+2+4+6+0)}{5}$$
$$= \frac{15}{5} = 3$$

Table 5-1 shows the remaining calculations for the sample covariance:

Table 5-1		Computing the Sample Covariance			
Year	Excelsior Corp Annual Return (percent)	Adirondack Corp Annual Return (percent)	$(X_i - \bar{X})$	$(Y_i - \bar{Y})$	$(X_i - \bar{X})(Y_i - \bar{Y})$
2008	1	3	$1 - 1 = 0$	$3 - 3 = 0$	$(0)(0) = 0$
2009	-2	2	$-2 - 1 = -3$	$2 - 3 = -1$	$(-3)(-1) = 3$
2010	3	4	$3 - 1 = 2$	$4 - 3 = 1$	$(2)(1) = 2$
2011	0	6	$0 - 1 = -1$	$6 - 3 = 3$	$(-1)(3) = -3$
2012	3	0	$3 - 1 = 2$	$0 - 3 = -3$	$(2)(-3) = -6$
Mean	1	3		**Sum**	**-4**

The $(X_i - \bar{X})$ column represents the differences between each return to Excelsior in the sample and the sample mean; similarly, the $(Y_i - \bar{Y})$ column represents the same calculations for Adirondack. The entries in the $(X_i - \bar{X})(Y_i - \bar{Y})$ column equal the product of the entries in the previous two columns. The sum of the $(X_i - \bar{X})(Y_i - \bar{Y})$ column gives the numerator in the sample covariance formula:

$$\sum_{i=1}^{n}(X_i - \bar{X})(Y_i - \bar{Y}) = -4$$

The denominator equals the sample size minus one, which is $5 - 1 = 4$. (Both samples have five elements, $n = 5$.) Therefore, the sample covariance equals

$$s_{XY} = \frac{\sum_{i=1}^{n}(X_i - \bar{X})(Y_i - \bar{Y})}{n-1}$$

$$= \frac{-4}{4} = -1$$

To calculate the sample correlation coefficient, divide the sample covariance by the product of the sample standard deviation of X and the sample standard deviation of Y:

$$r_{XY} = \frac{s_{XY}}{s_X s_Y}$$

You find the sample standard deviation of X by computing the sample variance of X and then taking the square root of the result (as I explain in Chapter 4). Table 5-2 shows the calculations for the sample variance of X.

Table 5-2   Computing the Sample Variance for Excelsior

Year	Excelsior Corp. Annual Return (percent)	$(X_i - \bar{X})$	$(X_i - \bar{X})^2$
2008	1	$1 - 1 = 0$	$(0)^2 = 0$
2009	-2	$-2 - 1 = -3$	$(-3)^2 = 9$
2010	3	$3 - 1 = 2$	$(2)^2 = 4$
2011	0	$0 - 1 = -1$	$(-1)^2 = 1$
2012	3	$3 - 1 = 2$	$(2)^2 = 4$
Mean	1	**Sum**	18

The $(X_i - \bar{X})$ column represents the differences between each return to Excelsior in the sample and the sample mean; the $(X_i - \bar{X})^2$ column represents the *squared* difference between each return to Excelsior and the sample mean. The sum of the $(X_i - \bar{X})^2$ column gives the numerator in the sample variance formula. You divide this number by the sample size minus one $(5 - 1 = 4)$ to get the sample variance of X:

$$s_X^2 = \frac{\sum_{i=1}^{n}(X_i - \bar{X})^2}{n-1}$$
$$= \frac{18}{4}$$
$$= 4.5$$

The sample standard deviation of X is the square root of 4.5, or $\sqrt{4.5} = 2.1213$.

Table 5-3 shows the calculations for the sample variance of Y.

Table 5-3   Computing the Sample Variance for Adirondack

Year	Adirondack Corp. Annual Return (percent)	$(Y_i - \bar{Y})$	$(Y_i - \bar{Y})^2$
2008	3	$3 - 3 = 0$	$(0)^2 = 0$
2009	2	$2 - 3 = -1$	$(-1)^2 = 1$
2010	4	$4 - 3 = 1$	$(1)^2 = 1$
2011	6	$6 - 3 = 3$	$(3)^2 = 9$
2012	0	$0 - 3 = -3$	$(-3)^2 = 9$
Mean	3	**Sum**	20

Based on the calculations in Table 5-3, the sample variance of Y equals

$$s_Y^2 = \frac{\sum\limits_{i=1}^{n}\left(Y_i - \bar{Y}\right)^2}{n-1}$$

$$= \frac{20}{4}$$

$$= 5$$

The sample standard deviation of Y equals the square root of 5, or $\sqrt{5} = 2.2361$.

Substituting these values into the sample correlation formula gives you

$$r_{XY} = \frac{s_{XY}}{s_X s_Y}$$

$$= \frac{-1}{(2.1213)(2.2361)}$$

$$= -0.2108$$

The negative result shows that there's a weak negative correlation between the stock returns of Excelsior and Adirondack. If two variables are *perfectly* negatively correlated (they *always* move in opposite directions), their correlation will be –1. If two variables are *independent* (unrelated to each other), their correlation will be 0. The correlation between the returns to Excelsior and Adirondack stock is a –0.2108, which indicates that the two variables show a slight tendency to move in opposite directions.

Population covariance and correlation coefficient

The population covariance measures the strength and the direction of the relationship between the elements of two populations. It's computed in a manner similar to the sample covariance.

You use the following formula to find the population covariance:

$$\sigma_{XY} = \frac{\sum\limits_{i=1}^{n}\left(X_i - \mu_X\right)\left(Y_i - \mu_Y\right)}{n}$$

The key terms here are

✔ σ_{XY} = the population covariance between variables X and Y

✔ μ_X = the population mean for X

✔ μ_Y = the population mean for Y

✔ n = the number of elements in both populations

✔ i = an *index* that assigns a number to each population element, ranging from 1 to n

✔ X_i = a single element in the population for X

✔ Y_i = a single element in the population for Y

✔ Σ = the uppercase Greek letter sigma that indicates a sum is being computed

The population correlation coefficient is based on the population covariance. You use the following formula to find the population correlation coefficient:

$$\rho_{XY} = \frac{\sigma_{XY}}{\sigma_X \sigma_Y}$$

The key terms here are

ρ_{XY} = the population correlation coefficient between variables X and Y

σ_{XY} = the population covariance between variables X and Y

σ_X = the population standard deviation of variable X

σ_Y = the population standard deviation of variable Y

For example, suppose that two new companies were created in 2008: Theta Corp. and Eta Corp. The returns to the two companies' stocks from 2008 to 2012 are shown in Table 5-4:

Table 5-4	Annual Returns to Theta and Eta	
Year	**Theta Corp. Annual Return (percent) (X)**	**Eta Corp. Annual Return (percent) (Y)**
2008	11	6
2009	9	5
2010	4	1
2011	2	9
2012	5	12

Because these companies have been in business only since 2008, each set of returns represents a *population* (the entire history of returns).

The population covariance and correlation between the returns to these stocks are computed as follows.

✔ The population mean of X is

$$\mu_X = \frac{\sum_{i=1}^{n} X_i}{n}$$

$$= \frac{(11+9+4+2+5)}{5}$$

$$= \frac{31}{5} = 6.2$$

The population mean is obtained by summing all the elements of the population and then dividing by the population size. In this case, the 5 population elements sum to 31, and the population size is 5. Dividing these numbers gives a population mean of 6.2.

✔ The population mean of Y is

$$\mu_Y = \frac{\sum_{i=1}^{n} Y_i}{n}$$

$$= \frac{(6+5+1+9+12)}{5}$$

$$= \frac{33}{5} = 6.6$$

Table 5-5 shows the remaining calculations for the population covariance:

Table 5-5	Computing the Population Covariance				
Year	Theta Corp. Annual Return (percent) (X)	Eta Corp. Annual Return (percent) (Y)	$(X_i - \mu_x)$	$(Y_i - \mu_y)$	$(X_i - \mu_x)(Y_i - \mu_y)$
2008	11	6	$11 - 6.2$ $= 4.8$	$6 - 6.6$ $= -0.6$	$(4.8)(-0.6)$ $= -2.88$
2009	9	5	$9 - 6.2$ $= 2.8$	$5 - 6.6$ $= -1.6$	$(2.8)(-1.6)$ $= -4.48$
2010	4	1	$4 - 6.2$ $= -2.2$	$1 - 6.6$ $= -5.6$	$(-2.2)(-5.6)$ $= 12.32$
2011	2	9	$2 - 6.2$ $= -4.2$	$9 - 6.6$ $= 2.4$	$(-4.2)(2.4)$ $= -10.08$
2012	5	12	$5 - 6.2$ $= -1.2$	$12 - 6.6$ $= 5.4$	$(-1.2)(5.4)$ $= -6.48$
Mean	6.2	6.6		Sum	-11.60

The sum of the $(X_i - \mu_X)(Y_i - \mu_Y)$ column gives the numerator in the population covariance formula:

$$\sum_{i=1}^{n}(X_i - \mu_X)(Y_i - \mu_Y) = -11.60$$

The denominator equals the population size, which is 5. Therefore, the population covariance equals

$$\sigma_{XY} = \frac{\sum_{i=1}^{n}(X_i - \mu_X)(Y_i - \mu_Y)}{n}$$
$$= \frac{-11.60}{5}$$
$$= -2.32$$

To calculate the population correlation coefficient, divide the population covariance by the product of the population standard deviation of X and the population standard deviation of Y:

$$\rho_{XY} = \frac{\sigma_{XY}}{\sigma_X \sigma_Y}$$

You find the population standard deviation of X by computing the population variance of X and then taking the square root of the result (as I explain in Chapter 4). Table 5-6 shows the calculations for the population variance of X.

Table 5-6	Computing the Population Variance for Theta		
Year	Theta Corp. Annual Return (%) (X)	$(X_i - \mu_X)$	$(X_i - \mu_X)^2$
2008	11	$11 - 6.2 = 4.8$	$(4.8)^2 = 23.04$
2009	9	$9 - 6.2 = 2.8$	$(2.8)^2 = 7.84$
2010	4	$4 - 6.2 = -2.2$	$(-2.2)^2 = 4.84$
2011	2	$2 - 6.2 = -4.2$	$(-4.2)^2 = 17.64$
2012	5	$5 - 6.2 = -1.2$	$(-1.2)^2 = 1.44$
Mean	6.2	**Sum**	54.80

The sum of the $(X_i - \mu_X)^2$ column gives the numerator in the population variance formula. You divide this number by the population size to get the population variance of X:

$$\sigma_X^2 = \frac{\sum_{i=1}^{n}(X_i - \mu_X)^2}{n}$$

$$= \frac{54.8}{5}$$

$$= 10.96$$

The population standard deviation of X is the square root of 10.96, or $\sqrt{10.96} = 3.3106$.

Table 5-7 shows the calculations for the population variance of Y.

Table 5-7	Computing the Population Variance for Eta Corporation		
Year	Eta Corp. Annual Return (percent) (Y)	$(Y_i - \mu_Y)$	$(Y_i - \mu_Y)^2$
2008	6	$6 - 6.6 = -0.6$	$(-0.6)^2 = 0.36$
2009	5	$5 - 6.6 = -1.6$	$(-1.6)^2 = 2.56$
2010	1	$1 - 6.6 = -5.6$	$(-5.6)^2 = 31.36$
2011	9	$9 - 6.6 = 2.4$	$(2.4)^2 = 5.76$
2012	12	$12 - 6.6 = 5.4$	$(5.4)^2 = 29.16$
Mean	6.6	Sum	69.2

Based on the calculations in Table 5-7, the population variance of Y equals

$$\sigma_Y^2 = \frac{\sum_{i=1}^{n}(Y_i - \mu_Y)^2}{n}$$

$$= \frac{69.2}{5}$$

$$= 13.84$$

The population standard deviation of Y equals the square root of 13.84, or $\sqrt{13.84} = 3.7202$.

Substituting these values into the population correlation formula gives you:

$$\rho_{XY} = \frac{\sigma_{XY}}{\sigma_X \sigma_Y}$$

$$= \frac{-2.32}{(3.3106)(3.7202)}$$

$$= -0.1884$$

The negative result shows that there's a weak negative correlation between the stock returns of Theta and Eta.

Comparing correlation and covariance

When trying to find the relationship between two variables, you see that the correlation coefficient has several advantages over the covariance, including the following:

- ✔ The covariance has no lower or upper limits, whereas the correlation coefficient ranges between –1 and 1, making it easier to interpret its meaning.

  In the example with the returns to Excelsior and Adirondack stock (in the earlier section "Sample covariance and correlation"), the covariance is –1. Although this negative number indicates a tendency for the stock returns to move in opposite directions, it's difficult to judge the *strength* of this relationship. On the other hand, the correlation coefficient is –0.2108; because the correlation coefficient ranges from –1 to 1, you can see that the relationship between the stock returns is negative but not very strong.

- ✔ Unlike the covariance, the value of the correlation isn't affected by the units in which X and Y are measured. For example, suppose that a sample of tuna is chosen from the catch of two different fishing boats. The covariance between the weights of the tuna caught by the two boats is computed. The value of the covariance is different if the weights are expressed in kilograms or in pounds; however, the correlation is the same whether weights are expressed in kilograms or pounds.

To illustrate the second point further, say you record a sample of the average temperatures (in Celsius and Fahrenheit) in two cities from 2008 to 2012 and come up with the following results.

Year	City 1 (Celsius)	City 2 (Celsius)	City 1 (Fahrenheit)	City 2 (Fahrenheit)
2008	0.0°C	–10.0°C	32.0°F	14.0°F
2009	20.0°C	15.0°C	68.0°F	59.0°F
2010	–8.0°C	22.0°C	17.6°F	71.6°F
2011	25.0°C	30.0°C	77.0°F	86.0°F
2012	14.0°C	25.0°C	57.2°F	77.0°F
Mean	10.2°C	16.4°C	50.4°F	61.5°F

Assume that X represents the temperature in City 1 and Y represents the temperature in City 2. Table 5-8 shows the calculations for the covariance between the temperatures in Celsius of both cities.

Year	City 1 (Celsius)	City 2 (Celsius)	$(X_i - \bar{X})$	$(Y_i - \bar{Y})$	$(X_i - \bar{X})(Y_i - \bar{Y})$
2008	0.0°C	−10.0°C	$\begin{aligned}0.0 - 10.2 \\ = -10.2\end{aligned}$	$\begin{aligned}-10.0 - 16.4 \\ = -26.4\end{aligned}$	$\begin{aligned}(-10.2)(-26.4) \\ = 269.3\end{aligned}$
2009	20.0°C	15.0°C	$\begin{aligned}20.0 - 10.2 \\ = 9.8\end{aligned}$	$\begin{aligned}15.0 - 16.4 \\ = -1.4\end{aligned}$	$\begin{aligned}(9.8)(-1.4) \\ = -13.7\end{aligned}$
2010	−8.0°C	22.0°C	$\begin{aligned}-8.0 - 10.2 \\ = -18.2\end{aligned}$	$\begin{aligned}22.0 - 16.4 \\ = 5.6\end{aligned}$	$\begin{aligned}(-18.2)(5.6) \\ = -101.9\end{aligned}$
2011	25.0°C	30.0°C	$\begin{aligned}25.0 - 10.2 \\ = 14.8\end{aligned}$	$\begin{aligned}30.0 - 16.4 \\ = 13.6\end{aligned}$	$\begin{aligned}(14.8)(13.6) \\ = 201.3\end{aligned}$
2012	14.0°C	25.0°C	$\begin{aligned}14.0 - 10.2 \\ = 3.8\end{aligned}$	$\begin{aligned}25.0 - 16.4 \\ = 8.6\end{aligned}$	$\begin{aligned}(3.8)(8.6) \\ = 32.7\end{aligned}$
Mean	**10.2°C**	**16.4°C**		**Sum**	**387.6**

Table 5-8   Covariance between Celsius Temperatures in City 1 and City 2

The $(X_i - \bar{X})$ column represents the differences between each temperature in City 1 and the sample mean. The $(Y_i - \bar{Y})$ column represents the differences between each temperature in City 2 and the sample mean. The $(X_i - \bar{X})(Y_i - \bar{Y})$ column is simply the product of the $(X_i - \bar{X})$ column and the $(Y_i - \bar{Y})$ column. The sum of the $(X_i - \bar{X})(Y_i - \bar{Y})$ column gives the numerator in the sample covariance formula, which is 387.6.

$$\sum_{i=1}^{n}(X_i - \bar{X})(Y_i - \bar{Y}) = 387.6$$

The denominator equals the sample size minus one, which is 5 – 1 = 4 (because both samples have five elements, n = 5.) Therefore, the sample covariance equals

$$S_{XY} = \frac{\sum_{i=1}^{n}(X_i - \bar{X})(Y_i - \bar{Y})}{n-1}$$
$$= \frac{387.6}{4}$$
$$= 96.9$$

You find the sample standard deviation of X by computing the sample variance of X and then taking the square root of the result (see Chapter 4). Table 5-11 shows the calculations for the sample variance of X (Celsius temperatures for City 1):

Table 5-9	Sample Variance of *City 1*		
Year	City 1 (Celsius)	$\left(X_i - \bar{X}\right)$	$\left(X_i - \bar{X}\right)^2$
2008	0.0°C	0.0 – 10.2 = –10.2	$(-10.2)^2 = 104.0$
2009	20.0°C	20.0 – 10.2 = 9.8	$(9.8)^2 = 96.0$
2010	–8.0°C	–8.0 – 10.2 = –18.2	$(-18.2)^2 = 331.2$
2011	25.0°C	25.0 – 10.2 = 14.8	$(14.8)^2 = 219.0$
2012	14.0°C	14.0 – 10.2 = 3.8	$(3.8)^2 = 14.4$
Mean	**10.2°C**	**Sum**	**764.8**

To finish the calculation for the sample variance of X, you divide the sum of the terms in the $\left(X_i - \bar{X}\right)^2$ column by the sample size minus one, like so:

$$s_X^2 = \frac{\sum_{i=1}^{n}\left(X_i - \bar{X}\right)^2}{n-1}$$
$$= \frac{764.8}{4}$$
$$= 191.2$$

The sample standard deviation is the square root of the sample variance, or $\sqrt{191.2} = 13.8275$.

Following the same steps, you can find the sample variance of Y with the calculations in Table 5-10.

Table 5-10	Sample Variance of *City 2*		
Year	City 2 (C)	$\left(Y_i - \bar{Y}\right)$	$\left(Y_i - \bar{Y}\right)^2$
2008	–10.0	–10.0 – 16.4 = –26.4	$(-26.4)^2 = 697.0$
2009	15.0	15.0 – 16.4 = –1.4	$(-1.4)^2 = 2.0$
2010	22.0	22.0 – 16.4 = 5.6	$(5.6)^2 = 31.4$
2011	30.0	30.0 – 16.4 = 13.6	$(13.6)^2 = 185.0$
2012	25.0	25.0 – 16.4 = 8.6	$(8.6)^2 = 74.0$
Mean	**16.4**	**Sum**	**989.2**

To get the sample variance, divide the sum of the terms in the $\left(Y_i - \bar{Y}\right)^2$ column by the sample size minus one:

$$s_Y^2 = \frac{\sum_{i=1}^{n}(Y_i - \bar{Y})^2}{n-1}$$
$$= \frac{989.2}{4}$$
$$= 247.3$$

The sample standard deviation is the square root of the sample variance, or $\sqrt{247.3} = 15.7258$.

Next, substitute these values into the sample correlation formula:

$$r_{XY} = \frac{s_{XY}}{s_X s_Y}$$
$$= \frac{96.9}{(13.8275)(15.7258)}$$
$$= 0.4456$$

Repeating these same calculations for the temperatures in Fahrenheit, the covariance is 313.96 (compared with 96.9 when measured in Celsius) and the correlation remains at 0.4456. The covariance increases with Fahrenheit temperatures because the magnitude of the temperatures is greater, whereas the correlation isn't affected. The fact that the results depend on the units involved is one of the major drawbacks of using covariance instead of correlation.

Interpreting the Correlation Coefficient

Interpreting the correlation coefficient is easier than interpreting the covariance. Consider these examples:

✔ A correlation of 0.9 (close to the maximum value of 1.0) indicates a strong positive relationship between X and Y; when X increases, Y nearly always increases, and vice versa.

A correlation of 0.2 (close to zero) indicates a weak positive relationship; when X increases, Y is somewhat more likely to increase than decrease, and vice versa.

✔ A correlation of –0.9 (close to the minimum value of –1.0) indicates a strong negative relationship between X and Y. Most of the time, when X increases, Y decreases; most of the time, when X decreases, Y increases.

A correlation of –0.2 (close to zero) indicates a weak negative relationship; when X increases, Y is somewhat more likely to decrease than increase, and vice versa.

✔ A correlation of 0 indicates that X and Y are unrelated. When X increases or decreases, it has no direct effect on Y increasing or decreasing, and vice versa.

In the Fahrenheit and Celsius temperatures example in the previous section, the covariance was 96.9 for Celsius temperatures and 313.96 for Fahrenheit temperatures. Although the positive values indicate that the temperatures in both cities tend to increase or decrease at the same time, using the covariance measure alone makes it difficult to judge the *strength* of this relationship. On the other hand, the correlation for both Celsius and Fahrenheit temperatures was 0.4456, showing that a moderately strong, positive relationship exists between the temperatures in the two cities, whether measured in Celsius or Fahrenheit degrees.

In the following sections, you see a type of graph known as a *scatter plot* to illustrate the relationship between two different variables. An extremely important application of correlation is introduced; correlation can be used to show the degree of diversification that is present in a portfolio of stocks. In other words, the correlation can be used to determine how much the addition of a stock to a portfolio will affect the overall risk of the portfolio.

Showing the relationship between two variables

As I discuss in detail in Chapter 2, a *scatterplot* is a special type of graph that shows the relationship between two variables X and Y. The values of X are shown on the horizontal axis, and the values of Y are shown on the vertical axis.

Suppose that X represents a corporation's sales and Y represents its profits. Then X and Y would normally have a positive correlation between them, because higher sales tend to be associated with higher profits and vice versa. Figure 5-1 shows the relationship between two variables with a strong positive correlation.

Each point on the graph represents a corporation's sales (X) and its profits (Y) during a given year. The graph shows that as X increases, there's a strong tendency for Y to also increase. The straight line is known as a *trend line*. A trend line shows the direction of the points on a scatter plot. It can have a positive slope, a negative slope, or a zero slope (which means that the line is perfectly flat.) In this example, the trend line is positively sloped, which indicates that the correlation between X and Y is also positive. Because the points are extremely close to the trend line, the relationship between X and Y is very strong. With a weaker relationship, the points would be more scattered around the trend line.

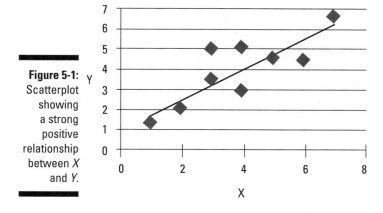

Figure 5-1:
Scatterplot
showing
a strong
positive
relationship
between *X*
and *Y*.

Suppose that *X* represents a corporation's costs of production and *Y* represents its profits; then *X* and *Y* would normally have a negative correlation between them, because higher costs tend to be associated with lower profits and vice versa. Figure 5-2 shows the relationship between two variables with a strong negative correlation.

Each point on the graph represents a corporation's costs of production (*X*) and its profits (*Y*) during a given year. The graph shows that as *X* increases, there's a strong tendency for *Y* to decrease. The trend line has a negative slope, which indicates that the correlation between *X* and *Y* is negative.

By contrast, suppose that *X* represents the average daily temperature and *Y* represents a corporation's profits. Unless the corporation produces goods and services with a seasonal demand, these two variables are likely unrelated. Therefore, the correlation between *X* and *Y* will also be close to zero.

Figure 5-2:
Scatterplot
showing
a strong
negative
relationship
between *X*
and *Y*.

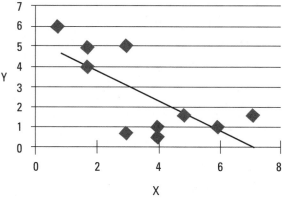

Figure 5-3 shows the relationship between two unrelated variables.

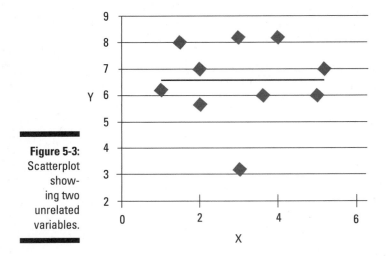

Figure 5-3:
Scatterplot show-ing two unrelated variables.

Each point on the graph represents the average daily temperature (*X*) and a corporation's profits (*Y*) during a given year. The graph shows that as *X* increases, *Y* sometimes increases and sometimes decreases; no real pattern occurs. The trend line is almost perfectly flat, which indicates that the correlation between *X* and *Y* is very close to zero.

Application: Correlation and the benefits of diversification

You can measure the risk of a stock with the standard deviation of its returns. The greater the standard deviation, the further away the returns are from the mean on average (that is, the more "spread out" they are.) This indicates more uncertainty over the actual return during a given year, so the risk is greater. You can measure the diversification benefits of adding a stock to a portfolio with the correlation coefficient. The lower the correlation coefficient between two stocks, the *greater* is the reduction in risk and therefore the greater are the benefits of diversification.

For a portfolio of stocks, the risk depends not only on the standard deviations of the individual stocks but also on the *correlations* between the stocks. With low or negative correlations, the portfolio can experience significant reductions in risk, which occurs because losses to some stocks tend to be offset by gains by other stocks at any given time. As a result, the variability of the portfolio's returns tends to be lower than the variability of the returns to the individual stocks.

The following data is a sample of returns to the stocks of Hilo, Inc., and Lohi Corp. during the past ten years.

Year	Hilo	Lohi
2003	0.03	0.10
2004	0.06	0.10
2005	0.07	0.08
2006	0.09	0.05
2007	0.08	0.04
2008	0.10	0.07
2009	0.09	0.01
2010	0.04	0.02
2011	0.02	0.10
2012	0.06	0.13

Table 5-11 summarizes the sample mean, variance, standard deviation, and coefficient of variation of the stock returns.

Table 5-11	Summary Measures for Hilo and Lohi	
	Hilo	**Lohi**
Mean	0.0640	0.0700
Variance	0.0007	0.0015
Standard deviation	0.0272	0.0392
Coefficient of variation (CV)	42.44 percent	55.94 percent

The sample covariance between the stocks is –0.0004, and the sample correlation coefficient is –0.4179.

Assume that an investor purchased $100,000 of each stock for his portfolio at the start of 2003. The returns to the portfolio during this sample period are listed here.

Year	Portfolio
2003	0.065
2004	0.080
2005	0.075
2006	0.070
2007	0.060
2008	0.085
2009	0.050
2010	0.030
2011	0.060
2012	0.095

Because the portfolio is composed of 50 percent Hilo stock and 50 percent Lohi stock, you calculate the returns to the portfolio by multiplying the returns to each individual stock by 0.5 and combining the results, like so:

Portfolio return = 0.5(return to Hilo) + 0.5(return to Lohi)

For example, in 2003, the portfolio return is computed as follows:

Portfolio return = 0.5(0.03) + 0.5(0.10) = 0.065. Table 5-12 summarizes the sample mean, variance, standard deviation, and coefficient of variation of the portfolio returns.

Table 5-12	Portfolio Summary Measures
	Portfolio
Mean	0.0670
Variance	0.0003
Standard deviation	0.0186
Coefficient of variation (CV)	27.74 percent

The mean return to the portfolio is halfway between the mean returns to Hilo (0.0640) and Lohi (0.0700). The risk of the portfolio, as measured by the standard deviation of the returns, is only 0.0186 compared with Hilo (0.0272) and Lohi (0.0392). As a result, the portfolio's coefficient of variation is only 27.74 percent compared with Hilo at 42.442 percent and Lohi at 55.94 percent.

This substantial reduction in risk is due to the fact that the portfolio is well diversified, as seen by the negative correlation (–0.4179) between the returns to the two stocks.

Part II
Probability Theory and Probability Distributions

Top 4 Advantages to Normal Distribution

Modeling the properties of asset returns requires the choice of an appropriate *probability distribution*. This distribution must have properties that match up with actual historical experience with asset returns. One of the most popular choices for this type of modeling is the *normal* distribution.

The normal distribution offers several advantages in this case:

✔ It's a *continuous* distribution, defined for an infinite number of values. This is important since the number of different returns that can occur is also infinite.

✔ It's *symmetrical* about the mean; there is a balance between the probability of returns that are below the mean and returns that are above the mean.

✔ The probability of extreme outcomes (outcomes well above or below the mean) is quite low; for financial returns, these occur quite infrequently.

✔ It's *additive*; the sum of normal random variables is also normal. This means that if the returns to a single asset are normal, the returns to a portfolio of assets are also normal.

Learn about normal distribution and more at www.dummies.com/extras/businessstatistics.

In this part...

- ✔ Review the foundations of probability theory; this is the foundation of all statistical analysis.

- ✔ Use random variables and probability distributions to determine if a random event will take place.

- ✔ Use binomial distribution to compute probabilities for processes where only one of two possible outcomes may occur. This could be something as simple as flipping a coin several times to see if the coin turns up heads or tails on each flip, or as complicated as a stock price increase.

- ✔ Describe the rates of return to financial assets, the distribution of corporate profits, and the prices of key commodities (such as oil) using normal distribution.

- ✔ Understand two key areas of statistics: sampling and sampling distributions. Most statistical analysis is based on samples randomly drawn from a population.

Chapter 6

Probability Theory: Measuring the Likelihood of Events

. . . .

In This Chapter

▶ Understanding sets and how they're related to each other

▶ Determining the possible outcomes

▶ Applying types of probabilities

▶ Using rules of probability

. . . .

*P*robability theory is a branch of mathematics that focuses on the analysis of random events and is the foundation of all statistical analysis. You can use probability theory to model a large number of situations that arise in practice. For example, you can use probability theory to estimate how likely it is that a new product will succeed in the marketplace, identify appropriate prices for an insurance company to charge its customers, and more.

This chapter reviews the mathematical foundations of probability theory, such as sets and events, defines types of probabilities, and introduces the rules of probability.

Working with Sets

Probability theory is based on the notion of a *set* — a collection of objects, such as numbers, letters, colors, names, and so on, individually called *elements*. You use mathematical operations, such as membership, subset, union, intersection, and complement, used to create new sets from existing ones according to specific rules. For example, you use the operation union to combine two different sets into one new set that contains all the elements from both sets. I explore each of these operations in the following sections.

Membership

Membership indicates whether an element belongs to a set. For example, suppose that set A contains the elements 1 through 6 (the numbers on a die), which is shown mathematically as $A = \{1, 2, 3, 4, 5, 6\}$.

As you can see, the elements or *members* in a set are listed only once, are separated by commas, and are enclosed within *braces:* { }.

In this example, the element 3 belongs to set A. To indicate that an element is part of a set, you use the symbol $\in$: $3 \in A$.

On the other hand, to indicate that an element is *not* part of a set, you use the symbol $\notin$. So in this case, the element 7 doesn't belong to set A, or $7 \notin A$, because it's not listed in the definition (between the braces) of set A.

Subset

A *subset* is a set that's completely contained within a larger set. For example, suppose that sets A and B are defined as follows:

$A = \{1, 2, 3, 4, 5, 6\}$

$B = \{1, 2, 3, 4, 5, 6, 7, 8, 9, 10\}$

Set A represents the numbers on a die; set B represents the numbers from 1 to 10. In this example, set A is a *subset* of set B because every element of set A is also an element of set B. The symbol $\subset$ represents that one set is a subset of another, as in $A \subset B$.

A *Venn diagram* is used to illustrate the relationship between sets. Sets are represented as circles so that it's easy to see how they're related to each other. If sets overlap, the area common to both sets is shaded.

The Venn diagram in Figure 6-1 shows the relationship between sets A and B. The diagram shows that set A is completely contained within set B — that is, A is a subset of B. A is completely shaded because the area of overlap between A and B is A itself.

As another example, suppose that set C contains the elements 1, 2, 3, 4, 5, and 6 (the numbers on a die), whereas set D contains the elements 1, 2, 3 and 7:

$D = \{1, 2, 3, 7\}$

$C = \{1, 2, 3, 4, 5, 6\}$

Set D is *not* a subset of set C because the element 7 belongs to set D but *not* to set C; in mathematical terms, $D \not\subseteq C$.

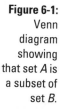

Figure 6-1:
Venn
diagram
showing
that set *A* is
a subset of
set *B*.

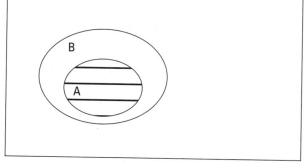

Illustration by Wiley, Composition Services Graphics

Union

Two sets can be combined with a mathematical operation known as *union*. The union of two sets *A* and *B* is a set that contains the following:

- All the elements in set *A*
- All the elements in set *B*

This definition also includes the elements that belong to *both* sets. As an example, suppose that set *A* contains all the students at a university who are majoring in mathematics; set *B* contains all the students who are majoring in finance. The union of sets *A* and *B* contains all students who are majoring in math *and* all students who are majoring in finance *and* all students who are majoring in *both* (for example, double majors).

As another example, suppose that sets *A* and *B* are defined as follows:

$A = \{2, 4, 6\}$

$B = \{1, 2, 3, 4\}$

The union of these sets is all the numbers on the face of a die except 5:

$A \cup B = \{1, 2, 3, 4, 6\}$

The symbol $\cup$ represents union.

The union shows all elements that appear in set *A*, set *B*, or both. Note that even though elements 2 and 4 appear in both sets *A* and *B*, they're not listed twice in the union; a set contains only *unique* values.

The Venn diagram in Figure 6-2 shows the relationship between sets *A* and *B*. The shaded region in the diagram represents the union.

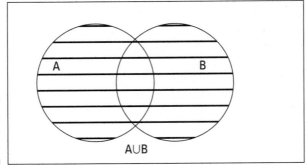

Figure 6-2:
Union of two
sets.

Illustration by Wiley, Composition Services Graphics

Note: The order in which you write the sets is irrelevant; for example, $B \cup A = A \cup B$.

Intersection

The *intersection* of two sets A and B is a set containing the elements that are in *both* sets. For example, suppose that sets A and B are defined as follows:

$A = \{1, 3, 5, 7\}$

$B = \{3, 6, 7\}$

The intersection of these sets is $A \cap B = \{3, 7\}$.

The intersection of A and B contains the elements 3 and 7 because these elements belong to *both* A and B. The symbol $\cap$ represents intersection.

The Venn diagram in Figure 6-3 shows the relationship between A and B. The shaded region in the diagram represents the intersection of these sets.

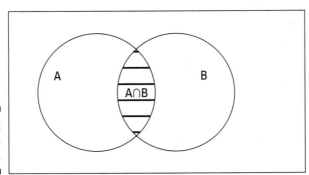

Figure 6-3:
Intersection
of two sets.

Illustration by Wiley, Composition Services Graphics

As another example, suppose that set *C* contains the elements 2, 4, 6:

$A = \{1, 3, 5, 7\}$

$C = \{2, 4, 6\}$

The intersection of these sets is $A \cap C = \{\ \}$.

The intersection of sets *A* and *C* contains *no elements* because the sets don't have any of the same elements. The set containing no elements, or { }, is known as an *empty set*. Two sets that have no elements in common are said to be *mutually exclusive*.

The Venn diagram in Figure 6-4 shows the relationship between sets *A* and *C*. This diagram has no shaded region because the intersection of sets *A* and *C* contains no elements.

Figure 6-4:
An inter-
section
containing
no elements
between
two sets.

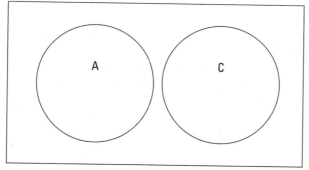

Illustration by Wiley, Composition Services Graphics

Complement

The mathematical operation *complement* is based on the notion of a *universal set* or *sample space* — all the elements a set may contain. For example, suppose that you roll a single die; the number that turns up may be any whole number between 1 and 6. Assume that set *A* contains the odd numbers that may turn up when you roll a die, and set *B* contains the even numbers:

$A = \{1, 3, 5\}$

$B = \{2, 4, 6\}$

In this case, the sample space contains all possible numbers that may turn up when you roll the die:

$S = \{1, 2, 3, 4, 5, 6\}$

The complement of set A is the set of all numbers that are elements of the sample space but *not* elements of A:

$$A^C = \{2, 4, 6\}$$

A^C is the set "A complement." It contains the elements 2, 4, and 6 because they *don't* belong to set A, and they *do* belong to the sample space.

Note that elements such as 7, 8, 9, and so on aren't elements of A^C because they're not elements of set A, but they're also not elements of the sample space.

The complement of A is shown in the Venn diagram in Figure 6-5. The shaded region shows all the elements in the sample space that don't belong to set A.

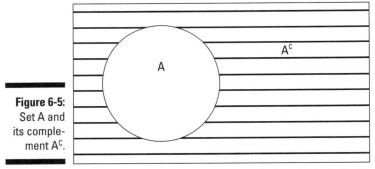

Figure 6-5: Set A and its complement A^C.

Illustration by Wiley, Composition Services Graphics

Similarly, the complement of B is $B^C = \{1, 3, 5\}$.

Betting on Uncertain Outcomes

Probability theory is based on the premise that a process generates uncertain (random) outcomes. This process is sometimes known as a *random experiment,* such as the following examples:

- ✔ A roulette wheel is spun. The outcome can be a 0, a 00 ("double zero"), or any number between 1 and 36.
- ✔ A lottery drawing results in a single winning number being chosen.
- ✔ A futures contract trades throughout the day, resulting in a settlement price at the close of trading.

In each case, the outcome isn't known in advance. Using probability, you can determine the likelihood of a specific outcome, such as the likelihood of getting an even number from a single spin of a roulette wheel.

In this section, I introduce several key terms, along with an introduction to computing probabilities.

The sample space: Everything that can happen

A *sample space* is another name for the universal set (described in the earlier section "Complement"); it contains all the outcomes that can result from a random experiment. For example, suppose you flip a coin two times. The possible outcomes of this random experiment are:

- ✔ Heads followed by heads (HH)
- ✔ Heads followed by tails (HT)
- ✔ Tails followed by heads (TH)
- ✔ Tails followed by tails (TT)

The sample space for this random experiment is S = {HH, HT, TH, TT}. It includes all the possible outcomes.

Event: One possible outcome

An *event* is one possible outcome of a random experiment. More formally, it is a *subset* of the sample space. For example, in the coin-flipping, the event E = "2 tails turn up." Event E is a set containing the element TT, or in mathematical terms, E = {TT}.

Event E is a subset of the sample space because it's completely contained within the sample space. As another example, the event F = "at least 1 head turns up." Event F is a set containing the elements HH, HT, TH, or F = {HH, HT, TH}.

In some cases, events may be related to each other. Two key ways in which events may be related to each other are known as mutually exclusive and independent.

These are described in the following section.

Mutually exclusive events

Two events are said to be *mutually exclusive* if they can't both happen at the same time. Here are two events that are mutually exclusive:

> A = The roll of a die is odd.

> B = The roll of a die is even.

Clearly, the roll of a die must result in a number that is either odd or even; it can't be both. Therefore, events A and B are mutually exclusive.

As another example, based on the coin-flipping experiment, suppose that two events are defined:

> G = Two heads turn up.

> H = Two tails turn up.

It's impossible for *both* two heads to turn up *and* two tails to turn up. This means that G and H are mutually exclusive. This result can be demonstrated using sets as follows:

G = {HH} and H = {TT}. These events have no elements in common; their intersection is the *empty set* $G \cap H = \{ \ \}$.

The probability of the empty set is zero; therefore, the event that both G and H occur is *impossible*. This means that G and H are mutually exclusive.

Independent events

Two events A and B are said to be *independent* if the outcome of event A doesn't affect the outcome of event B and vice versa. For example, suppose that based on the coin-flipping experiment, event A is defined as the event that the first flip is a head, and event B is defined as the event that the second flip is a head. In other words:

> A = {HH, HT}

> B = {HH, TH}

Because the outcome of the first flip has no influence over the outcome of the second flip, events A and B are *independent* events. (See a more formal test of independence in the next section.)

Note that A and B are *not* mutually exclusive; both A and B can occur.

Computing probabilities of events

If a sample space contains elements that are all equally likely to occur, then computing the probabilities of events is straightforward. For example, for the coin-flipping experiment in the earlier sections "The sample space: Everything that can happen" and "Event: One possible outcome," these probabilities exist:

- ✔ $P(HH) = 0.25$
- ✔ $P(HT) = 0.25$
- ✔ $P(TH) = 0.25$
- ✔ $P(TT) = 0.25$

For example, the probability of getting two consecutive heads is ¼ (which equals 0.25.) This is because HH is one of four possible outcomes when a coin is flipped twice. Furthermore, each outcome is equally likely to occur (because heads and tails are equally likely). Therefore, each outcome has a probability of ¼ = 0.25.

> One possible outcome ÷ 4 possibilities = 0.25.

As an example, suppose that the event K is defined as "at least one tail turns up." Then event K contains the elements HT, TH and TT, or K = {HT, TH, TT}.

You find the probability of event K with this formula:

$$P(K) = \frac{\text{elements in } K}{\text{elements in } S}$$

Because event K contains three elements and the total number of elements in the sample space is four, $P(K) = 3/4 = 0.75$.

Based on this formula, the probability of the empty set is 0, and the probability of the entire sample space is 1. For example, suppose that event A is an impossible event. It is represented by a set containing no elements (the empty set). The sample space contains the elements 1, 2, and 3. The probability of A is, therefore,

$$P(A) = \frac{\text{elements in } A}{\text{elements in } S} = \frac{0}{3} = 0$$

The probability of S is:

$$P(S) = \frac{\text{elements in } S}{\text{elements in } S} = \frac{3}{3} = 1$$

Looking at Types of Probabilities

The three basic types of probabilities are:

  ✔ **Unconditional (marginal) probabilities:** When events are independent

  ✔ **Joint probabilities:** When two things happen at once

  ✔ **Conditional probabilities:** When one event depends on another

In this section, you find out about each of these types of probabilities, and you also discover how you can use conditional probabilities to determine whether two events are independent.

Unconditional (marginal) probabilities: When events are independent

The *unconditional (marginal) probability* of an event is found as a row total or a column total in a joint probability table. As an example, Table 6-1 is a joint probability table, representing the distribution of students in a business school according to major and whether they're working on a bachelor's degree or a master's degree. In this section, I show you how to use data like this to find unconditional probabilities.

Table 6-1	Joint Probability Table Showing the Distribution of Business Students			
	Majoring in Finance	**Majoring in Accounting**	**Majoring in Marketing**	**Total**
Bachelor's degree	0.26	0.36	0.18	**0.80**
Master's degree	0.09	0.07	0.04	**0.20**
Total	**0.35**	**0.43**	**0.22**	**1.00**

Based on Table 6-1, the following events are defined:

  ✔ *B* = pursuing a bachelor's degree

  ✔ *M* = pursuing a master's degree

  ✔ *F* = majoring in finance

✔ A = majoring in accounting

✔ T = majoring in marketing

You can find the unconditional probabilities of the following events directly from Table 6-1:

✔ $P(B)$ = the probability of pursuing a bachelor's degree

✔ $P(M)$ = the probability of pursuing a master's degree

✔ $P(F)$ = the probability of majoring in finance

✔ $P(A)$ = the probability of majoring in accounting

✔ $P(T)$ = the probability of majoring in marketing

Say you want to find the probability that a randomly chosen business student is pursuing a bachelor's degree. In other words, you want to calculate $P(B)$.

Referring to Table 6-1, you look at the first row (which refers to students pursuing their bachelor's degrees). The row total is 0.80. This is the probability that a randomly chosen student is pursuing a bachelor's degree.

Suppose you want to know the probability that a randomly chosen student is majoring in finance. In other words, you want to calculate $P(F)$.

Referring to Table 6-1, you look at the first column (which refers to students majoring in finance). The column total is 0.35. This is the probability that a randomly chosen student is majoring in finance.

You can find the remaining unconditional probabilities in the same way. These are:

$P(M) = 0.20$

$P(A) = 0.43$

$P(T) = 0.22$

Joint probabilities: When two things happen at once

The probability that two different events occur at the same time is known as a *joint probability*. For example, the probability that a student is working on a bachelor's degree *and* is majoring in finance is a joint probability.

As you study Table 6-1, you can see that the intersection of two different events can determine joint probabilities. For example, to find the probability that a randomly chosen business student is pursuing a bachelor's degree *and* is majoring in finance, take the intersection of events B and F. This equals $P(B \cap F) = 0.26$.

You find the remaining joint probabilities in the same way:

$P(B \cap A) = 0.36$

$P(B \cap T) = 0.18$

$P(M \cap F) = 0.09$

$P(M \cap A) = 0.07$

$P(M \cap T) = 0.04$

Conditional probabilities: When one event depends on another

The *conditional probability* of an event is defined as the probability of an event *given that* another event has occurred. For example, the probability that a student is working on a bachelor's degree *given that* he or she is majoring in accounting is a conditional probability. This is written as follows:

$P(B \mid A)$

The symbol "|" is used to indicate a conditional probability. (You pronounce this expression as "the probability of B *given* A.")

To find the conditional probability of an event, you set up the ratio of a joint probability to an unconditional (marginal) probability (see previous sections on these types of probabilities). For example, say you want to find out what the probability is that a student who's known to be pursuing a bachelor's degree is majoring in marketing. Referring to Table 6-1, you first calculate the joint probability of pursuing a bachelor's degree and majoring in marketing, as follows:

$P(B \cap T) = 0.18$

Then you find that the unconditional probability of pursuing a bachelor's degree equals $P(B) = 0.80$. Therefore,

$$\frac{P(B \cap T)}{P(B)} = \frac{0.18}{0.80} = 0.225$$

As another example, to find the probability that an accounting major is pursuing a master's degree you take the joint probability of these two events:

$P(M \cap A) = 0.07$

The unconditional probability of majoring in accounting equals $P(A) = 0.43$. Therefore,

$$P(M \mid A) = \frac{P(M \cap A)}{P(A)} = \frac{0.07}{0.43} = 0.163$$

Determining independence of events

You can use conditional probabilities to determine whether two events are independent. Two events are independent if the probability of one event occurring doesn't influence the probability of the other occurring, and vice versa.

To prove independence, the following two conditions must be met:

$P(A|B) = P(A)$

$P(B|B) = P(B)$

Using the business students example from the earlier section "Joint probabilities: When two things happen at once" and referring to Table 6-1, you can determine whether the events "majoring in accounting" (A) and "pursuing a bachelor's degree" (B) are independent events.

The first step is to compute the conditional probabilities $P(A|B)$ and $P(B|A)$:The joint probability of events A and B is $P(A \cap B) = 0.36$.

The unconditional probabilities of events A and B are

$P(A) = 0.43$

$P(B) = 0.80$

Therefore,

$$P(A \mid B) = \frac{P(A \cap B)}{P(B)} = \frac{0.36}{0.80} = 0.45$$

$$P(B \mid A) = \frac{P(A \cap B)}{P(A)} = \frac{0.36}{0.43} = 0.84$$

because $P(A \mid B)$ must equal $P(A)$ *and* $P(B \mid A)$ must equal $P(B)$ for the two events to be independent. The results show that $P(A \mid B) = 0.45$, $P(A) = 0.43$, $P(B \mid A) = 0.84$, and $P(B) = 0.80$, so *both* conditions fail. Events A and B are *not* independent of each other; in other words, they're *dependent* on each other. Therefore, the decision to pursue a bachelor's or a master's degree appears to influence the choice of major.

Following the Rules: Computing Probabilities

In addition to computing joint, conditional, and unconditional probabilities (discussed in the previous sections), the following three rules can help you determine other probabilities:

 ✔ The **addition rule** shows the probability of the union of two events.

 ✔ The **complement rule** determines the probability of the complement of an event.

 ✔ The **multiplication rule** identifies the probability of the intersection of events.

I discuss these three rules and how to use them in the following sections.

Addition rule

You use the addition rule to compute the probability of the union of two events. Mathematically speaking, for events A and B, the addition rule states that $P(A \cup B) = P(A) + P(B) - P(A \cap B)$.

This shows that the probability of the union of events A and B equals the sum of the probability of A and the probability of B, from which the probability of *both* events is subtracted. Subtracting the probability of both events is necessary to avoid to problem of *double-counting*. This is shown in the following example:

Suppose that event A contains the elements 1, 2, 3 and event B contains the elements 3, 4, 5. The sample space contains the elements 1, 2, 3, 4, 5.

$$A = \{1,2,3\}$$

$$B = \{3,4,5\}$$

$$S = \{1,2,3,4,5\}$$

The corresponding probabilities are:

$$P(A) = 3/5$$

$$P(B) = 3/5$$

$$P(S) = 5/5 = 1$$

The union of A and B contains all the elements in the sample space:

$$A \cup B = \{1,2,3\} \cup \{3,4,5\} = \{1,2,3,4,5\} = S$$

As a result, the probability of A union B equals 1. (Recall that the sample space always has a probability of 1.) If you simply combine the probabilities of A and B, though, you will get a surprising result; they sum to 6/5, which is greater than one.

$$P(A) + P(B) = 3/5 + 3/5 = 6/5$$

This result occurs because the element 3 appears in both A and B:

$$A \cap B = \{3\}$$

The probability of 3 was counted *twice*, one in set A and once in set B, which accounts for the sum of the probabilities being greater than one. By subtracting the probability of the element 3, the correct probability of one is found.

$$P(A \cup B) = P(A) + P(B) - P(A \cap B)$$

$$P(A \cup B) = 3/5 + 3/5 - 1/5 = 5/5 = 1$$

Table 6-2 shows the distribution of coffees (measured in pounds) the Big Bean Corporation produces during a given day.

Table 6-2	Joint Probability Distribution for Coffee Styles			
	Special Reserve Blend (S)	**Kona Hawaii Blend (K)**	**Aromatic Blend (A)**	**Total**
Decaffeinated (D)	0.12	0.80	0.22	0.42
Regular (R)	0.24	0.12	0.22	0.58
Total	0.36	0.20	0.44	1.00

If you choose a pound of coffee randomly from the daily output of the Big Bean Corporation, what's the probability that it's either the *Special Reserve Blend (S)* or the *Regular (R)* (or both)?

In this example, you use the addition rule because you're being asked to compute the probability of a union. You combine the probability of S with the probability of R, subtracting the intersection between them to avoid the problem of double-counting.

$$P(S \cup R) = P(S) + P(R) - P(S \cap R)$$

From Table 6-2, you can determine that $P(S) = 0.36$; that $P(R) = 0.58$; $P(S \cap R) = 0.24$. Therefore,

$$P(S \cup R) = P(S) + P(R) - P(S \cap R)$$
$$= 0.36 + 0.58 - 0.24 = 0.70$$

Seventy percent of the coffee produced by Big Bean is either the special reserve blend, regular, or both.

When two events A and B are *mutually exclusive* (that is, they can't both occur at the same time), the addition rule simplifies to $P(A \cup B) = P(A) + P(B)$ because $P(A \cap B) = 0$.

For example, if you choose a pound of coffee randomly from the daily output of the Big Bean Corporation, what's the probability that it's either the *Kona Hawaii Blend (K)* or the *Aromatic Blend (A)*?

Because a pound of coffee can't be both the Kona Hawaii Blend *and* the Aromatic Blend, events K and A are mutually exclusive. This means that you can use the simplified version of the addition rule:

$$P(K \cup A) = P(K) + P(A)$$

$$P(K \cup A) = 0.20 + 0.44 = 0.64$$

Complement rule

The complement rule is expressed as follows:

$$P(A^C) = 1 - P(A)$$

A^C is the complement of event A.

Two events are said to be complements if they are mutually exclusive *and* their union equals the entire sample space. Here's an example: Suppose that an experiment consists of choosing a single card from a standard deck. Event A = "the card is red." Event B = "the card is black." Events A and B are complements because A and B are mutually exclusive (no card can be *both* red and black). The union of A and B is the sample space (the entire deck, because all cards must be either red or black, so the union of A and B equals the entire sample space.)

In the Big Bean example from the previous section, the complement of event D (decaffeinated coffee) is event R (regular coffee) because all coffee must be either decaffeinated or regular, and no coffee can be *both*. You can find the probability of the complement of *D* as follows:

$$P(D^C) = 1 - P(D)$$

Referring to Table 6-2, you can see that $P(D) = 0.42$. Therefore, $P(D^C) = 1 - P(D) = 1 - 0.42 = 0.58$, which is equal to $P(R)$.

Multiplication rule

To figure out the probability of the intersection of two events, you use the multiplication rule. This is used to determine the probability that two events are *both* true. For example, suppose an experiment consists of choosing a card from a standard deck. Event *A* = "the card is red." Event *B* = "the card is a king." The multiplication rule could be used to determine the probability that the card is *both* red and a king (for example, a red king.)

The multiplication rule can be written in two equivalent ways:

$$P(A \cap B) = P(A \mid B)P(B)$$

$$P(A \cap B) = P(B \mid A)P(A)$$

Note that these formulas are simply algebraic rearrangements of the definition of conditional probability:

$$P(A \mid B) = \frac{P(A \cap B)}{P(B)}$$

$$P(B \mid A) = \frac{P(A \cap B)}{P(A)}$$

Suppose the Omega Corporation has been the subject of takeover rumors for several months. The takeover is far more likely to occur if the economy rebounds next year. Omega's chief economist estimates that the likelihood of strong growth next year is 5 percent, the likelihood of weak growth is 35 percent, and the likelihood of negative growth is 60 percent. The likelihood of a takeover during a period of strong growth is estimated to be 40 percent; during a period of weak growth, this falls to 20 percent; and during a period of negative growth, it's assumed to be only 5 percent. What is the probability that there is strong growth next year *and* Omega is taken over?

The following events are defined:

- ✔ S = "strong growth"
- ✔ W = "weak growth"
- ✔ N = "negative growth"
- ✔ T = "Omega is taken over"

The probability of the events S and T can be determined as follows:

$$P(T \cap S) = P(T \mid S)P(S)$$

Because there's a 5 percent chance of strong growth next year, $P(S)$ = 0.05. The likelihood of a takeover during a period of strong growth is estimated to be 40 percent. Therefore, $P(T \mid S)$ = 0.40. So the probability that there's strong growth next year *and* that Omega is taken over is

$$P(T \cap S) = P(T \mid S)P(S) = (0.40)(0.05) = 0.02$$

When two events A and B are *independent,* the multiplication rule simplifies to

$$P(A \cap B) = P(A)P(B)$$

$$P(A \cap B) = P(B)P(A)$$

This is because $P(A \mid B)$ = $P(A)$ and $P(B \mid A)$ = $P(B)$.

Chapter 7

Probability Distributions and Random Variables

. . . .

In This Chapter

▶ Understanding the concept of the random variable

▶ Describing the behavior of a random variable with a probability distribution

▶ Summarizing the properties of a random variable with moments

. . . .

*T*his chapter introduces two new concepts that are used to determine the probability that a random event takes place — random variables and probability distributions.

These concepts are closely related to the notion of the *random experiment* (defined in Chapter 6). A random experiment is a *process* in which events unfold in an unpredictable way. A random variable is used to assign numerical values to all the possible outcomes of a random experiment. A probability distribution assigns probabilities to these numerical values.

In this chapter, I also define summary measures of a probability distribution, known as *moments*, such as expected value and variance. Random variables and probability distributions are used by economists, financial analysts, researchers, and others to model the behavior of economic and financial variables, such as interest rates, inflation rates, corporate earnings, and so on.

Defining the Role of the Random Variable

A random variable is based on a *random experiment,* a process that generates outcomes that aren't known in advance (see Chapter 6). For example, suppose that a game of chance consists of spinning a wheel with four colors — red, blue, green, and yellow — each color results in a prize ranging from $1.00 to $10.00. A random variable may be used to assign a prize value to each color.

For example, you could define X to represent the prize that is received for each color, as follows:

red	$X = \$1$
blue	$X = \$2$
green	$X = \$5$
yellow	$X = \$10$

In this example, the random experiment consists of spinning the wheel. For each possible outcome (color), X assigns a numerical value that represents the prize received.

It may seem like a paradox, but a random variable is neither random nor a variable! In fact, a random variable is a *function*. It assigns a single numerical value to each outcome of a random experiment. Random variables may represent a large number of different financial and economic variables, including the following:

- ✔ A corporation's profits during the upcoming quarter
- ✔ The number of new customers resulting from a new advertising campaign
- ✔ The value of the Dow Jones Industrial Average at the end of next year

As another example, suppose you conduct a simple random experiment by flipping a coin three times. The set of all possible outcomes, known as the *sample space,* consists of the following elements. (*H* represents a head turning up on a single flip of the coin, and *T* represents a tail turning up.)

$$S = \{HHH, HHT, HTH, THH, HTT, THT, TTH, TTT\}$$

S represents the sample space. Each element in the sample space is a single sequence of three flips; for example, *HTH* refers to a head followed by a tail followed by another head.

Because a head and a tail are equally likely to occur on each flip, each outcome of this random experiment is also equally likely to occur. For example, *HHT* is just as likely to happen as *THT*. With eight equally likely outcomes, each has a probability of 1/8 or 0.125.

An *event* is one outcome or a combination of outcomes of a random experiment. For example, suppose that you want to calculate the probability of the event E, where two or more heads turn up. This outcome can occur in four ways:

- ✔ Three consecutive heads (*HHH*)
- ✔ Two heads followed by one tail (*HHT*)
- ✔ A head followed by a tail followed by another head (*HTH*)
- ✔ A tail followed by two heads (*THH*)

You can express these possible outcomes more compactly with set notation:

$$E = \{HHH,\ HHT,\ HTH,\ THH\}$$

To compute the probability of the event E, you count the number of elements that correspond to event E and divide by the number of elements in the entire sample space (S):

$$P(E) = \frac{\text{elements in } E}{\text{elements in } S} = \frac{4}{8} = \frac{1}{2}$$

$P(E)$ is the probability of event E.

This approach can be extremely cumbersome if the sample space contains a large number of elements. As an alternative, you can define a random variable to represent the number of heads that turn up during the random experiment. You can then determine the probability of event E from the probabilities of the different possible values of the random variable.

For example, let the random variable X equal the number of heads that turn up when a coin is flipped three times. X has a numerical value for each outcome of this experiment. Here are the outcomes of the experiment and the corresponding values of X.

Outcome	X
HHH	3
HHT	2
HTH	2
THH	2
HTT	1
THT	1
TTH	1
TTT	0

For example, *HHT* represents two heads followed by a tail; therefore, the value of X for *HHT* is 2. Similarly, for the outcome *TTH*, the value of X is 1.

Suppose that a marketing firm conducts a survey of customers to determine whether they're satisfied with the customer service received from the local cable company. Each customer answers yes or no. The survey yielded the following replies:

yes	no	no	yes
no	yes	yes	yes
yes	yes	yes	yes
yes	yes	no	yes
no	no	no	no

For the results, X is defined as follows:

$X = 0$: the customer reply is no

$X = 1$: the customer reply is yes

The results are shown in Table 7-1.

Table 7-1	Survey Responses
Number of Responses	*X (0 = no, 1 = yes)*
8	0
12	1

By organizing the results this way, you can easily see the proportion of the customers who are satisfied with their cable service.

Assigning Probabilities to a Random Variable

Although random variables may provide useful information, their greatest advantage is that they simplify the calculation of probabilities. For example, in the case of the coin-flipping experiment in the previous section, computing probabilities directly from the values of a random variable is simpler than counting up all the ways in which an event can occur.

You can assign probabilities to each possible value of a random variable by using a *probability distribution* — a table or formula that shows these probabilities. A probability distribution has two important properties:

✔ The probability of each value of a random variable is between 0 and 1.

✔ The sum of the probabilities equals 1.

In the following sections, I show you how to construct a probability distribution. I also show you how to illustrate the properties of a probability distribution with a special type of graph known as a *histogram*.

Calculating the probability distribution

Based on the coin flip example in the earlier section, "Defining the Role of the Random Variable," the range of possible values for X (the number of heads that turn up) is 0 to 3. Here is the number of ways in which each possible value of X may occur:

X	*Outcomes*
0	*TTT*
1	*HTT, THT, TTH*
2	*HHT, HTH, THH*
3	*HHH*

Because eight equally likely outcomes of this experiment can occur, the probability for each value of X equals the number of outcomes divided by the size of the sample space. Table 7-2 shows this probability distribution.

Table 7-2	**Probability Distribution for the Coin-Flipping Experiment**
X	$P(X)$
0	1/8 = 0.125
1	3/8 = 0.375
2	3/8 = 0.375
3	1/8 = 0.125

The probability distribution in Table 7-2 shows that

✔ The probability of getting no heads ($X = 0$) is 0.125.

✔ The probability of getting one head ($X = 1$) is 0.375.

✔ The probability of getting two heads ($X = 2$) is 0.375.

✔ The probability of getting three heads ($X = 3$) is 0.125.

Now, suppose that you want to calculate the probability of the event F, where two or more tails turn up. This outcome can occur in four ways:

✔ Three consecutive tails (*TTT*)

✔ Two tails followed by a head (*TTH*)

✔ A tail followed by a head followed by another tail (*THT*)

✔ A head followed by two tails (*HTT*)

The event F corresponds to a set containing four elements:

$F = \{TTT, TTH, THT, HTT\}$

For two or more tails to turn up, the experiment must result in either zero heads or one head. Therefore, you can calculate the probability of F as follows:

$$P(F) = P(X = 0) + P(X = 1) = 0.125 + 0.375 = 0.500$$

Visualizing probability distribution with a histogram

You can express the probability distribution for the coin-flipping experiment graphically with a *histogram*. A histogram is a graph in which you place individual values or ranges of values on the horizontal axis and the frequency of occurrence for each value or range of values on the vertical axis.

The histogram for the probability distribution of the coin-flipping experiment is shown in Figure 7-1. The vertical axis shows the probability of X, and the horizontal axis shows the value of X (that is, the number of heads.)

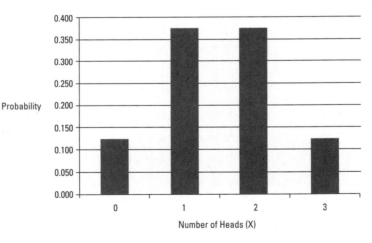

Probability Distribution for the Number of Heads

Figure 7-1:
Histogram
showing the
probability
distribution
of the
number of
heads.

The histogram shows that the two most likely outcomes of this experiment are one head or two heads ($X = 1$ or $X = 2$); these are equally likely to occur. The least likely outcomes are no heads or three heads ($X = 0$ or $X = 3$); these are also equally likely to occur.

Characterizing a Probability Distribution with Moments

Recall from Chapters 3 through 5 that the properties of samples and populations may be summarized in a convenient form with a series of numerical *measures*, including the mean, variance, standard deviation, and so on.

The properties of a probability distribution can also be summarized with a set of numerical measures known as *moments*.

In this section, I cover the most important of these moments: expected value (mean) and the variance. (The standard deviation isn't a separate moment; it's the square root of the variance.) First, though, I explain the role of the summation operator in calculating these moments.

Understanding the summation operator (Σ)

The summation operator is used to indicate that a set of values should be added together. (The summation operator was introduced in Chapter 3.) The formulas used to compute moments for a probability distribution are based on the summation operator. This is because each calculation must be repeated for each possible value of a random variable and the results must be summed.

As an example of the summation operator, suppose a data set contains five elements. The summation operator tells you to perform the following calculations:

$$\sum_{i=1}^{n} X_i = X_1 + X_2 + X_3 + X_4 + X_5$$

X_i represents a single element in a data set; i is an *index*, and n is the number of elements to be summed.

Expected value

The *expected value* of a random variable X represents the average value of X that occurs if the random experiment is repeated a large number of times. You can think of the expected value as the *center* of the distribution.

The expected value is a *weighted average* of its possible values, with weights equal to probabilities. The formula for computing expected value of X is

$$E(X) = \sum_{i=1}^{n} X_i P(X_i)$$

Here are the key terms in this formula:

- $E(X)$ = the expected value of X
- n = the number of possible values of X
- i = an index
- X_i = one possible value of X
- $P(X_i)$ = the probability of X_i
- Σ = the summation operator used to indicate that a sum is being computed

Suppose that a biopharmaceutical firm is planning to release several new drugs during the coming year, depending on whether or not the patents are approved. You can use the random variable X to represent the number of new drugs that will be released.

Table 7-3 shows the probability distribution of these results.

Table 7-3	Probability Distribution for Release of New Drugs
X	**P(X)**
0	0.10
1	0.25
2	0.50
3	0.15

You can then use the probability distribution to determine the expected (average) value of X by setting up the possible values of X and the corresponding probabilities, like so:

$$X_1 = 0 \ \ P(X_1) = 0.10$$
$$X_2 = 1 \ \ P(X_2) = 0.25$$
$$X_3 = 2 \ \ P(X_3) = 0.50$$
$$X_4 = 3 \ \ P(X_4) = 0.15$$

The corresponding histogram is shown in Figure 7-2.

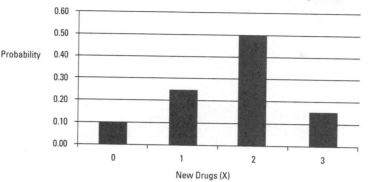

Probability Distribution for the Number of New Drugs Released

Figure 7-2:
Probability
distribu-
tion for the
number of
new drugs
released.

Illustration by Wiley, Composition Services Graphics

Next, you substitute these numbers into the expected value formula:

$$E(X) = \sum_{i=1}^{n} X_i P(X_i)$$
$$= X_1 P(X_1) + X_2 P(X_2) + X_3 P(X_3) + X_4 P(X_4)$$
$$= (0)(0.10) + (1)(0.25) + (2)(0.50) + (3)(0.15)$$
$$= 0.00 + 0.25 + 1.00 + 0.45$$
$$= 1.70$$

This result shows that the expected (average) number of new drugs that will be released during the coming year is 1.7. Although it's physically impossible to release 1.7 new drugs (since 1.7 is not an *integer* or whole number), if this experiment is repeated many times, the average number of new drugs released will be 1.7.

Variance and standard deviation

The *variance* of a random variable X is the average squared distance between the values of X and the expected value of X. In other words, variance is the amount of "spread" among the different values of X. The standard deviation is simply the square root of the variance. Note that the variance and standard deviation of a random variable are equivalent to the variance and standard deviation of a sample or population (discussed in Chapter 4).

The formula for computing the variance of X is

$$\sigma^2 = \sum_{i=1}^{n} [X_i - E(X)]^2 P(X_i)$$

σ^2 represents the variance of X.

This expression tells you to perform the following calculations:

- ✔ For each possible value of X (X_i), subtract the expected value of X.
- ✔ Square the result.
- ✔ Multiply this expression by the probability of X_i.
- ✔ Compute the sum of these products.

For the example of the biopharmaceutical company (in the earlier section, "Understanding the summation operator [Σ]") you compute the variance like so:

$$\sigma^2 = \sum_{i=1}^{n}\left[X_i - E(X)\right]^2 P(X_i)$$

$$= \left[X_1 - E(X)\right]^2 P(X_1) + \left[X_2 - E(X)\right]^2 P(X_2) + \left[X_3 - E(X)\right]^2$$
$$P(X_3) + \left[X_4 - E(X)\right]^2 P(X_4)$$

$$= \left[0 - 1.7\right]^2(0.10) + \left[1 - 1.7\right]^2(0.25) + \left[2 - 1.7\right]^2(0.50) + \left[3 - 1.7\right]^2(0.15)$$

$$= \left(-1.7\right)^2(0.10) + \left(-0.7\right)^2(0.25) + \left(0.3\right)^2(0.50) + \left(1.3\right)^2(0.15)$$

$$= \left(2.89\right)(0.10) + \left(0.49\right)(0.25) + \left(0.09\right)(0.50) + \left(1.69\right)(0.15)$$

$$= 0.2890 + 0.1225 + 0.0450 + 0.2535$$

$$= 0.7100$$

One of the major drawbacks to the variance is that it's measured in *squared units*, which makes interpretation difficult. In this example, the variance of the number of new drugs that will be released next year is 0.7100 *drugs squared*. It's hard to visualize what "drugs squared" actually means. As a result, the standard deviation is normally used in place of variance as a measure of spread. By taking the square root of 0.7100 drugs squared, you get a result of 0.8426 drugs, which is much more intuitively clear.

$$\sigma = \sqrt{\sum_{i=1}^{n}\left[X_i - E(X)\right]^2 P(X_i)}$$

$$= \sqrt{0.7100}$$

$$= 0.8426$$

For the example of the biopharmaceutical company, the standard deviation of the number of new drugs released next year equals $\sigma = \sqrt{0.7100} = 0.8426$.

The standard deviation is 0.8426 new drugs. You can think of the standard deviation as a measure of how much *uncertainty* is associated with the expected value.

σ represents the standard deviation of X.

Chapter 8

The Binomial, Geometric, and Poisson Distributions

In This Chapter

▶ Finding probabilities when only two things can happen with the binomial distribution

▶ Seeing how many "successes" or" failures" occur first with the geometric distribution

▶ Using the Poisson distribution to calculate the probability of events occurring during a given time frame

*Y*ou can model many complex business problems by using probability distributions. These distributions help provide answers to questions such as, "What's the likelihood that oil prices will rise during the coming year?" "What's the probability of a stock market crash next month?" "How likely is it that a corporation's earnings will fall below expectations this year?" "What is the likelihood that three oil wells will have to be drilled before oil is found?"

A *probability distribution* defines the statistical properties of a variable. Accurate modeling of financial variables requires that you pick the appropriate distribution for a given situation. Some of the more widely used probability distributions in business are the binomial, geometric, and Poisson distributions. These are examples of *discrete distributions,* in which only a countable number of values are possible.

This chapter covers the key properties of the binomial, geometric, and Poisson distributions and explains the circumstances under which you may apply them. For each distribution, I give you formulas for computing probabilities and also provide tables as alternatives to doing the computing yourself.

This chapter also introduces summary measures of probability distributions, known as *moments,* which are closely related to the mean, variance, and standard deviation of samples and populations (described in Chapter 3). Then I wrap up the chapter by covering simplified formulas for computing the moments of the binomial, geometric, and Poisson distributions.

Looking at Two Possibilities with the Binomial Distribution

You use the *binomial distribution* to compute probabilities for processes where only one of two possible outcomes may occur. (The fact that only two possible outcomes can occur is what gives the distribution its name.) Here are some examples of processes you can model with the binomial distribution:

- When you flip a coin several times, the outcome of interest is whether the coin turns up heads or tails on each flip.

- When you roll a die multiple times, the outcome of interest is whether the number that turns up on each roll is odd (1, 3, or 5) or even (2, 4, or 6).

- When you look at the closing price of a stock each day for one year, the outcome of interest is whether the stock price increased or not.

As another example, suppose you hold a portfolio of stocks. During the coming year, it's possible that some of these stocks may split. (A stock split results in additional shares being distributed to existing shareholders.) For each stock, only two possible outcomes may occur: The stock splits, or it doesn't split. As a result, you can use the binomial distribution to compute the probability of a given number of splits in your portfolio over the coming year.

The binomial distribution is based on several specialized assumptions, which I explain in detail in the next section. If these assumptions aren't true, using the binomial distribution to compute probabilities for a given situation is likely to give inaccurate results.

Checking out the binomial distribution

You generate a binomial distribution by a special type of random experiment, known as a *binomial process*. This consists of a fixed number of repeated trials, each with only *two* possible outcomes and the following distinguishing features:

- **Each trial results in either a success or a failure.** On each trial of a binomial process, two possible outcomes may take place — and they're designated as "success" and "failure." For example, if you're doing a series of coin flips, you may call the outcome of the coin landing with "heads" up a success and the outcome of "tails" up a failure.

- **The trials are *independent* of each other.** Each trial of a binomial process is independent of previous trials; in other words, the outcome of one trial has no influence over the outcome of the other trials. For example, the probability of heads turning up on a coin flip doesn't depend on the outcomes of flips that have taken place in the past.

✔ **The probability of success remains constant for all trials.** The probability of success in a binomial process doesn't change from one trial to the next; instead, it remains constant throughout the entire process. For example, the probability of a head turning up on a flip of a coin is always one-half (50 percent), no matter how many times the coin is flipped.

Computing binomial probabilities

You can compute the probability that a specified number of successes will occur during a fixed number of trials by using the binomial formula. For example, with this formula, you can determine the probability that five odd numbers turn up when a die is rolled ten times. The formula is:

$$P(X = x) = \frac{n!}{x!(n-x)!} p^x (1-p)^{n-x}$$

Here's what each element of this formula means:

✔ X = a binomial random variable whose value is determined by the number of successes that occur during a series of trials

✔ x = the number of successes whose probability you are computing

✔ n = the number of trials that take place

✔ p = the probability of success on a single trial

✔ $(1 - p)$ = the probability of failure on a single trial

✔ ! = the factorial operator

The capital X is a binomial random variable (discussed in Chapter 7), and the lowercase x is a specific value, which refers to the number of successes whose probability you're calculating.

Factorial: counting how many ways you can arrange things

The exclamation point (!) doesn't just mean you're excited. The symbol is also the mathematical operator _factorial_. You pronounce $n!$ as "n factorial," which is the product of all positive integers less than or equal to n. For example:

$0! = 1$ (looks odd, but it's true)

$1! = 1$

$2! = (2)(1) = 2$

$3! = (3)(2)(1) = 6$

$4! = (4)(3)(2)(1) = 24$

A general description is $n! = (n)(n-1)(n-2) \ldots (2)(1)$. The factorial is a handy tool, but you can apply it only to 0 and positive integers.

You can use the factorial operator to count the number of ways you can arrange a group of objects. For example, suppose that a small bookshelf has enough room for three titles: *Algebra and Its Applications; Baseball: A History;* and *Chemistry in Everyday Life.* You can label these titles A, B, and C and then set up the possibilities for how many ways you can you arrange these books on the shelf like this:

ABC

ACB

BAC

BCA

CAB

CBA

This list covers every possibility. Each entry in the list is an *arrangement* of the three titles. Counting the number of elements in this list shows that you can arrange the books in six ways.

Fortunately, a much easier way to get this same result is to simply compute 3! (because three books are being arranged), giving a total number of arrangements of $3! = (3)(2)(1) = 6$.

Many calculators contain a built-in function for the factorial operator. It typically appears as *x*! In Microsoft Excel, you can compute factorial with the function FACT.

Combinations: Counting how many choices you have

You use the combinations formula to count the number of *combinations* that can be created when choosing *x* objects from a set of *n* objects:

$$\frac{n!}{x!(n-x)!}$$

One distinguishing feature of a combination is that the order of objects is irrelevant.

For example, you can use this formula to count the number of ways you choose two elective classes from a set of eight for the upcoming semester. The order in which you choose the electives is immaterial; each possible selection is a *combination* of two objects.

As another example, suppose that you're painting your house with two colors from a set of four: green, blue, white, and yellow. Because the order in which you choose the colors is irrelevant, each pair of colors is a combination. How many different color schemes are possible with the given set of choices? You can answer this question by simply listing all the possible combinations:

green, white

green, blue

green, yellow

white, yellow

white, blue

blue, yellow

This list shows that you have six possible choices of pairs of colors.

The quicker way to answer this question is to substitute these values into the combinations formula; in this case, x represents the number of colors to choose (2), and n represents the total number of colors you can choose from (4).

$$\frac{n!}{x!(n-x)!} = \frac{4!}{2!(4-2)!} = \frac{4!}{2!2!} = \frac{24}{(2)(2)} = 6$$

The formula for computing the number of combinations is sometimes expressed as

$$\binom{n}{x}$$

Read or say this expression as "n choose x." This function appears on many calculators as nCr. In Microsoft Excel, you can compute combinations with the function COMBIN.

When you're selecting x objects from a group of n objects in such a way that the order of selection *does* matter, the choices are known as *permutations* instead of combinations.

Binomial formula: Computing the probabilities

Combinations are useful for computing binomial probabilities. You can find the probability of x successes during n trials with the binomial formula:

$$P(X = x) = \frac{n!}{x!(n-x)!} p^x (1-p)^{n-x}$$

Here,

$$\frac{n!}{x!(n-x)!}$$

is the total number of ways you can get exactly x successes during n trials, and

$$p^x(1-p)^{n-x}$$

is the probability of a sequence consisting of x successes and $(n-x)$ failures.

For example, say 40 percent of all published books are fiction, so the remaining 60 percent are nonfiction. If you pick six books at random from a bookstore, what's the probability that either none or one of them is fiction?

First, define fiction as a *success*. The probability of success on a single trial is $p = 0.4$, because 40 percent of all books are fiction. Each book you choose is a single trial of an experiment, so if you pick six books, you're conducting $n = 6$ trials for this experiment. You then figure the probability of getting one or fewer fiction books by calculating the probabilities of getting none and one fiction book and then adding them together:

- ✔ Based on the binomial formula, the probability of choosing *no* fiction books from a selection of six books is

$$P(X=0) = \frac{6!}{0!(6-0)!}(0.40)^0(0.60)^6$$
$$P(X=0) = (1)(1)(0.0467)$$
$$P(X=0) = 0.0467$$

- ✔ Based on the binomial formula, the probability of choosing one fiction book from a selection of six is

$$P(X=1) = \frac{6!}{1!(6-1)!}(0.40)^1(0.60)^5$$
$$P(X=1) = (6)(0.40)(0.07776)$$
$$P(X=1) = 0.1866$$

Now add the probabilities together. The probability of getting either no fiction book or one is $0.0467 + 0.1866 = 0.2333$. Alternatively, you can get these results from a binomial table for six trials ($n = 6$), such as Table 8-1.

Table 8-1   Binomial Probabilities that Result from 6 Trials ($n = 6$)

	$p = 0.1$	$p = 0.2$	$p = 0.3$	$p = 0.4$	$p = 0.5$
$x = 0$	0.5314	0.2621	0.1176	0.0467	0.0156
$x = 1$	0.3543	0.3932	0.3025	0.1866	0.0938
$x = 2$	0.0984	0.2458	0.3241	0.3110	0.2344
$x = 3$	0.0146	0.0819	0.1852	0.2765	0.3125
$x = 4$	0.0012	0.0154	0.0595	0.1382	0.2344
$x = 5$	0.0001	0.0015	0.0102	0.0369	0.0938
$x = 6$	0.0000	0.0001	0.0007	0.0041	0.0156

Table 8-1 shows the probability of success (p) at the top of each column. In this example, because $p = 0.4$, the probability of choosing zero fiction books is $P(X = 0) = 0.0467$ (found in the $x = 0$ row and the $p = 0.4$ column). The probability of choosing one fiction book is $P(X = 1) = 0.1866$ (found in the $x = 1$ row and the $p = 0.4$ column). The probability of getting no fiction books or one fiction book is the sum of $0.0467 + 0.1866$, or 0.2333.

Check out a binomial table with 19 values for n at www.statisticshowto.com/tables/binomial-distribution-table.

If you simply don't like using formulas or tables to compute binomial probabilities, or if you want to triple-check your numbers, you can also use a specialized calculator, such as the Texas Instruments TI-83 or TI-84, which contains built-in functions that compute these probabilities quickly and easily. Or you can use the function BINOMDIST in Microsoft Excel 2007 and older versions, or BINOM.DIST in Excel 2010. If you need help with Excel, visit http://office.microsoft.com/en-us/excel-help.

Moments of the binomial distribution

Moments are summary measures of a probability distribution. The expected value represents the mean or average value of a distribution. The expected value is sometimes known as the *first moment* of a probability distribution. You calculate the expected value by taking each possible value of the distribution, weighting it by its probability, and then summing the results. The expected value is comparable to the mean of a population or sample (see Chapter 3).

The variance and standard deviation represent the dispersion among the possible values of a probability distribution. The variance and standard deviation of a probability distribution are equivalent to the variance and standard deviation of a population or sample. (The general formulas for computing moments for a discrete probability distribution are given in Chapter 7.) The variance is sometimes known as the *second central moment* of a probability distribution; the standard deviation isn't a separate moment, but simply the square root of the variance.

Luckily, for the binomial distribution, you can reduce computation time by using a series of simplified formulas, which I discuss in the following sections.

Binomial distribution: Calculating the expected value

The *expected value* of a probability distribution is its average value. You get it by weighting each possible value by its probability of occurring. For the binomial distribution, the calculation of the expected value can be simplified to

$$E(X) = np$$

For example, suppose that 10 percent of all people are left-handed, and 90 percent are right-handed (which happens to be true). In a class of 40 students, what's the expected number of left-handed students? You can calculate the expected value by thinking of each student as a "trial," with a 10 percent chance of being left-handed (a "success") and 90 percent chance of being right-handed (a "failure"). Therefore, $n = 40$ and $p = 0.10$. The expected number of left-handed students in the class is $E(X) = np = (40)(0.10) = 4$.

Binomial distribution: Computing variance and standard deviation

The *variance* of a distribution is the average squared distance between each possible outcome and the expected value. For the binomial distribution, you may compute the variance with the following simplified formula:

$$\sigma^2 = np(1 - p)$$

The *standard deviation* of a distribution equals the square root of the variance. For the binomial distribution, you calculate the standard deviation as

$$\sigma = \sqrt{np(1-p)}$$

For the example of left-handed students in the previous section,

- ✔ The expected value is $E(X) = np = (40)(0.10) = 4$.
- ✔ The variance is $\sigma^2 = np(1 - p) = 40(0.10)(0.90) = 3.6$.
- ✔ The standard deviation is $\sqrt{3.6} = 1.9$.

Graphing the binomial distribution

You may want to illustrate the binomial distribution with a *histogram*. A histogram shows the possible values of a probability distribution as a series of vertical bars. The height of each bar reflects the probability of each value occurring. A histogram is a useful tool for visually analyzing the properties of a distribution, and (by the way) all discrete distributions may be represented with a histogram. (See Chapter 2 for more about histograms and other types of graphs.)

For example, suppose that a candy company produces both milk chocolate and dark chocolate candy bars. The product mix is 50 percent of the candy bars are milk chocolate and 50 percent are dark chocolate. Say you choose ten candy bars at random, and choosing milk chocolate is defined as a success. The probability distribution of the number of successes during these ten trials with $p = 0.5$ is shown in Figure 8-1.

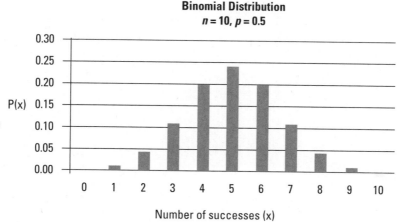

Figure 8-1: Binomial distribution: ten trials with $p = 0.5$.

Figure 8-1 shows that when $p = 0.5$, the distribution is *symmetric* about its expected value of 5 ($np = 10[0.5] = 5$), where the probabilities of X being below the mean match the probabilities of X being the same distance above the mean.

For example, with $n = 10$ and $p = 0.5$,

$P(X = 4) = 0.2051$ and $P(X = 6) = 0.2051$

$P(X = 3) = 0.1172$ and $P(X = 7) = 0.1172$

If the probability of success is less than 0.5, the distribution is *positively skewed*, meaning probabilities for X are greater for values below the expected value than above it.

For example, with $n = 10$ and $p = 0.2$,

$P(X = 4) = 0.0881$ and $P(X = 6) = 0.0055$

$P(X = 3) = 0.2013$ and $P(X = 7) = 0.0008$

Figure 8-2 shows the probability distribution for $n = 10$ and $p = 0.2$.

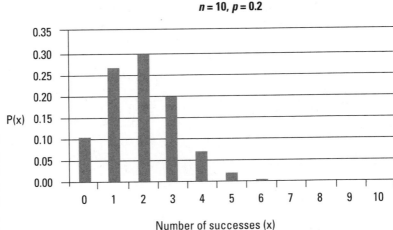

Figure 8-2:
Binomial
distribution:
ten trials
with $p = 0.2$.

If the probability of success is greater than 0.5, the distribution is *negatively skewed* — probabilities for X are greater for values above the expected value than below it.

For example, with $n = 10$ and $p = 0.8$,

$P(X = 4) = 0.0055$ and $P(X = 6) = 0.0881$

$P(X = 3) = 0.0008$ and $P(X = 7) = 0.2013$

Figure 8-3 shows the probability distribution for the same situation when $p = 0.8$.

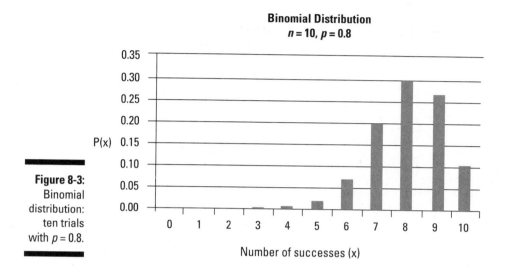

Figure 8-3:
Binomial
distribution:
ten trials
with $p = 0.8$.

Determining the Probability of the Outcome That Occurs First: Geometric Distribution

The geometric distribution is based on the binomial process. (That is, a series of independent trials with two possible outcomes. See the earlier section "Checking out the binomial distribution.") You use the geometric distribution to determine the probability that a specified number of trials will take place before the first success occurs. Alternatively, you can use the geometric distribution to figure the probability that a specified number of failures will occur before the first success takes place.

The following section explains how to compute geometric probabilities and also how to compute the moments of the geometric distribution. You also see graphs that illustrate the properties of the geometric distribution.

Computing geometric probabilities

To calculate the probability that a given number of trials take place until the first success occurs, use the following formula:

$$P(X = x) = (1 - p)^{x-1}p \text{ for } x = 1, 2, 3, \ldots$$

Here, x can be any whole number (*integer*); there is no maximum value for x.

X is a geometric random variable, x is the number of trials required until the first success occurs, and p is the probability of success on a single trial.

For example, suppose you want to flip a coin until the first heads turns up. The probability that it takes four flips for the first heads to occur (that is, three tails followed by one heads) is $P(X = x) = (1 - p)^{x-1}p$. In this example, $x = 4$ and $p = 0.5$:

$$P(X = 4) = (1 - 0.5)^3(0.5) = (0.125)(0.5) = 0.0625$$

To calculate the probability that a given number of failures occur before the first success, the formula is

$$P(X = x) = (1 - p)^x p$$

x now represents the number of failures that occur before the first success. In addition, x can assume values 0, 1, 2, . . . instead of 1, 2, 3, . . .

For example, suppose you flip a coin until the first heads turns up. The probability that there will be three tails before the first heads turns up is $P(X = x) = (1 - p)^x p$. In this example, $x = 3$ and $p = 0.5$:

$$P(X = 3) = (1 - 0.5)^3(0.5) = (0.5)^3(0.5) = (0.125)(0.5) = 0.0625$$

Both situations refer to getting three tails followed by a heads, so both formulas provide the same result.

Moments of the geometric distribution

The moments (see the earlier section "Moments of the binomial distribution" for a definition) of the geometric distribution depend on which of the following situations is being modeled:

- The number of trials required before the first success takes place
- The number of failures that occur before the first success

Just as with the binomial distribution discussed earlier in this chapter, the geometric distribution has a series of simplified formulas for computing these moments, which I explore in the following sections.

Geometric distribution: Calculating the expected value

The expected value of the geometric distribution when determining the number of trials required until the first success is

$$E(X) = \frac{1}{p}$$

The expected value of the geometric distribution when determining the number of failures that occur before the first success is

$$E(X) = \frac{1-p}{p}$$

For example, when flipping coins, if success is defined as "a heads turns up," the probability of a success equals $p = 0.5$; therefore, failure is defined as "a tails turns up" and $1 - p = 1 - 0.5 = 0.5$. On average, there'll be $(1 - p)/p = (1 - 0.5)/0.5 = 0.5/0.5 = 1$ tails before the first heads turns up.

Notice how the two results provide the same information; it takes an average of two flips to get the first heads, or on average there should be one tails before the first heads turns up.

Geometric distribution: Computing variance and standard deviation

The variance and standard deviation of the geometric distribution when determining the number of trials required until the first success or when determining the number of failures that occur before the first success are

$$\sigma^2 = \frac{1-p}{p^2}$$

$$\sigma = \sqrt{\frac{1-p}{p^2}}$$

For example, suppose you flip a coin until the first heads turns up. The expected number of trials required until the first heads turns up is

$$E(X) = \frac{1}{p} = \frac{1}{0.5} = 2$$

The variance is

$$\sigma^2 = \frac{1-p}{p^2} = \frac{1-0.5}{0.5^2} = \frac{0.5}{0.25} = 2$$

The standard deviation (σ) is $\sqrt{2} = 1.414$.

Graphing the geometric distribution

You can illustrate the geometric distribution with a histogram. For example, say you do a series of ten trials. On each trial, the probability of success is 0.2. Figure 8-4 shows the probability distribution of the number of trials required to reach the first success.

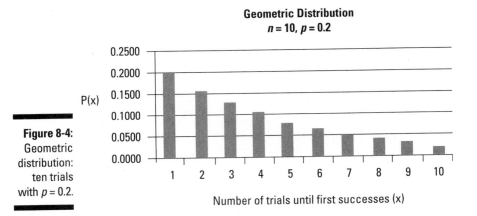

Geometric Distribution
$n = 10, p = 0.2$

Figure 8-4:
Geometric
distribution:
ten trials
with $p = 0.2$.

Unlike the binomial distribution, the geometric distribution is positively skewed for any value of p.

Keeping the Time: The Poisson Distribution

The *Poisson distribution* is useful for measuring how many events may occur during a given time horizon, such as the number of customers that enter a store during the next hour, the number of hits on a website during the next minute, and so forth. The *Poisson process* takes place over time instead of a series of trials; each interval of time is assumed to be *independent* of all other intervals.

For example, suppose that a bank counts the number of customers who enter each hour. If the number of customers that enter during a given hour is independent of the number that enter during all other hours (while the bank is open), you can use the Poisson distribution to find the probability that a specific number of customers enter the bank during the next hour.

The Poisson distribution is named for Siméon Denis Poisson who was a French mathematician, physicist, and genius. He was wrong about only one major thing: He opposed the wave theory of light.

The following section shows you how to compute Poisson probabilities and how to compute moments for the Poisson distribution. Graphs are used to illustrate the key properties of the Poisson distribution.

Computing Poisson probabilities

You calculate Poisson probabilities with the following formula:

$$P(X = x) = e^{-\lambda} \frac{\lambda^x}{x!}$$

Here's what each element of this formula represents:

- ✔ X = a Poisson random variable

- ✔ x = number of events whose probability you are calculating

- ✔ λ = the Greek letter "lambda," which represents the average number of events that occur per time interval

- ✔ e = a *constant* that's equal to approximately 2.71828

  e is a constant that's widely used in financial applications. One of the most important uses is in computing present values of sums of money when interest rates are *continuously compounded* — compounded an *infinite* number of times. Most calculators have a key labeled e^x that you can use to calculate the value of e raised to a specified power. In Excel, the appropriate function for determining the value of e is EXP.

For example, suppose that the number of messages that a person receives on his cellphone averages one per hour and that the number of messages received each hour is independent of all other hours. What's the probability of his receiving two messages in the next hour?

In this case, the value of lambda (λ) is equal to 1, because the average number of messages each hour equals 1. The probability of receiving two messages during the next hour is

$$P(X = 2) = e^{-1} \frac{1^2}{2!} = 0.1839$$

Alternatively, you can get results from a Poisson table set up like Table 8-2.

Table 8-2   Poisson Probabilities for Different Values of λ

	$\lambda = 0.5$	$\lambda = 1$	$\lambda = 1.5$	$\lambda = 2$	$\lambda = 2.5$	$\lambda = 3$
x = 0	0.6065	0.3679	0.2231	0.1353	0.0821	0.0498
x = 1	0.3033	0.3679	0.3347	0.2707	0.2052	0.1494
x = 2	0.0758	0.1839	0.2510	0.2707	0.2565	0.2240
x = 3	0.0126	0.0613	0.1255	0.1804	0.2138	0.2240
x = 4	0.0016	0.0153	0.0471	0.0902	0.1336	0.1680
x = 5	0.0002	0.0031	0.0141	0.0361	0.0668	0.1008
x = 6	0.0000	0.0005	0.00035	0.0120	0.0278	0.0504
x = 7	0.0000	0.0001	0.0008	0.0034	0.0099	0.0216
x = 8	0.0000	0.0000	0.0001	0.0009	0.0031	0.0081

Table 8-2 shows the Poisson probabilities for different values of λ. In the cellphone example, because $x = 2$ and $\lambda = 1$, the appropriate probability $P(X = 2)$ is found in the $x = 2$ row and the $\lambda = 1$ column. The probability is 0.1839.

If you don't care for using formulas or a table, try a specialized calculator or Excel. For Excel 2007 and older versions, use the POISSON function; for Excel 2010, use the POISSON.DIST function.

The moments of the Poisson distribution are used to represent the average value of the distribution and the dispersion of the distribution. As with the binomial and geometric distribution, these moments may be computed with simplified formulas.

Poisson distribution: Calculating the expected value

As with the binomial and geometric distributions (discussed earlier in this chapter), you can use simple formulas to compute the moments of the Poisson distribution. The expected value of the Poisson distribution is

$$E(X) = \lambda$$

For example, say that on average three new companies are listed in the New York Stock Exchange (NYSE) each year. The number of new companies listed during a given year is independent of all other years. The number of new listings per year, therefore, follows the Poisson distribution, with a value of $\lambda = 3$. As a result, the expected number of new listings next year is $\lambda = 3$.

Poisson distribution: Computing variance and standard deviation

Compute the variance and the Poisson distribution as $\sigma^2 = \lambda$; the standard deviation (σ) equals $\sqrt{\lambda}$.

Based on the NYSE listing example in the previous section, the variance equals 3 and the standard deviation equals $\sqrt{3} = 1.732$.

Graphing the Poisson distribution

As with the binomial distribution, the Poisson distribution can be illustrated with a histogram. In Figures 8-5 through 8-7, the results are shown for three values of λ: 2 (Figure 8-5), 5 (Figure 8-6) and 7 (Figure 8-7).

For $\lambda = 2$ (Figure 8-5), the distribution is skewed to the right; for $\lambda = 5$ (Figure 8-6), the distribution is nearly symmetric about the mean of 5; for $\lambda = 7$ (Figure 8-7), the distribution is skewed to the left.

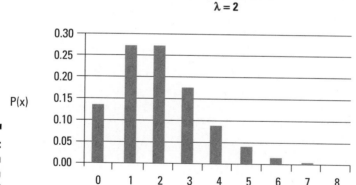

Figure 8-5: Poisson distribution with $\lambda = 2$

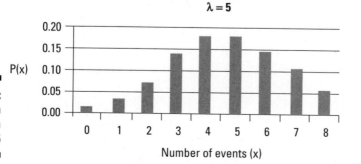

Figure 8-6: Poisson distribution with $\lambda = 5$

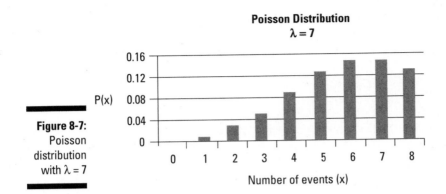

Figure 8-7:
Poisson
distribution
with λ = 7

Chapter 9

The Uniform and Normal Distributions: So Many Possibilities!

....

In This Chapter

▶ Understanding the differences between discrete and continuous distributions

▶ Discovering the properties of the uniform distribution

▶ Checking out normal distribution probabilities

....

*T*his chapter introduces two important new probability distributions: the uniform and the normal. The normal distribution is especially important in business applications; it can be used to describe the behavior of many financial variables, such as the rate of return to an investment, a corporation's annual profits, consumer spending on new products, and so on.

The uniform and the normal distributions have one important feature in common: they assign probabilities to *ranges* of values instead of individual values. This contrasts with the distributions found in Chapter 8: the binomial, geometric, and Poisson; these distributions assign probabilities to *individual* values.

The *uniform* distribution is used to describe a situation where all possible outcomes of a random experiment are equally likely to occur. For example, suppose that a manufacturer produces one-liter bottles of soda. The goal is to fill each bottle with exactly one liter of soda, but in actual practice, the acceptable range is between 0.99 and 1.01 liters. Any bottles that fall outside of this range are discarded. Suppose that for each acceptable bottle, the content is equally likely to be any value between 0.99 and 1.01 liters. In this case, the uniform distribution could be used to answer questions such as:

What is the likelihood that a randomly chosen bottle contains between 0.992 and 0.994 liters?

What is the likelihood that a randomly chosen bottle contains more than 1 liter?

What is the average content of the acceptable bottles?

In this chapter I demonstrate how uniform probabilities may be determined with a graph or with an algebraic formula. I also show how the moments of the uniform distribution may be computed.

The *normal* distribution is the most widely used distribution in business because you can use it to model many variables. For example, you can use the normal distribution to describe the rates of return to financial assets, the distribution of corporate profits, the prices of key commodities (such as oil), and so forth.

Suppose that the returns to the stocks in the Standard and Poor's 500 (S&P 500) index are normally distributed. The normal distribution could then be used to answer questions such as:

What is the probability that the S&P 500 will increase by at least 5 percent next year?

What is the probability that the S&P 500 will fall next year?

How much risk is associated with investing in the S&P 500?

Due to the complexity of the normal distribution, I show you how to compute normal probabilities with standard tables in this chapter instead of formulas.

The following sections explain the differences between the two basic types of probability distributions: discrete and continuous. There is a detailed look at the properties of the uniform and normal distributions, including techniques for computing probabilities and moments.

Comparing Discrete and Continuous Distributions

Discrete and continuous distributions are the two standard types of *probability distributions*, which you use to compute probabilities for possible outcomes of a random experiment. (For more about random experiments and probability distributions, see Chapter 7.)

✔ You use the **discrete distribution** with a random experiment that can generate a *finite* (countable) number of outcomes. (You see three examples of discrete distributions — binomial, geometric, and Poisson — in Chapter 8.)

✔ You use the **continuous distribution** with a random experiment that can generate an *infinite* (uncountable) number of outcomes.

Intuitively, a random experiment can generate a finite (countable) number of outcomes if it's possible to make up a list of all the possible outcomes of the experiment. For example, if a coin is flipped ten times, and *heads turns up* is the variable of interest, then there are 11 possible outcomes: 0, 1, 2, ..., 10. These outcomes could be easily listed. On the other hand, if an experiment consists of observing the length of time until the next phone call arrives, the number of possible times until the next phone call is *infinite (uncountable)*. This is because the times are not restricted to whole numbers. The time could be 2.3 seconds, 1.41742 seconds, 8.19444212 seconds, and so on. A list containing all possible times until the next phone call is impossible to construct, because there are an unlimited number of entries.

Computing probabilities for continuous distributions is more complex than for a discrete distribution; often, your best resources are tables or specialized calculators. For an example, visit www.solvemymath.com/online_math_calculator/statistics/continuous_distributions/index.php.

Aside from the number of possible outcomes, one of the most important differences between discrete and continuous distributions is this: With a continuous distribution, the probability that a random variable (X) equals a specific constant (x) is defined as *zero*. With an infinite number of possibilities, the likelihood of X being equal to a specific value is infinitesimally small.

For example, the probability of tomorrow's temperature at noon being exactly 72.141712987 degrees is pretty much zero. As a result, for any value x, $P(X \le x)$ equals $P(X < x)$. A statement such as "the probability that the temperature at noon tomorrow will be less than or equal to 72 degrees" has the same interpretation as "the probability that the temperature at noon tomorrow will be less than 72 degrees."

To demonstrate this statement mathematically, you can write $P(X \le x)$ as $P(X < x) + P(X = x)$, because the probability that X is less than or equal to x consists of the sum of two different probabilities — the probability that X is strictly less than x and the probability that X is exactly equal to x. With a continuous distribution, $P(X = x) = 0$; therefore,

$$P(X \le x) = P(X < x) + P(X = x)$$
$$P(X \le x) = P(X < x) + 0$$
$$P(X \le x) = P(X < x)$$

Based on this reasoning, $P(X \geq x) = P(X > x)$ is also true.

With a discrete distribution, $P(X \leq x)$ does *not* equal $P(X < x)$, and $P(X \geq x)$ does *not* equal $P(X > x)$ unless $P(X = x) = 0$.

For example, suppose that a coin is flipped three times. The outcome of interest is whether a head turns up on each flip.

The probability that two or fewer heads turns up is computed as:

$$P(X \leq 2) = P(X = 0) + P(X = 1) + P(X = 2)$$

The probability that fewer than two heads turn up is computed as:

$$P(X < 2) = P(X = 0) + P(X = 1)$$

Therefore, unless $P(X = 2) = 0$, $P(X \leq 2)$ and $P(X < 2)$ gives different results.

In the continuous case, though, $P(X \leq 2)$ and $P(X < 2)$ is always equal.

Working with the Uniform Distribution

The *uniform distribution* is a continuous distribution that assigns only positive probabilities within a specified interval (a, b) — that is, all values between a and b. (a and b are two constants; they may be negative or positive.)

For example, suppose that the U.S. Postal Service offers a special new delivery service; it's guaranteed that the time required for a package to be delivered from New York City to Los Angeles is no more than 72 hours. (It also takes at least 24 hours for the package to be delivered.) If the delivery time is equally likely to be any value between 24 and 72 hours, then the uniform distribution can be used to compute probabilities for the delivery time. For example, suppose that a customer wants to know the likelihood that the package will be delivered between 24 and 36 hours after mailing; this can be computed with the uniform distribution.

In this case, the uniform distribution is defined over the interval (24, 72). (In other words, a = 24 and b = 72.) This implies that the probability of a package arriving in less than 24 hours or more than 72 hours equals 0. Furthermore, the probability of the package arriving within any given interval between 24 and 72 hours depends only on the *width* of the interval. For example, the package is just as likely to arrive in 24 to 28 hours as it is to arrive in 68 to 72 hours, because both of these intervals have a width of four hours.

Although the uniform distribution may be defined for an infinite number of different intervals, if the distribution is defined over the interval (0, 1) it's known as the *standard uniform distribution.* This indicates that all values between 0 and 1 are equally likely to occur.

The standard uniform distribution is used for random experiments where the outcome is equally likely to be any value between 0 and 1. For example, because probabilities are always between 0 and 1, the standard uniform distribution can be used to describe a random process that generates probabilities.

The standard uniform distribution is often used for *simulation* studies, in which the value of a variable is estimated by repeatedly choosing random numbers and substituting them into a mathematical model. For example, the sales of a new product could be estimated by choosing values from the standard uniform distribution and substituting the results into a model of consumer demand.

The uniform distribution and the standard uniform distribution are discussed at www.en.wikipedia.org/wiki/Uniform_distribution.

In the following sections, I explore the uniform distribution and all it has to offer, including how to visualize its intervals on a graph, how to calculate its moments, and how to work with its probabilities.

Graphing the uniform distribution

A discrete distribution may be described with a *histogram,* which is a special type of graph consisting of a series of vertical bars. Each bar represents a value or range of values, and the height of each bar represents the probability of that value or range of values. (Histograms are introduced in Chapter 7.)

A continuous distribution can't be illustrated with a histogram, because this would require an *infinite* number of bars. Instead, a continuous distribution may be illustrated with a line or a curve. Areas under the line or the curve correspond to probabilities.

With the uniform distribution, all values over an interval (a, b) are equally likely to occur. As a result, the graph that illustrates this distribution is a *rectangle.* Figure 9-1 shows the uniform distribution defined over the interval (0, 10).

The horizontal axis shows the range of values for X (0 to 10). The distribution assigns a probability of 0 to any value of X outside of the interval from 0 to 10.

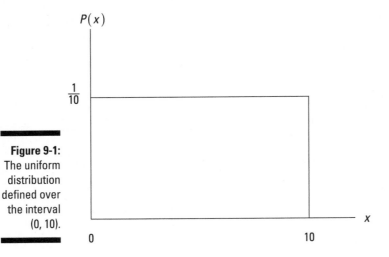

Figure 9-1:
The uniform
distribution
defined over
the interval
(0, 10).

The *width* of this interval equals the upper limit (*b*) minus the lower limit (*a*), which equals *b* − *a*. So in Figure 9-1, the width equals 10 − 0 = 10. The width of this interval represents the *base* of the rectangle. The *height* of the rectangle equals 1 divided by the base (1/10 in this case). The height always equals 1 divided by the base; this ensures that the area of the rectangle always equals 1. As discussed in the later section "Computing uniform probabilities," areas under this rectangle represent probabilities. The total probability for any distribution is 1; therefore, the area under the rectangle must equal 1.

The area of a rectangle equals the base times the height, or in mathematical terms, $A = b \times h$.

Discovering moments of the uniform distribution

Moments are a set of summary measures that express the properties of the probability distribution of a random variable. (For more about the moments of a probability distribution, see Chapter 7.) The moments include expected value (mean) and variance. Standard deviation is not a separate moment, but is instead the square root of the variance.

As discussed in Chapter 7, the expected value represents the average value of all the possible values of a probability distribution, weighted by the probabilities of these values. The variance and standard deviation measure the "spread" among the possible values of the distribution.

For example, suppose that an art gallery sells two types of art work: inexpensive prints and original paintings. The length of time that the prints remain in inventory is uniformly distributed over the interval (0,40). For example, some prints are sold immediately; no print remains in inventory for more than 40 days. For the paintings, the length of time in inventory is uniformly distributed over the interval (5, 105). For example, each painting requires at least 5 days to be sold and may take up to 105 days to be sold.

The expected value, variance, and standard deviation are much lower for the prints because the range of possible values is much smaller. On average, prints sell much faster than paintings. In addition, the inventory times of the prints are much closer to each other than for the paintings. The uniform distribution has simple formulas for calculating the moments, which I describe in the following sections.

Uniform distribution: Calculating the expected value

For any probability distribution, the expected value represents the *average* value of the distribution. For the uniform distribution, you calculate the expected value as the midpoint of the interval over which the distribution is defined.

For example, suppose that the uniform distribution is defined over the interval (a, b). You calculate the expected value as

$$E(X) = \frac{b+a}{2}$$

The key terms in this formula are

- ✔ X = a uniformly distributed random variable defined over the interval (a, b)
- ✔ $E(X)$ = the expected value of X
- ✔ a = the lower limit of the interval
- ✔ b = the upper limit of the interval

The expected value formula for the uniform distribution is illustrated in Figure 9-2.

The graph in Figure 9-2 shows that the expected value is the *midpoint* of the interval (a,b). In other words, it's half-way between a and b.

As an example, the expected value of the uniform distribution defined over the interval (1,5) is computed as follows:

$$E(X) = \frac{b+a}{2}$$

$$E(X) = \frac{5+1}{2} = 3$$

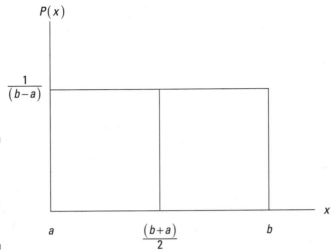

Figure 9-2:
The
expected
value of the
uniform
distribution.

Uniform distribution: Computing variance and standard deviation

In addition to the expected value, a probability distribution can be characterized by the variance and the standard deviation. These values measure the degree of *dispersion* (spread) among the values of a probability distribution.

For the uniform distribution defined over the interval from a to b, the variance equals

$$\sigma^2 = \frac{(b-a)^2}{12}$$

The standard deviation is the square root of the variance:

$$\sigma = \frac{(b-a)}{\sqrt{12}}$$

For example, the variance of the uniform distribution defined over the interval (1, 5) is computed as follows:

$$\sigma^2 = \frac{(b-a)^2}{12}$$
$$= \frac{(5-1)^2}{12}$$
$$= \frac{16}{12}$$
$$= 1.333$$

The standard deviation is:

$$\sigma = \frac{(b-a)}{\sqrt{12}}$$
$$= \frac{(5-1)}{\sqrt{12}}$$
$$= \frac{4}{\sqrt{12}}$$
$$= 1.1547$$

Computing uniform probabilities

You can compute probabilities for the uniform distribution with formulas or graphs. When using graphs to compute uniform probabilities, you are computing areas within the rectangle that describes the uniform distribution.

Computing uniform probabilities with formulas

For example, suppose the random variable X is uniformly distributed over the interval (a, b). You compute the probability that X is less than or equal to a specified value of x, using this formula:

$$P(X \le x) = \frac{x-a}{b-a}$$

If, for example, X is a uniform random variable with $a = 0$ and $b = 10$. You find the probability that X is less than or equal to 7 by these calculations:

$$P(X \le x) = \frac{x-a}{b-a}$$
$$P(X \le 7) = \frac{7-0}{10-0}$$
$$P(X \le 7) = 0.7$$

To determine the probability that X is greater than or equal to x, use the following formula:

$$P(X \ge x) = 1 - \frac{x-a}{b-a}$$

This is true because with a continuous random variable,
$$P(X \le x) + P(X \ge x) = 1$$

For a continuous random variable X, either $X \le x$ or $X \ge x$ must be true; therefore, the probabilities of these events must sum to 1. (Recall from Chapter 6 that these events are *complements*.) So rearranging algebraically gives you the following:

$$P(X \geq x) = 1 - P(X \leq x)$$

$$P(X \geq x) = 1 - \left(\frac{x-a}{b-a}\right)$$

As an example, to calculate the probability that a uniform random variable X defined over the interval (0, 10) is greater than or equal to 2, apply the formula and solve:

$$P(X \leq x) = 1 - \left(\frac{x-a}{b-a}\right)$$

$$P(X \leq 2) = 1 - \left(\frac{2-0}{10-0}\right)$$

$$P(X \leq 2) = 1 - 0.2 = 0.8$$

$$P(X \leq 0.2) = 0.8$$

To calculate the probability that X is *between* two constants a and b, use the following formula:

$$P(a \leq X \leq b) = P(X \leq b) - P(X \leq a)$$

For example, you compute the probability that a uniform random variable X defined over the interval (0, 10) is between 3 and 6 as

$$P(3 \leq X \leq 6) = P(X \leq 6) - P(X \leq 3)$$

and follow these steps:

1. **Determine the probability that X is less than or equal to 6:**

$$P(X \leq x) = \frac{x-a}{b-a}$$

$$P(X \leq 6) = \frac{6-0}{10-0}$$

$$P(X \leq 6) = 0.6$$

2. **Compute the probability that X is less than or equal to 0.3:**

$$P(X \leq x) = \frac{x-a}{b-a}$$

$$P(X \leq 3) = \frac{3-0}{10-0}$$

$$P(X \leq 3) = 0.3$$

3. **Combine the results:**

$$P(3 \le X \le 6) = 0.6 - 0.3$$
$$P(3 \le X \le 6) = 0.3$$

One of the unique properties of the uniform distribution is that the probability that X falls within a given range of values depends only on the *width* of the range. For example, for the *standard* uniform distribution, the following probabilities are equal:

$$P(0.1 \le X \le 0.2)$$
$$P(0.3 \le X \le 0.4)$$
$$P(0.7 \le X \le 0.8)$$

Each of these probabilities equals 0.1, which you can compute as
$$P(0.1 \le X \le 0.2) = P(X \le 0.2) - P(X \le 0.1)$$

Then follow these steps:

1. **Determine the probability that X is less than or equal to 0.2:**

$$P(X \le x) = \frac{x-a}{b-a}$$
$$P(X \le 0.2) = \frac{0.2 - 0}{1 - 0}$$
$$P(X \le 0.2) = 0.2$$

2. **Compute the probability that X is less than or equal to 0.1:**

$$P(X \le x) = b - a$$
$$P(X \le 0.1) = \frac{0.1 - 0}{1 - 0}$$
$$P(X \le 0.1) = 0.1$$

3. **Combine the results:**

$$P(0.1 \le X \le 0.2) = 0.2 - 0.1$$
$$P(0.1 \le X \le 0.2) = 0.1$$

Computing uniform probabilities with graphs

You can also compute probabilities graphically for the uniform distribution by computing areas under a rectangle (see the earlier section "Graphing the uniform distribution"). For example, Figure 9-3 shows the probability that a standard uniform random variable X is between 0.3 and 0.6.

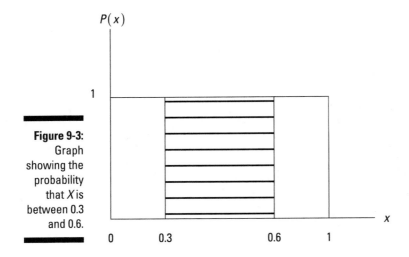

Figure 9-3:
Graph
showing the
probability
that *X* is
between 0.3
and 0.6.

The horizontal axis shows that the distribution is defined over the interval from 0 to 1. The width of this interval, which is the base of the rectangle, equals $1 - 0 = 1$. The height of the rectangle equals 1 divided by the base, or $1/1 = 1$. The area of the rectangle equals the base times the height, which is $1 \times 1 = 1$.

To find the probability that *X* is between 0.3 and 0.6, you compute an area within the rectangle (see the shaded region in Figure 9-3). The base of this shaded region equals $0.6 - 0.3 = 0.3$. The height equals 1. Therefore, the area equals 0.3 (0.3×1). The probability that *X* is between 0.3 and 0.6 is 0.3, which matches the result found with the algebraic formula.

Understanding the Normal Distribution

The normal distribution is a continuous probability distribution that can be used to describe a large number of different situations, not just in business applications but in a wide variety of other disciplines, such as psychology, sociology, biology, and so on. The normal distribution, sometimes called the *Gaussian distribution*, is named after scientist and mathematician Johann Carl Friedrich Gauss who introduced the concept.

The normal distribution has several useful properties that can be used to describe real-world events. For example, under the normal distribution, there is a balance or *symmetry* between the likelihood of a value being below the mean of the distribution and being above the mean of the distribution.

As an example, suppose that researchers have determined that the heights of all men in a country are normally distributed with a mean of 69 inches and a standard deviation of 2 inches. Based on the normal distribution, the following events are equally likely:

A randomly chosen man is no more than 67 inches tall

A randomly chosen man is at least 71 inches tall

These events are equally likely because:

A height of 67 inches is one standard deviation below the mean (69 – 1(2) = 67)

A height of 71 inches is one standard deviation above the mean (69 + 1(2) = 71)

Similarly, the following events are equally likely:

A randomly chosen man is no more than 65 inches tall

A randomly chosen man is at least 73 inches tall

These events are equally likely because:

A height of 65 inches is two standard deviations below the mean (69 – 2(2) = 65)

A height of 73 inches is two standard deviations above the mean (69 + 2(2) = 73)

Because the normal distribution is a *continuous* distribution, it's defined for an infinite number of values. Unlike the uniform distribution, the normal distribution is defined for *all* values between negative infinity and positive infinity.

In the following sections, I show you how you can express the normal distribution graphically, I introduce you to the standard normal distribution, and I walk you through calculating probabilities for the normal distribution.

Graphing the normal distribution

The normal distribution can be graphed with a special type of curve, which is usually described as a *bell-shaped curve*. Normal probabilities can be determined by computing areas under this curve.

The bell-shaped curve has several key features. It's defined over the entire range of values between negative and positive infinity; it's *symmetrical* about the mean (for example, the area below the mean is a *mirror image* of the area above the mean); and most of the area under the normal distribution is close to the mean. The area declines rapidly for values that are several standard deviations away from the mean.

As an example, the distribution of heights from the previous example is illustrated with a bell-shaped curve as shown in Figure 9-4.

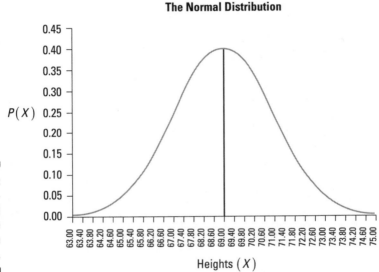

The Normal Distribution

Figure 9-4:
The bell-shaped curve of the distribution of heights.

The mean of 69 inches is at the center of the distribution; the area to the left of the mean is a mirror image of the area to the right of the mean. Most of the area under the curve is close to the mean; the area falls off rapidly for large and small values of X. (The extreme right and left ends of the curve are known as the *tails* of the distribution.)

Figure 9-5 shows that the probability of a randomly chosen man's height being between 67 inches and 71 inches is 68.27 percent.

The shaded region under the curve represents heights between 67 and 71 inches. This covers 68.27 percent of the area under the curve; therefore, the probability that a randomly chosen man's height is between 67 inches and 71 inches is 0.6827 or 68.27 percent.

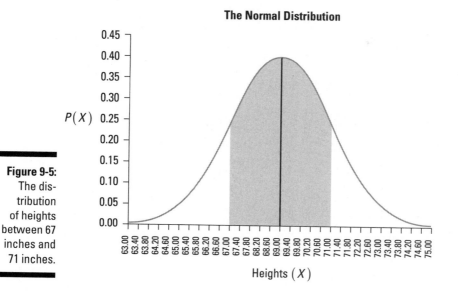

Figure 9-5:
The distribution of heights between 67 inches and 71 inches.

The normal distribution is uniquely characterized by two values:

- The expected value (mean), represented by μ (the Greek letter "mu")
- The standard deviation, represented by σ (the Greek letter "sigma")

There are an infinite number of different possible normal distributions, each with a different value of the mean and standard deviation.

The normal distribution in statistical analysis

The normal distribution is used in conjunction with many statistical techniques. It plays a key role in a lot of applications, such as the following:

- Computing confidence intervals
- Testing hypotheses about the mean of a population
- Testing hypotheses about the means of two populations
- Regression analysis

In many business applications, variables are assumed to be normally distributed. For example, returns to stocks are often assumed to be normally distributed by investors, portfolio managers, financial analysts, risk managers, and so on. The assumption of normality is not only convenient, but many standard statistical techniques require it in order to generate valid results. For example, computing a confidence interval for the mean of a population may be based on the normal distribution. Many of the techniques used in regression analysis to check the validity of the results are based on the normal distribution. As a result, even when the assumption of normality is not perfectly accurate, the normal distribution is often used to perform statistical analyses due to its convenience.

Getting to know the standard normal distribution

The *standard normal distribution* is the special case where $\mu = 0$ and $\sigma = 1$.

For example, suppose that the daily returns to a stock follow the standard normal distribution. The mean return over a single trading day is 0 percent, and the standard deviation is 1 percent; as a result:

The probability that tomorrow's return will be between -1 percent and +1 percent is 0.6827 or 68.27 percent. –1 percent represents one standard deviation below the mean, while +1 percent represents one standard deviation above the mean.

The probability that tomorrow's return will be between –2 percent and +2 percent is 0.9544 or 95.44 percent. –2 percent represents two standard deviations below the mean, while +2 percent represents two standard deviations above the mean.

The probability that tomorrow's return will be between –3 percent and +3 percent is 0.9973 or 99.73 percent. –3 percent represents three standard deviations below the mean, while +3 percent represents three standard deviations above the mean.

By convention, the letter Z represents a standard normal random variable, whereas the letter X represents any other normal random variable.

Computing standard normal probabilities

One approach to computing probabilities for the standard normal distribution is to use statistical tables. (For the mathematically inclined, the tables result from applying calculus to the normal distribution.)

The standard normal table is designed to show *cumulative* probabilities; i.e., the probability that a standard normal random variable Z is less than or equal to a specified value, such as $P(Z \leq 2.50)$. Standard normal tables are divided into two parts; the first shows positive values for Z, and the second shows negative values for Z.

Computing other types of probabilities, such as $P(Z \geq 1.70)$, can be accomplished by using the properties of the standard normal distribution to rearrange these probabilities in a more convenient form.

The following sections illustrate how to compute any time of normal probabilities using the standard normal tables.

Computing "Less Than or Equal to" Standard Normal Probabilities

Table 9-1 shows a portion of the standard normal table for positive values of Z. (The actual table typically shows Z values between 0 and 3.)

Table 9-1	Standard Normal Table — Positive Values			
Z	0.00	0.01	0.02	0.03
0.9	0.8159	0.8186	0.8212	0.8238
1.0	0.8413	0.8438	0.8461	0.8485
1.1	0.8643	0.8665	0.8686	0.8708
1.2	0.8849	0.8869	0.8888	0.8907

The table shows the probability that a standard normal random variable Z is *less than or equal to* a specific value. For example, to express the probability that Z is less than or equal to 1, you write $P(Z \leq 1.00)$. Here's how you find this probability:

1. **Take the first digits before and after the decimal point (1.0 in 1.00) from the Z column, second row.**

2. **Take the second digit after the decimal point (0.00 in 1.00) from the corresponding column (*0.00* in this case).**

3. **Find the appropriate probability at the intersection of this row and column.**

    Using this technique, the table shows that $P(Z \leq 1.00) = 0.8413$. Figure 9-6 shows this expression graphically.

The shaded region to the left of 1 represents 84.13 percent of the area under the curve; therefore, $P(Z \leq 1.00) = 0.8413$ or 84.13 percent.

Negative probabilities also have a corresponding standard normal table. Take a look at Table 9-2. This shows several negative values for Z; the actual table typically shows values ranging from 0 to –3.

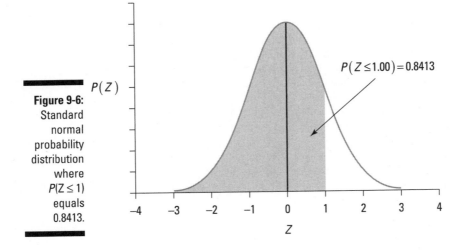

Standard Normal Probability Distribution

$P(Z \leq 1.00) = 0.8413$

$P(Z)$

Figure 9-6:
Standard
normal
probability
distribution
where
$P(Z \leq 1)$
equals
0.8413.

Table 9-2	Standard Normal Table — Negative Values			
Z	0.00	0.01	0.02	0.03
−1.3	0.0968	0.0951	0.0934	0.0918
−1.2	0.1151	0.1131	0.1112	0.1093
−1.1	0.1357	0.1335	0.1314	0.1292
−1.0	0.1587	0.1562	0.1539	0.1515

Say you want to compute the probability that Z is less than −1.23, which you write as $P(Z \leq -1.23)$. The first digits before and after the decimal point (−1.2 in −1.23) are in the Z column, second row. The second digit after the decimal point (0.03 in −1.23) is in the far right column. You find the probability at the intersection of the row and column, so the table shows that $P(Z \leq -1.23) = 0.1093$. This is shown in Figure 9-7.

One of the drawbacks to using tables to compute standard normal probabilities is that they show only cumulative probabilities for Z; for example, Z is less than or equal to a specific value. But you can figure all other cases by combining the properties of the standard normal distribution with the tables.

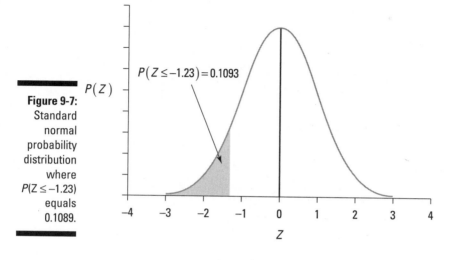

Standard Normal Probability Distribution

$P(Z \le -1.23) = 0.1093$

$P(Z)$

Figure 9-7:
Standard normal probability distribution where $P(Z \le -1.23)$ equals 0.1089.

Z

Property 1: The area under the standard normal curve equals 1

The first of these properties is that the entire area under the standard normal curve equals 1. Because the curve covers the entire area between negative and positive infinity (∞), you can express this result as $P(-\infty \le Z \le \infty) = 1$. So the probability that a standard normal random variable Z falls between negative infinity and positive infinity is 1; in other words, Z will fall within this interval with *certainty*.

When you consider all possible outcomes in any given situation, you can be certain that one outcome will occur. A probability of 1 indicates that an event will occur with *certainty*. A probability of 0 indicates that an event is *impossible*. All other probabilities fall between 0 and 1. (Probability theory is covered in Chapter 6.)

Property 2: The standard normal curve is symmetrical about the mean

The next key property of the standard normal distribution is *symmetry*, where the area to the left of the mean is a mirror image of the area to the right. As a result, the probability that Z is less than the mean is 0.5, and you write it as $P(Z \le 0) = 0.5$ (because half of the area under this distribution is to the left of the mean, and half is to the right of the mean; the total area is 1), as shown in the Figure 9-8.

Because $P(Z \le 0) = 0.5$, due to the symmetry of the standard normal probability distribution, it's also true that $P(Z \ge 0) = 0.5$, as illustrated in Figure 9-9.

Standard Normal Probability Distribution

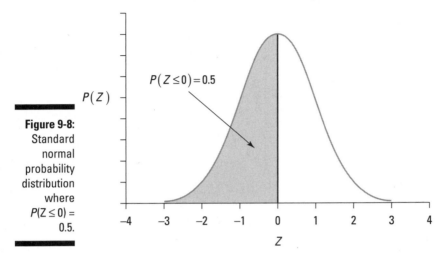

Standard Normal Probability Distribution

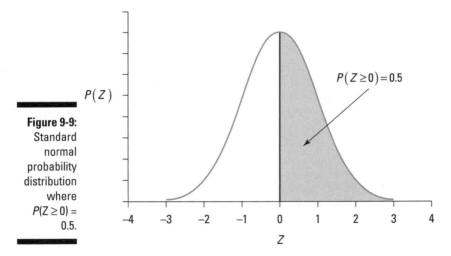

Other examples of symmetry include

$$P(Z \leq -1) = P(Z \geq 1) = 0.1587$$
$$P(Z \leq -2) = P(Z \geq 2) = 0.0228$$

Computing "greater than or equal to" standard normal probabilities

One type of probability you can't compute directly from a table is the case where a standard normal random variable Z is *greater than or equal to* a specified value z: $P(Z \geq z)$. Instead, you rearrange the identity to yield a very useful result:

$$P(Z \leq z) + P(Z \geq z) = 1$$

This is a consequence of the first property of the standard normal distribution: The area under the standard normal curve equals 1.

Rearranging this equation gives you

$$P(Z \geq z) = 1 - P(Z \leq z)$$

For example, to determine the probability that a standard normal random variable is greater than 1 (for example, $P(Z \geq 1)$, the first step is to rewrite the probability in a form that enables you to use the standard normal tables. This is shown as:

$$P(Z \geq 1) = 1 - P(Z \leq 1)$$
$$P(Z \leq 1) = 0.8413$$
$$P(Z \geq 1) = 1 - 0.8413$$
$$= 0.1587$$

The result is shown in Figure 9-10.

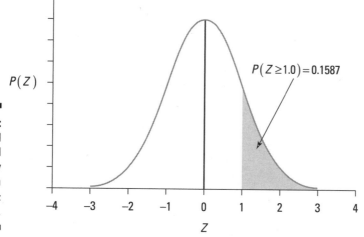

Standard Normal Probability Distribution

$P(Z \geq 1.0) = 0.1587$

$P(Z)$

Figure 9-10:
Standard
normal
probability
distribution
where $P(Z \geq 1) = 0.1587$.

Z

Computing "in between" standard normal probabilities

Another type of probability that you can't compute directly from a standard normal table is the case where a standard normal random variable Z is *between* two constants: c and d: $P(c \le Z \le d)$. But, lucky for you, you can work around this with the following identity:

$$P(c \le Z \le d) = P(Z \le d) - P(Z \le c)$$

You can now compute this probability by looking up $P(Z \le c)$ and $P(Z \le d)$ in the standard normal table and computing the difference between them.

For example, suppose that you want to know the probability that Z is between one and two standard deviations above the mean. In this case, c = 1.00 and d = 2.00. This probability can be expressed as follows:

$$P(1.00 \le Z \le 2.00)$$

Algebraically, this can be rearranged in a form that involves two "less than or equal to" probabilities that can be looked up in the standard normal tables:

$$P(1.00 \le Z \le 2.00)$$
$$= P(Z \le 2.00) - P(Z \le 1.00)$$

From the standard normal table (Table 9-1):

$$P(Z \le 2.00) = 0.9772$$
$$P(Z \le 1.00) = 0.8413$$

As a result, you calculate the probability:

$$P(1.00 \le Z \le 2.00) = 0.9772 - 0.8413 = 0.1359$$

Figure 9-11 illustrates this probability.

Note that you can use this approach for negative values, too. For example, from the standard normal table (Table 9-2),

$$P(-2.00 \le Z \le -1.00)$$
$$= P(Z \le -1.00) - P(Z \le -2.00),$$

$$P(Z \le -2.00) = 0.0228$$
$$P(Z \le -1.00) = 0.1587$$

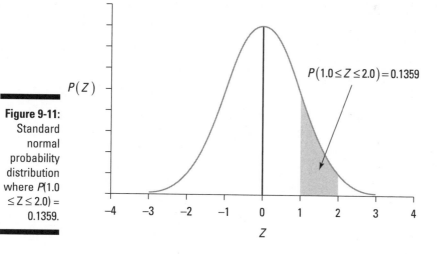

Figure 9-11:
Standard
normal
probability
distribution
where $P(1.0 \le Z \le 2.0) = 0.1359$.

As a result:

$$P(-2.00 \le Z \le -1.00)$$
$$= P(Z \le -1.00) - P(Z \le -2.00)$$
$$= 0.1587 - 0.0228$$
$$= 0.1359$$

Computing normal probabilities other than standard normal

Many variables in business applications are assumed to be normally distributed, including rates of returns to stocks and other financial assets. Although these variables are normal, they're usually not *standard* normal. As a result, you can't compute probabilities for these variables from the standard normal tables without first transforming them into the equivalent standard normal form, as shown with the following formula:

$$Z = \frac{X - \mu}{\sigma}$$

In this expression, Z is a standard normal random variable, and X is a normal random variable with mean μ and standard deviation σ.

For example, suppose that the annual return of the stock of the Gamma Corporation is normally distributed with a mean of 5 percent and a standard deviation of 2 percent. What's the probability that the return from this stock over the coming year will be 4 percent or less?

Let X be a random variable that represents "the annual return for the stock of Gamma Corporation." X is a normally distributed random variable with a mean (μ) of 0.05 and a standard deviation (σ) of 0.02. X is *not* standard normal, because the mean isn't 0 and the standard deviation isn't 1.

To compute this probability, convert the rate of return X into a standard normal random variable Z as follows:

$$P(X \le 0.04) = P\left(Z \le \frac{X - \mu}{\sigma}\right) = P\left(Z \le \frac{0.04 - 0.05}{0.02}\right) = P(Z \le -0.5)$$

Based on the standard normal tables (refer to Tables 9-1 and 9-2 in the earlier section "Computing standard normal probabilities"), $P(Z \le -0.5) = 0.3085$, so the probability that the stock's return will be 4 percent or less is 0.3085 or 30.85 percent.

Similarly, you can determine the probability that the stock's return next year will be 8 percent or more like so:

$$P(X \ge 0.08) = P\left(Z \ge \frac{X - \mu}{\sigma}\right) = P\left(Z \ge \frac{0.08 - 0.05}{0.02}\right) = P(Z \ge 1.5)$$

Recall from the earlier section "Computing "greater than or equal to" standard normal probabilities" the following key property for the standard normal distribution:

$$P(Z \le z) + P(Z \ge z) = 1$$

Rearranging this algebraically gives:

$$P(Z \ge z) = 1 - P(Z \le z)$$

Therefore,

$$P(Z \ge 1.5) = 1 - P(Z \le 1.5)$$

Based on the standard normal table (Table 9-1):

$$P(Z \le 1.5) = 0.9332$$

Therefore,

$$1 - P(Z \leq 1.5)$$
$$= 1 - 0.9332$$
$$= 0.0668$$
$$= 6.68\%$$

the probability that the stock's return next year will be between 7 percent and 10 percent as follows:

$$P(0.07 \leq X \leq 0.10) = P\left(\frac{0.07 - 0.05}{0.02} \leq Z \leq \frac{0.10 - 0.05}{0.02}\right)$$
$$= P(1.00 \leq Z \leq 2.50)$$
$$= P(Z \leq 2.50) - P(Z \leq 1.00)$$
$$= 0.9938 - 0.8413$$
$$= 0.1525$$
$$= 15.25\%$$

As another example, imagine that the scores on a standardized test are normally distributed with a mean score of 80 and a standard deviation of 10. If a student receives a score of 90, he was outperformed by what proportion of all other students taking the test?

In other words, what is the probability of receiving a score of more than 90 on this test? Let X represent the random variable "score on the exam." X is a normally distributed random variable with a mean of 80 and a standard deviation of 10. Because X isn't a standard normal random variable, you must convert it:

$$P(X \geq 90) = P\left(Z \geq \frac{X - \mu}{\sigma}\right) = P\left(Z \geq \frac{90 - 80}{10}\right) = P(Z \geq 1.00)$$

Due to the symmetry of the standard normal distribution,

$$P(Z \geq 1.00) = 1 - P(Z \leq 1.00)$$

From the standard normal table (Table 9-1),

$$P(Z \leq 1.00) = 0.8413$$

Therefore,

$$P(Z \geq 1.00)$$
$$= 1 - P(Z \leq 1.00)$$
$$= 1 - 0.8413$$
$$= 0.1587$$

or only 15.87 percent of the students taking the exam scored better than 90.

These techniques can be used to compute *any* normal probability, whether it is expressed as greater than, less than, or between, and regardless of the mean and standard deviation of the distribution.

Chapter 10

Sampling Techniques and Distributions

A *population* is a collection of data that we are interested in studying; a *sample* is a selection of data randomly chosen from a population. The use of sample data is the basis for a wide variety of business applications. This is because obtaining information about an entire population is likely to be very time-consuming and costly. Instead, samples may be used to understand the behavior of the underlying population.

For example, if a department store wants to know which types of new products customers are willing to buy, the store may not have the resources to survey every single one of its customers. Instead, if the store can choose representative samples of its customers to survey, it could potentially obtain the same information at a fraction of the cost.

One of the requirements of using samples to draw conclusions about a population is that the samples accurately mirror the population; otherwise, any conclusions that are reached about the population are bound to be inaccurate.

Several different types of sampling techniques have been developed to accurately capture the properties of a population. The choice of technique depends on several factors, such as:

What are the demographic characteristics of interest?

How easy will it be to obtain sample data?

How much data is needed to ensure accurate results?

For example, suppose that the New York State government wants to analyze the distribution of ages of everyone living in the state. This helps determine what type of funding is needed for various programs in the future. Although the ages of every single resident could be collected, this could be very time consuming and costly.

Instead, suppose the government decides to randomly sample residents throughout the state and use this information to estimate the distribution of ages. Clearly, it makes no sense to focus only on high school students, because their ages are substantially lower than the overall population. Instead, samples are chosen that ideally match the demographic characteristics of the entire state. For example, questionnaires could be mailed to randomly chosen addresses throughout the state.

In this chapter, I introduce several types of sampling techniques that may be used for various types of studies. I also show you a special type of probability distribution, known as a *sampling distribution.* This is a special type of probability distribution that describes the properties of a *sample statistic.* (Sample statistics are summary measures of a sample; these include the sample mean, sample variance and sample standard deviation. Sample statistics are discussed in Chapters 3 and 4.) Due to its widespread use in statistical analysis, I focus on the sampling distribution of the *sample mean.*

Sampling Techniques: Choosing Data from a Population

Statistical inference is a methodology that lets you draw conclusions about a population from sample data. One of the most important challenges in statistical inference is choosing samples that accurately reflect the characteristics of the underlying population. Although you can choose from many sampling techniques, the appropriate technique depends on the type of information you're studying and your resources.

You can classify the two basic approaches to sampling as probability sampling and nonprobability sampling. Probability sampling is used when it is important to ensure that each member of a population has a chance of being chosen. Nonprobability sampling is a more subjective approach, and is often used when it would be difficult or impossible to use probability sampling. I explore both of these approaches in the following sections.

Probability sampling

When you use *probability sampling*, each member of the population has a chance of being chosen for the sample. In some of these techniques, each population member is *equally likely* to be chosen; in others, this is not the case. With probability sampling, it's possible to determine the probability that a given member of the population will be chosen.

Within the category of probability sampling, you can choose from four types of sampling techniques, which I discuss in the following sections.

Simple random samples

In a *simple random sample,* each member in the population is equally likely to be chosen. There are several different ways in which population members may be chosen with equal probability. One approach is to assign a numerical value to each population member and then randomly choose numbers that correspond to these members.

For example, suppose a population consists of the following ten members of the finance faculty at a prestigious university:

1. Benjamin Harrison
2. Martin Van Buren
3. John Tyler
4. Millard Fillmore
5. Grover Cleveland
6. Chester Arthur
7. James Polk
8. Zachary Taylor
9. James Buchanan
10. Franklin Pierce

You would like to randomly choose five of these faculty members for a newly formed committee. You assign each faculty member a number from one to ten. (This could be done alphabetically or in any number of other ways.) To choose a simple random sample of five of these faculty members, you can use a random number generator.

A random number generator is a function that can be used to randomly choose numbers within a specified interval. As an example, you can use

Excel's RANDBETWEEN function; this generates whole numbers that are randomly chosen between any two values you specify.

For this example, you would need to generate a random number between 1 and 10. You would then enter RANDBETWEEN(1,10) into Excel and record the resulting number. You would repeat this process until you have five unique numbers. The faculty members associated with these numbers are then chosen for the new committee.

In this example, you don't want to choose the same number twice; if this happens, you simply discard the result and choose another random number until you have five unique numbers. The process you are using is known as sampling *without* replacement. If you are willing to choose the same number more than once, then no results would be discarded; the process that you would be using is known as sampling *with* replacement.

Suppose the following sequence of random numbers is chosen:

RANDBETWEEN(1,10) = 1

RANDBETWEEN(1,10) = 4

RANDBETWEEN(1,10) = 5

RANDBETWEEN(1,10) = 8

RANDBETWEEN(1,10) = 6

Your simple random sample would then consist of the following faculty members:

1. Benjamin Harrison

4. Millard Filmore

5. Grover Cleveland

8. Zachary Taylor

6. Chester Arthur

These are the lucky members of the new committee.

Systematic samples

With *systematic samples,* population members are assigned a numerical value, as is the case with simple random samples. Instead of using random numbers to choose population members, though, you will instead use a specific *sequence* of numbers.

For example, suppose an economist wants to study the distribution of 100 household incomes in a small town and wants to draw a sample size of ten. In this case, the economist draws every tenth population member (because the number of households divided by the sample size equals 100/10 = 10). One way she can draw every tenth member is to start with a random number (between 1 and 10) and then add ten to each number to get the desired sequence.

For example, you could use RANDBETWEEN(1,10) to obtain the starting value for the sequence. If this turns out to be a 3, then the appropriate sequence of random numbers would be:

3, 13, 23, 33, 43, 53, 63, 73, 83, 93

If instead the function RANDBETWEEN(1,10) generates a 5, then the appropriate sequence of random numbers would be:

5, 15, 25, 35, 45, 55, 65, 75, 85, 95

Other techniques could be used to randomly choose the first value, such as the flip of a coin, the roll of a die, and so on. Similarly, if a population contains 1,200 members and the economist wants a sample size of ten, the numbering sequence includes every 120th member (1,200/10 = 120). One way she can draw every 120th member is to start with a random number (between 1 and 120) and then add 120 to each number to get the sequence.

In this case, suppose that the function RANDBETWEEN(1,120) results in a value of 57; then the sequence would consist of the following values:

57, 177, 297, 417, 537, 657, 777, 897, 1017, 1137

As another example, suppose that a marketing firm wants to find out whether consumers are responding favorably to a newly launched advertising campaign. A researcher could choose a busy mall and ask every 20th customer that walks by how he or she feels about the new advertising campaign. In this case, though, the researcher wouldn't have a specific sequence of numbers, because it's impossible to determine in advance how many people are in the mall at any given time.

In this case, systematic samples are chosen based on incomplete knowledge of the underlying population. This approach is useful when the size of the entire population is not known.

Stratified samples

When using *stratified samples,* you divide a population into *strata* (levels or layers). The strata may reflect any of a wide variety of characteristics of the population data, such as ages, incomes, levels of education, and so on.

Basically, you choose a stratified sample in such a way that you ensure that the proportion of sample members in each stratum (singular of *strata*) matches the distribution found in the population.

For example, suppose a college wants to conduct a survey of student attitudes toward the building of a costly new sports stadium as an alternative to expanding the current antiquated library. Instead of surveying every single student in the school, the college chooses stratified samples. It divides the entire student body by class: freshmen, sophomores, juniors, and seniors. (Assume for this example that the school doesn't offer any graduate programs, so all students belong to one of these four classes.) Here's how the classes break down:

Class	Number of Students
Freshmen	800
Sophomores	1,200
Juniors	1,000
Seniors	1,000

And the percentages of students in each class are as follows:

Class	Number of Students	Percentage of Total
Freshmen	800	20 percent
Sophomores	1,200	30 percent
Juniors	1,000	25 percent
Seniors	1,000	25 percent

If the college chooses a stratified sample of 200 students, the sample consists of the following:

40 freshmen (20 percent of 200)

60 sophomores (30 percent of 200)

50 juniors (25 percent of 200)

50 seniors (25 percent of 200)

Within each stratum, a simple random sample of the appropriate number of students is chosen. This selection method ensures that no class is under- or overrepresented in the sample data.

One of the advantages of the stratified sample approach is that you can draw conclusions about each individual stratum. For example, the college can analyze the attitudes of freshmen separately from the attitudes of sophomores, juniors, and seniors. On the other hand, one of the disadvantages of this approach is that you need more information about the characteristics of the population than with other approaches, such as the simple random sampling approach discussed earlier. In this example, you need to know the distribution of students among the freshman, sophomore, junior, and senior classes.

Cluster samples

With *cluster samples,* you subdivide a population into groups based on common characteristic (such as location, age, income level, and so forth). You choose groups randomly, and then you choose samples from those groups randomly.

Say you're a researcher conducting a national survey about attitudes toward proposed national legislation. You divide the entire voting age population of the United States into groups according to state of residency. You decide to choose a sample of eight states; you believe that this is sufficient to represent the entire country.

In this case, you would first assign a number to each state in the United States. Next, you could use the function RANDBETWEEN(1,50) until you choose eight different states.

Within each selected state, voting age residents are randomly chosen using a simple random sample. This may be accomplished by assigning a number to each registered voter and then using a random number generator to randomly pick the desired number of voters.

Suppose that the following states are chosen:

> Wisconsin
>
> Rhode Island
>
> Michigan
>
> Utah
>
> Illinois
>
> South Carolina
>
> Arizona
>
> Oregon

Within each state, you choose simple random samples of voters.

The advantage of using cluster sampling is that it can be implemented more quickly and cheaply than stratified sampling. In this example, stratified sampling requires voters to be randomly chosen from each of the 50 states. The disadvantage of using cluster sampling is that it may not be as accurate as stratified sampling.

Nonprobability sampling

Unlike probability sampling, *nonprobability sampling* doesn't guarantee that each population member has a chance of being chosen. And with nonprobability sampling, you have to use subjective judgment.

One of the major drawbacks to nonprobability samples is that the results aren't as reliable for drawing conclusions about the overall population. It may be easier to get the samples, but there's a price — they're less useful than probability samples.

I discuss four of the nonprobability sampling techniques in the following sections, including convenience samples, quota samples, purposive samples, and judgment samples.

Convenience samples

When you choose population members primarily because they're accessible, you're using *convenience samples.* For example, if a marketing firm needs to study consumer attitudes toward new products, it may be forced to rely on the input of people who are willing to participate; they are not necessarily representative of the overall population.

Suppose for example a marketing firm decides to conduct a series of interviews at a mall to determine which new movies are likely to do well at the box office. The interviews are conducted at 3:00 in the afternoon on a Wednesday. Although there may be many volunteers who are willing to take part in the interviews, most or all of them are likely to be students and/or retirees, which doesn't reflect the overall population. Unless the marketing firm is only interested in the views of these groups, the results are not likely to be accurate.

Quota samples

Quota samples are closely related to stratified samples; in both cases, you divide population members into separate groups. The main difference is that with a quota sample, the number of sample members in each stratum may not exactly represent the numbers in the underlying population.

For example, suppose that a college is interested in comparing the GPA of its male and female students. Assume that the proportion of male students at this college is 60 percent, so the proportion of female students is 40 percent. A stratified sample would ensure that 60 percent of the sample members are male, and 40 percent are female. With a quota sample, any number of males and females may be chosen. Suppose that the college doesn't know the exact proportion of male and female students, so it decides to choose an equal mix of male and female students for the sample. Clearly, this doesn't reflect the proportions in the actual population.

Purposive samples

With *purposive samples,* you choose members of the population because they're *not* typical in some important way. For example, a company that produces a new product may be concerned that the product is too expensive for the average consumer to buy. The company may target students (who presumably have low incomes) to determine whether they'd consider buying the product. The logic is that if the product isn't too expensive to people with relatively low incomes, it won't be too expensive to people with higher incomes.

As another example, suppose that a snack foods company manually inspects all the potato chips that it produces before they are sold to the public. Any chips that appear to be burned are automatically discarded. This process is very time consuming and costly; the company wants to try a different approach.

Suppose that the smallest chips are most likely to be burned. Rather than inspecting every single potato chip, the company decides to save time by only inspecting the chips that appear to be unusually small. If these are not burned, the remaining chips are probably acceptable. The company is now using purposive samples to represent the entire population.

Judgment samples

When conducting a study with a *judgment sample,* you chose members based on your subjective judgment. You choose these members because they offer specific characteristics of interest. For example, suppose that half of the residents of a city are male (and, therefore, half are female). A handbag manufacturer wants to determine which features are most important to consumers in this city. If the company chooses to survey customers in the local mall, it may go out of its way to question a larger number of female customers (rather than male customers) because most handbags are purchased by women.

Sampling Distributions

A *statistic* is a summary measure of a sample, and a *parameter* is a summary measure of a population. (I discuss both summary measures of samples and populations in Chapters 3, 4, and 5.) The probability distribution of a statistic is known as a *sampling distribution,* which is what this section is all about.

Some examples of statistics include

- Sample mean ($\bar{X}$)
- Sample variance (s^2)
- Sample standard deviation (s)

Some examples of parameters are

- Population mean (μ)
- Population variance (σ^2)
- Population standard deviation (σ)

Note: Latin letters represent statistics; Greek letters represent parameters.

In many cases, a *population parameter* is costly and time-consuming to calculate. For example, figuring out the average age of everyone living in the United States would be very time-consuming! In these cases, the statistician uses sample statistics instead. The sample mean ($\bar{X}$) estimates the population mean (μ). The researcher can use a representative sample of U.S. residents to compute a sample mean, which would serve as an estimated value of the average age of all U.S. residents.

If you repeatedly draw samples from a population, the value of a statistic is most likely different for each sample. As a result, it's useful to think of a statistic as a *random variable* whose properties can be described with a *probability distribution.* (See Chapter 7 for details.)

In the following sections, I explore the characteristics of sampling distributions, including how to represent data from a sampling distribution graphically and how to compute the moments of a sampling distribution. The focus is on the sampling distribution of the sample mean $\bar{X}$.

Portraying sampling distributions graphically

As I explain in Chapter 2, a *histogram* is a graphical representation of data in which ranges of values, known as *classes,* appear on the horizontal axis (the *x*-axis) and probabilities on the vertical axis (the *y*-axis). Each class is shown as a single bar whose height equals the probability of that class.

A histogram shows at a glance how the values of a variable are distributed. In this section, histograms are used to describe the properties of the sampling distribution of $\bar{X}$.

One of the benefits of using histograms to analyze a sampling distribution is that it is easy to see if the sampling distribution is symmetrical about the mean, negatively skewed, or positively skewed.

A distribution is symmetrical about the mean if values below the mean occur as frequently as the values an equal distance above the mean. A negatively skewed distribution is one in which there are a small number of extremely small values; a positively skewed distribution is one in which there are a small number of extremely large values. (Skewness and symmetry are discussed in Chapter 3.)

A distribution is symmetrical about the mean if the mean equals the median. A distribution is negatively skewed if the mean is less than the median and positively skewed if the mean is greater than the median.

A histogram also shows at a glance the center or mean of a distribution, and how "spread out" are the members of the distribution. (Recall from Chapter 4 that the spread of a distribution is measured by its variance and its standard deviation.)

A histogram can be used to compare the properties of different sampling distributions or to observe the effect of different sample sizes on a sampling distribution. For example, suppose that a manufacturer of computer chips has found from experience that its assembly line produces two defective chips per hour, and that the number of defective chips produced during a given hour is independent of the number produced during any other hour. In other words, the distribution of defective chips follows the Poisson distribution with an average value of two per hour — in other words, $\lambda = 2$. (The Poisson distribution is discussed in detail in Chapter 8.)

The distribution of defective chips is shown in Figure 10-1.

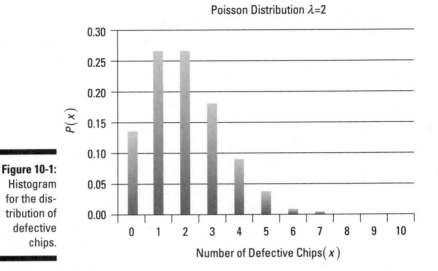

Figure 10-1:
Histogram
for the dis-
tribution of
defective
chips.

Suppose that a sample of five computer chips is randomly chosen, and the number of defective chips in each sample is recorded. This process is repeated 300 times. The resulting distribution consists of 300 sample means, ranging from a low of 0.6 to a high of 4.2.

Figure 10-2 shows the distribution of the mean number of defective chips among the 300 samples of size 5.

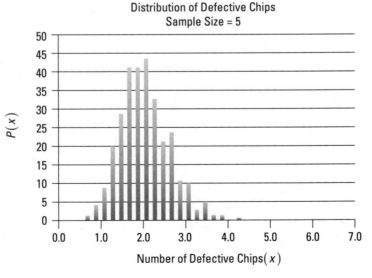

Figure 10-2:
Histogram
of a
sampling
distribution
of defective
computer
chips with a
sample size
of 5.

Note that the distribution of sample means with a sample size of 5 strongly resembles the Poisson distribution.

Suppose now that a sample of 30 computer chips is randomly chosen, and the number of defective chips in each sample is recorded. This process is repeated 300 times. The resulting distribution consists of 300 sample means, ranging from a low of 1.3 to a high of 3.

Figure 10-3 shows the distribution of the mean number of defective chips among the 300 samples of size 30.

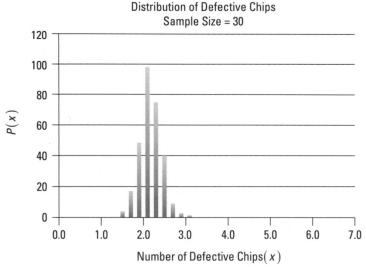

Figure 10-3:
Histogram of a sampling distribution of defective computer chips with a sample size of 30.

Note that the distribution of sample means with a sample size of 30 much more closely resembles the normal distribution than the Poisson distribution.

Figures 10-2 and 10-3 show that the sample mean remains centered on 2 regardless of the sample size, but the mean number of defectives is far less *dispersed* around the mean with a sample size of 30 compared with a sample size of 5. (You can tell that this is the case because the sample mean ranges from 0.6 to 4.2 with a sample size of 5, compared with 1.3 to 3 for a sample size of 30.)

In addition, the figures show that as the sample size grows from 5 to 30, the sampling distribution looks more like the normal distribution.

Moments of a sampling distribution

A sampling distribution is described by a series of summary measures known as *moments,* which include expected value (mean) and variance. The standard deviation is not a separate moment; it is the square root of the variance. The standard deviation of a sampling distribution is often referred to as the *standard error.*

For the sampling distribution of $\bar{X}$, the expected value is $\mu_{\bar{x}}$, which equals the mean of the underlying population (μ). The variance is $\sigma^2_{\bar{x}}$, and the standard deviation, also known as the *standard error,* is $\sigma_{\bar{x}}$.

The values of the variance and standard error depend on the relationship between the size of the sample (n) drawn from the population and the size of the population (N).

> ✔ If the sample size is less than or equal to 5 percent of the population size, the sample is small, relative to the size of the population. In this case, the variance of $\bar{X}$ equals
>
> $$\sigma^2_{\bar{x}} = \frac{\sigma^2}{n}$$
>
> Here, σ^2 is the variance and σ is the standard deviation of the underlying population; n is the sample size.
>
> The square root of the variance of $\bar{X}$ is the standard error of $\bar{X}$:
>
> $$\sigma_{\bar{x}} = \frac{\sigma}{\sqrt{n}}$$
>
> ✔ If the sample size is greater than 5 percent of the population size, the sample is large, relative to the size of the population. In this case, the standard error of $\bar{X}$ equals
>
> $$\sigma_{\bar{x}} = \frac{\sigma}{\sqrt{n}} \sqrt{\frac{N-n}{N-1}}$$

The term $\sqrt{\frac{N-n}{N-1}}$ is known as the *finite population correction factor,* which always assumes a value of less than or equal to 1 (it equals 1 only if the sample size is 1). You use the finite population correction factor to reduce the size of the standard error to reflect the fact that less variability from one sample mean to the next occurs when the sample size is large relative to the population.

The Central Limit Theorem

According to the Central Limit Theorem, the sampling distribution of $\bar{X}$ is normal if the underlying population is normal. If not, the sampling distribution of $\bar{X}$ is at least approximately normal if the sample size is at least 30. Under these circumstances, you can use the normal distribution to determine the probability that the sample mean will fall within a specified range of values. (See Chapter 9 for techniques on using the normal distribution.)

For example, suppose you choose a sample of 50 gasoline prices from gas stations in a major city. You can use the normal distribution to determine the probability that the sample mean gas price is between $3.50 and $4.00 per gallon.

If the Central Limit Theorem fails to hold, you can't use the normal distribution to compute probabilities for the sample mean; instead, you need to find an alternative probability distribution that closely resembles the population that you are studying.

Converting $\bar{X}$ to a standard normal random variable

Based on the Central Limit Theorem, if you draw samples from a population of $n \geq 30$, then $\bar{X}$ is a normally distributed random variable. To determine probabilities for $\bar{X}$, you may use the standard normal probability tables. (These are discussed in Chapter 9.) Use the standard normal tables, which require you to convert $\bar{X}$ to a standard normal random variable.

The standard normal distribution is the special case where the mean (μ) equals 0, and the standard deviation (σ) equals 1.

For any normally distributed random variable X with a mean μ and a standard deviation σ, you find the corresponding standard normal random variable (Z) with the following equation:

$$Z = \frac{X - \mu}{\sigma}$$

For the sampling distribution of $\bar{X}$, the corresponding equation is

$$Z = \frac{\bar{X} - \mu_{\bar{X}}}{\sigma_{\bar{X}}}$$

As an example, say that there are 10,000 stocks trading each day on a regional stock exchange. It's known from historical experience that the returns to these stocks have a mean value of 10 percent per year, and a standard deviation of 20 percent per year.

An investor chooses to buy a random selection of 100 of these stocks for his portfolio. What's the probability that the mean rate of return among these 100 stocks is greater than 8 percent?

The investor's portfolio can be thought of as a sample of stocks chosen from the population of stocks trading on the regional exchange. The first step to finding this probability is to compute the moments of the sampling distribution.

✔ **Compute the mean:** $\mu_{\bar{x}} = \mu = 0.10$.

The mean of the sampling distribution equals the population mean.

✔ **Determine the standard error:** This calculation is a little trickier because the standard error depends on the size of the sample relative to the size of the population. In this case, the sample size (n) is 100, while the population size (N) is 10,000. So you first have to compute the sample size relative to the population size, like so:

$n/N = 100/10,000 = 0.01 = 1\%$

Because 1 percent is less than 5 percent, you don't use the finite population correction factor to compute the standard error. Note that in this case, the value of the finite population correction factor is:

$$\sqrt{\frac{N-n}{N-1}} = \sqrt{\frac{10,000-100}{10,000-1}} = \sqrt{\frac{9,900}{9,999}} = 0.995$$

Because this value is so close to 1, using the finite population correction factor in this case would have little or no impact on the resulting probabilities.

And because the finite population correction factor isn't needed in this case, the standard error is computed as follows:

$$\sigma_{\bar{x}} = \frac{\sigma}{\sqrt{n}}$$
$$= \frac{0.20}{\sqrt{100}}$$
$$= \frac{0.20}{10}$$
$$= 0.02$$

To determine the probability that the sample mean is greater than 8 percent, you must now convert the sample mean into a standard normal random variable using the following equation:

$$Z = \frac{\bar{X} - \mu_{\bar{X}}}{\sigma_{\bar{X}}}$$

To compute the probability that the sample mean is greater than 8 percent, you apply the previous formula as follows:

$$P(\bar{X} \geq 0.08) = P\left(Z \geq \frac{0.08 - \mu_{\bar{X}}}{\sigma_{\bar{X}}}\right)$$

Because $\mu_{\bar{X}} = 0.10$ and $\sigma_{\bar{X}} = 0.02$, these values are substituted into the previous expression as follows:

$$P\left(Z \geq \frac{0.08 - \mu_{\bar{X}}}{\sigma_{\bar{X}}}\right) = P\left(Z \geq \frac{0.08 - 0.10}{0.02}\right) = P(Z \geq -1.00)$$

You can calculate this probability by using the properties of the standard normal distribution along with a standard normal table such as Table 10-1.

Table 10-1	Standard Normal Table — Negative Values			
Z	0.00	0.01	0.02	0.03
−1.3	0.0968	0.0951	0.0934	0.0918
−1.2	0.1151	0.1131	0.1112	0.1093
−1.1	0.1357	0.1335	0.1314	0.1292
−1.0	0.1587	0.1562	0.1539	0.1515

Table 10-1 shows the probability that a standard normal random variable (designated Z) is *less than or equal to* a specific value. For example, you can write the probability that $Z \leq -1.00$ (one standard deviation below the mean) as $P(Z \leq -1.00)$. You find the probability from the table with these steps:

1. Locate the first digit before and after the decimal point (−1.0) in the first (Z) column.

2. Find the second digit after the decimal point (0.00) in the second (*0.00*) column.

3. See where the row and column intersect to find the probability: $P(Z \leq -1.00) = 0.1587$.

Because you're actually looking for the probability that Z is *greater than* or equal to –1, one more step is required.

Due to the *symmetry* of the standard normal distribution, the probability that Z is greater than or equal to a negative value equals one minus the probability that Z is less than or equal to the same negative value.

For example,

$$P(Z \geq -2.0) = 1 - P(Z \leq -2.0)$$

This is because $Z \geq -2.00$ and $Z \leq -2.00$ are *complementary* events. (Complementary events are discussed in Chapter 6.) This means that Z must either be greater than or equal to –2 or less than or equal to –2. Therefore,

$$P(Z \geq -2.0) + P(Z \leq -2.0) = 1$$

This is true because the occurrence of one of these events is *certain,* and the probability of a certain event is 1. (Probability and certain events are covered in Chapter 6.)

After algebraically rewriting this equation, you end up with the following result:

$$P(Z \geq -2.0) = 1 - P(Z \leq -2.0)$$

For the portfolio example,

$$P(Z \geq -1.0) = 1 - P(Z \leq -1.0)$$

$$P(Z \geq -1.0) = 1 - 0.1587 = 0.8413$$

The result shows that there's an 84.13 percent chance that the investor's portfolio will have a mean return greater than 8 percent. As another example, suppose that it is known that there are 120 surviving paintings by a well-known 19th century artist. These works have an average price of $1 million and a standard deviation of $120,000. Say that an art collector acquires a random selection of ten of these paintings. What's the probability that the mean price of these paintings is between $975,000 and $1,025,000?

In this case, the size of the population is $N = 120$. The sample size is $n = 10$. Therefore, the sample size represents $n/N = 10/120 = 0.08333$, which is 8.333 percent of the population. Because the sample size is *greater than* 5 percent, you use the finite population correction factor to compute the standard error, like so:

$$\sqrt{\frac{N-n}{N-1}} = \sqrt{\frac{120-10}{120-1}} = 0.96144$$

You then find the mean ($\mu_{\bar{X}} = \mu = 1,000,000$) and standard error of $\bar{X}$:

$$\sigma_{\bar{X}} = \frac{\sigma}{\sqrt{n}}\sqrt{\frac{N-n}{N-1}} = \frac{120,000}{\sqrt{10}}(0.96144) = 36,484$$

To calculate probabilities for $\bar{X}$, the first step is to convert the values of $\bar{X}$ into standard normal random variables:

$$P\left(975,000 \le \bar{X} \le 1,025,000\right)$$

$$= P\left(\frac{975,000-1,000,000}{36,484} \le Z \le \frac{1,025,000-1,000,000}{36,484}\right)$$

$$= P(-0.69 \le Z \le 0.69) = P(Z \le 0.69) - P(Z \le -0.69)$$

The next step is to find the values of $P(Z \le 0.69)$ and $P(Z \le -0.69)$, and subtract one from the other. The art collector can get these values from standard normal tables, such as Table 10-2 and Table 10-3.

Table 10-2	Standard Normal Table — Positive Values			
Z	0.06	0.07	0.08	0.09
0.5	0.7123	0.7157	0.7190	0.7224
0.6	0.7454	0.7486	0.7517	0.7549
0.7	0.7764	0.7794	0.7823	0.7852
0.8	0.8051	0.8078	0.8106	0.8133

Table 10-3	Standard Normal Table — Negative Values			
Z	0.06	0.07	0.08	0.09
−0.8	0.1949	0.1922	0.1894	0.1867
−0.7	0.2236	0.2206	0.2177	0.2148
−0.6	0.2546	0.2514	0.2483	0.2451
−0.5	0.2877	0.2843	0.2810	0.2776

Table 10-2 shows that $P(Z \leq 0.69) = 0.7549$. This value is at the intersection of the *0.6* row for Z and the *0.09* column. Table 10-3 shows that $P(Z \leq -0.69) = 0.2451$. This value is at the intersection of the –0.6 row for Z and the 0.09 column.

Therefore, $P(Z \leq 0.69) - P(Z \leq -0.69) = 0.7549 - 0.2451 = 0.5098$.

The result is that there's a 50.98 percent chance that the sample mean falls somewhere between \$975,000 and \$1,025,000.

Part III
Drawing Conclusions from Samples

Anova: Single Factor						
SUMMARY						
Groups	*Count*	*Sum*	*Average*	*Variance*		
Electrica	4	9.2	2.3	0.446667		
Readyforever	4	7.4	1.85	0.043333		
Voltagenow	4	8.6	2.15	0.016667		
ANOVA						
Source of Variation	*SS*	*df*	*MS*	*F*	*P-value*	*F crit*
Between Groups	0.45	2	0.21	1.243421	0.333571	4.256495
Within Groups	1.52	9	0.168889			
Total	1.94	11				

Learn how hypothesis testing can be used to test many different kinds of propositions at www.dummies.com/extras/businessstatistics.

In this part...

- Use confidence intervals to provide a range of possible values for a population parameter; these can be constructed for any population parameter: mean, variance, standard deviation, and so on.

- Use t-distribution to describe the statistical properties of sample means that are estimated from *small* samples; use standard normal distribution is for *large* samples.

- Draw conclusions about population properties — from a single population variance to multiple population variances — with hypothesis testing

- Test multiple population means with a special new technique called Analysis of Variance (ANOVA). This technique can be used to evaluate claims about the effectiveness of competing products, or identify the most profitable products to produce.

Chapter 11

Confidence Intervals and the Student's t-Distribution

In This Chapter
▶ Getting familiar with the t-distribution
▶ Developing techniques for constructing confidence intervals

A *confidence interval* is a range of numbers that's likely to contain the true value of an unknown population *parameter*, such as the population mean. (Parameters are numerical values that describe the properties of a population; they are discussed in Chapter 10.)

Here's an example. Suppose you are asked to estimate how long it takes to commute to work each day. You respond by saying, "On average, it takes about 20 minutes to get to work." This estimate may be useful, but it doesn't give any indication how much your commuting time may vary from one day to the next.

Suppose instead you respond by saying "Most days, it takes between 15 and 25 minutes to get to work." This range of values is more meaningful than the estimated average time of 20 minutes. With this interval, it's clear that the average commute time is 20 minutes (because this is halfway between 15 and 25 minutes.) In addition, the numbers tell you that it'll be an unusual day if your commuting time is more than 25 minutes or fewer than 15 minutes.

This range of estimated values is known as a *confidence interval*. The starting point in constructing a confidence interval is the estimated mean or average, which is 20 minutes in this example. The next step is to construct a *margin of error*, which represents the degree of uncertainty associated with the estimated mean. In this example, the margin of error is five minutes.

Confidence intervals may be constructed for any population parameter: mean, variance, standard deviation, etc. This chapter covers the techniques that are used to estimate confidence intervals for the population mean. These techniques are based on one of two probability distributions. One of these is the standard normal distribution (which I cover in detail in Chapter 9). The other is known as the *Student's t-distribution* (also known simply as the *t-distribution*) — which I introduce in this chapter.

Almost Normal: The Student's t-Distribution

The purpose of the t-distribution is to describe the statistical properties of sample means that are estimated from *small* samples; the standard normal distribution is used for *large* samples.

The means of small samples are likely to vary more dramatically from one sample to the next than the means of large samples. (In a small sample, a single observation that is unusually large or small will have a greater impact on the sample mean than it would in a larger sample.) It therefore makes sense that different probability distributions should be used to describe the properties of small and large sample means.

Properties of the t-distribution

The t-distribution shares a few key properties with the standard normal distribution (which is discussed in Chapter 9).

Properties shared by the t-distribution and the standard normal distribution

The properties shared by the t-distribution and the standard normal distribution are as follows:

✔ They have a mean of 0.

✔ They're *symmetric* about the mean (that is, the area below the mean is a mirror image of the area above the mean).

✔ They can be described graphically with a bell-shaped curve.

Several key differences also exist between the two distributions, including the following:

✔ The t-distribution has more area in the "tails," and less area near the mean than the standard normal distribution.

✔ The variance and standard deviation of the t-distribution are larger than those of the standard normal distribution.

The larger variance and standard deviation in the t-distribution reflect that much more variability occurs among the means of small samples than among the means of large samples.

Degrees of freedom

As with the normal distribution, the t-distribution is an infinite family of distributions. Whereas the mean and standard deviation uniquely identify each normal distribution, each t-distribution is characterized by a value known as *degrees of freedom* (df).

When you're estimating the sample mean, the number of degrees of freedom for the t-distribution equals the number of sample members that can *vary*. For example, if you choose a sample of size n to estimate the sample mean $\bar{X}$, the corresponding t-distribution has $n - 1$ degrees of freedom because the combination of $n - 1$ elements in the sample plus the sample mean uniquely identify the last element in the sample. Therefore, you have only $n - 1$ independent variables in the sample.

Suppose you choose a sample of three students to estimate the mean GPA of a university. If the sample mean, $\bar{X}$, equals 3.0, the first student's GPA is 2.5, the second student's GPA is 3.5, and the third student's GPA must be 3.0 because the sum of the GPAs must be 9.0 for the sample mean to be 3.0. As a result, the GPAs of any two students in this sample, along with the value of $\bar{X}$, uniquely determine the value of the third student's GPA. Therefore, the corresponding t-distribution has two degrees of freedom.

Moments of the t-distribution

A *moment* is a summary measure of a probability distribution (see Chapter 7 for a detailed explanation on moments). Probability distributions, including the t-distribution, have several moments, including:

- The first moment of a distribution is the expected value, $E(X)$, which represents the mean or average value of the distribution.

  For the t-distribution with ν degrees of freedom, the mean (or expected value) equals $\mu = E(X) = 0$. μ represents the mean of a population or a probability distribution, and ν commonly designates the number of degrees of freedom of a distribution.

- The second central moment is the variance (σ^2), and it measures the spread of the distribution about the expected value. The more spread out a distribution is, the more "stretched out" is the graph of the distribution. In other words, the tails will be further from the mean, and the area near the mean will be smaller. For example, based on Figures 11-1 and 11-3, it can be seen that the t-distribution with 2 degrees of freedom is far more spread out than the t-distribution with 30 degrees of freedom.

  You use the formula $\sigma^2 = \dfrac{\nu}{\nu - 2}$ to calculate the variance of the t-distribution.

As an example, with 10 degrees of freedom, the variance of the t-distribution is computed by substituting 10 for v in the variance formula:

$$\sigma^2 = \frac{v}{v-2}$$
$$= \frac{10}{10-2}$$
$$= \frac{10}{8}$$
$$= 1.25$$

With 30 degrees of freedom, the variance of the t-distribution equals

$$\sigma^2 = \frac{v}{v-2}$$
$$= \frac{30}{30-2}$$
$$= \frac{30}{28}$$
$$= 1.07$$

These calculations show that as the degrees of freedom increases, the variance of the t-distribution declines, getting progressively closer to 1.

✔ The standard deviation is the square root of the variance (σ). (It is not a separate moment.)

For the t-distribution, you find the standard deviation with this formula:

$$\sigma = \sqrt{\frac{v}{v-2}}$$

 For most applications, the standard deviation is a more useful measure than the variance because the standard deviation and expected value are measured in the same units while the variance is measured in *squared* units. For example, suppose you assume that the returns on a portfolio follow the t-distribution. You measure both the expected value of the returns and the standard deviation as a percentage; you measure the variance as a *squared* percentage, which is a difficult concept to interpret.

Graphing the t-distribution

One of the interesting properties of the t-distribution is that the greater the degrees of freedom, the more closely the t-distribution resembles the standard normal distribution. As the degrees of freedom increases, the area in the tails of the t-distribution decreases while the area near the center increases. (The tails consists of the extreme values of the distribution, both negative and positive.) Eventually, when the degrees of freedom reaches 30 or more, the t-distribution and the standard normal distribution are extremely similar.

Figures 11-1, 11-2, and 11-3 illustrate the relationship between the t-distribution with different degrees of freedom and the standard normal distribution. Figure 11-1 shows the standard normal and the t-distribution with two degrees of freedom (df). Notice how the t-distribution is significantly more spread out than the standard normal distribution.

The graph in Figure 11-1 shows that the t-distribution has more area in the tails and less area around the mean than the standard normal distribution. (The standard normal distribution curve is shown with square markers.) As a result, more extreme observations (positive and negative) are likely to occur under the t-distribution than under the standard normal distribution.

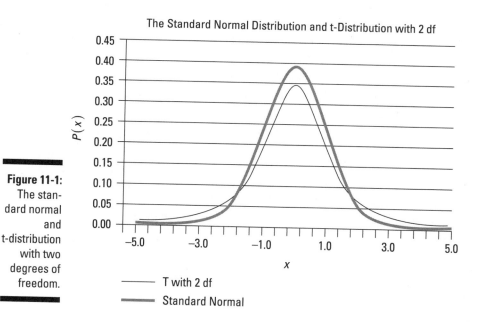

Figure 11-1: The standard normal and t-distribution with two degrees of freedom.

Figure 11-2 compares the standard normal distribution with the t-distribution with ten degrees of freedom. The two are much closer to each other here than in Figure 11-1.

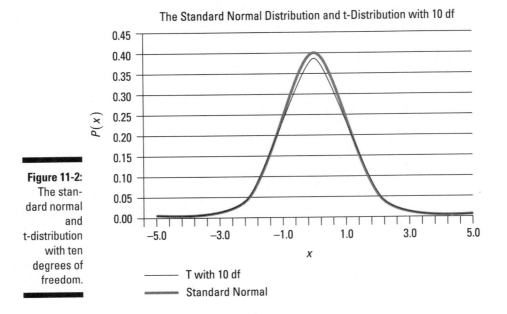

The Standard Normal Distribution and t-Distribution with 10 df

Figure 11-2:
The standard normal and t-distribution with ten degrees of freedom.

As you can see in Figure 11-3, with 30 degrees of freedom, the t-distribution and the standard normal distribution are almost indistinguishable.

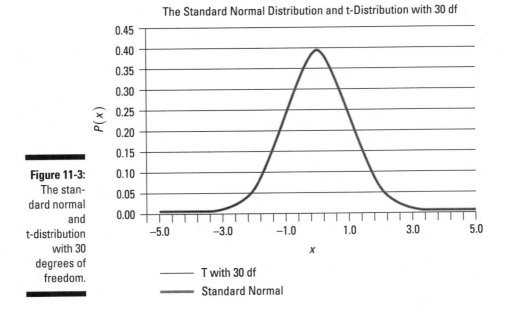

The Standard Normal Distribution and t-Distribution with 30 df

Figure 11-3:
The standard normal and t-distribution with 30 degrees of freedom.

Probabilities and the t-table

The t-table is used to show probabilities for the t-distribution. The top row of the t-table lists different values of $t\alpha$, where the right tail of the t-distribution has a probability (area) equal to α ("alpha"). Table 11-1 is an excerpt from the full t-table.

Table 11-1	The t-Table				
Degrees of Freedom	$t_{0.10}$	$t_{0.05}$	$t_{0.025}$	$t_{0.01}$	$t_{0.005}$
8	1.397	1.860	2.306	2.896	3.355
9	1.383	1.833	2.262	2.821	3.250
10	1.372	1.812	2.228	2.764	3.169

Table 11-1 shows that with ten degrees of freedom and with $\alpha = 0.05$, $t\alpha = 1.812$. So the right 5 percent tail of the distribution is located 1.812 standard deviations above the mean.

Alternatively, assume X is a *random variable* that follows the t-distribution with 10 degrees of freedom. (Random variables are discussed in Chapter 7.) In this case, $P(X \geq 1.812) = 0.05$. This is equivalent to saying the area under the curve to the right of 1.812 is 0.05, or 5 percent of the total area (see Figure 11-4).

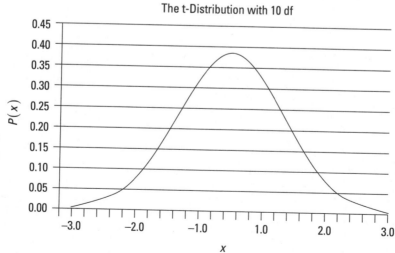

Figure 11-4: The t-distribution with 10 degrees of freedom.

The t-Distribution with 10 df

The shaded region starts at 1.812, which represents 1.812 standard deviations above the mean. The total area of the shaded region is 0.05 or 5 percent; therefore, the probability that a t-distributed random variable with 10 degrees of freedom exceeds 1.812 is 5 percent.

Point estimates vs. interval estimates

When you don't know the mean, standard deviation, variance, and other summary measures of a population, you need to estimate them from a sample.

To estimate the mean of a population, you use the mean of a sample drawn from the population. You express the sample mean as $\bar{X}$ ("X bar"). In a similar manner, to estimate the variance of a population, you use the sample variance, s^2. And you estimate the standard deviation of a population with the sample standard deviation, s. (I cover techniques for estimating the sample variance and standard deviation in Chapter 4.)

These sample measures are formally known as *point estimators* — formulas that help estimate a population measure. For example, $\bar{X}$ is a point estimator of the population mean μ. The numerical value of $\bar{X}$ is a *point estimate*.

The distinction between *estimator* and *estimate* seems very subtle — an estimator is a formula, and an estimate is a numerical value.

The usefulness of a point estimator (formula) is limited by the fact that it produces only a single number. Suppose a portfolio manager wants to estimate the mean annual return of a stock he holds by choosing a sample of historical returns and calculating the sample mean. Say the sample mean turns out to be 8 percent. This info is useful, but it's difficult to judge how much the stock's returns may fluctuate from one year to the next based on this result.

Instead, suppose that the portfolio manager can estimate, with 95 percent certainty, that the return on the stock is between 6 and 10 percent, showing the stock's returns are relatively stable over time — the stock isn't extremely risky. The estimated range from 6 to 10 percent is an *interval estimate*.

In general, you compute an interval estimate with this formula:

point estimate ± margin of error

This can be written as:

(point estimate − margin of error, point estimate + margin of error)

The symbol ± indicates that two values exist: point estimate − margin of error, and point estimate + margin of error.

The margin of error depends on several factors, such as the type of point estimate being used, the size of the sample being used to construct the point estimate, and so forth. The margin of error is a measure of the degree of uncertainty associated with the point estimate.

Calculate an interval estimate of the population mean (μ) with this formula:

$$\bar{X} \pm \text{margin of error}$$

The margin of error is a measure of how much uncertainty is associated with the value of $\bar{X}$. Its value is closely related to the standard deviation of the underlying population and the size of the sample used to estimate $\bar{X}$.

Estimating confidence intervals for the population mean

A confidence interval is a specific type of interval estimate characterized by:

- A confidence coefficient, expressed as $(1 - \alpha)$

  α is known as the *level of significance*. For example, if you choose the level of significance to be 0.05, then the corresponding confidence coefficient equals $(1 - \alpha) = (1 - 0.05) = 0.95$.

- A confidence level, expressed as $100(1 - \alpha)$

  For example, if the confidence coefficient equals 0.95, then the corresponding confidence level equals $100(0.95) = 0.95 = 95$ percent.

Suppose that a 95 percent confidence interval is constructed for the population mean age in the United States based on the ages of people randomly chosen throughout the country. If this process is repeated 100 times (for example, 100 samples are drawn and a new confidence interval is estimated in each case), then you would expect that the true population mean age is contained in 95 of these 100 confidence intervals.

Two possible situations may arise when constructing a confidence interval for the population mean: A known population standard deviation and an unknown population standard deviation that you must estimate with the sample standard deviation(s). I discuss these situations in the following sections.

Known population standard deviation

If you know the population standard deviation, then the confidence interval is based on the *standard normal* distribution (which I discuss in detail in Chapter 9). Here's the formula for constructing this confidence interval:

$$\bar{X} \pm Z_{\alpha/2} \frac{\sigma}{\sqrt{n}}$$

where:

$\bar{X}$ is the sample mean.

σ is the population standard deviation.

n is the sample size.

α is the level of significance.

$Z_{\alpha/2}$ is a *quantile* or *critical value,* which represents the location of the right tail of the standard normal distribution with an area of $\alpha/2$.

$Z_{\alpha/2} \dfrac{\sigma}{\sqrt{n}}$ is the margin of error.

The confidence interval can also be written as:

$$\left(\bar{X} - Z_{\alpha/2}\frac{\sigma}{\sqrt{n}}, \bar{X} + Z_{\alpha/2}\frac{\sigma}{\sqrt{n}} \right)$$

The two values contained in this interval are known as:

✔ The *lower limit* of the confidence interval: $\bar{X} - Z_{\alpha/2}\dfrac{\sigma}{\sqrt{n}}$

✔ The *upper limit* of the confidence interval: $\bar{X} + Z_{\alpha/2}\dfrac{\sigma}{\sqrt{n}}$

For example, suppose you want to construct a 95 percent confidence interval. This implies that $\alpha = 0.05$ (or 5 percent) so that $\alpha/2 = 0.025$ or 2.5 percent.

You can find the value of $Z_{\alpha/2}$ from a standard normal probability table, such as shown in Table 11-2. The standard normal table shows probabilities below of a specific value. Because the area above $Z_{\alpha/2} = 0.025$, the area below $Z_{\alpha/2} = 1 - 0.025 = 0.975$ (due to the *symmetry* of the standard normal distribution).

By searching in the body of the standard normal table for the area 0.9750, you get the appropriate value of $Z_{\alpha/2}$. See Table 11-2 for this result.

Table 11-2		The Standard Normal Table	
z	*0.05*	*0.06*	*0.07*
1.7	0.9599	0.9608	0.9616
1.8	0.9678	0.9686	0.9693
1.9	0.9744	0.9750	0.9756
2.0	0.9798	0.9803	0.9812

Table 11-2 shows that the appropriate value of $Z_{\alpha/2}$ is 1.96. (You find the value 1.9 in the first [Z] column and the value 0.06 in the third [0.06] column.)

You construct many confidence intervals using a 90 percent confidence level, a 95 percent confidence level, or a 99 percent confidence level. In these three cases, the value of $Z_{\alpha/2}$ is as follows:

Confidence Level	$Z_{\alpha/2}$
90 percent	1.645
95 percent	1.960
99 percent	2.576

These results indicate that for a standard normal random variable Z, the following expressions are true:

$$P(Z \le 1.645) = 0.9500$$

$$P(Z \ge 1.645) = 0.0500$$

$$P(Z \le 1.960) = 0.9750$$

$$P(Z \ge 1.960) = 0.0250$$

$$P(Z \le 2.576) = 0.9950$$

$$P(Z \ge 2.576) = 0.0050$$

The resulting confidence interval may then be expressed as follows:

$$P\left(\bar{X} - Z_{\alpha/2}\frac{\sigma}{\sqrt{n}} \le \mu \le \bar{X} + Z_{\alpha/2}\frac{\sigma}{\sqrt{n}} \right) = 1 - \alpha$$

This expression shows that the population mean is contained within this interval with a level of confidence equal to $100(1 - \alpha)$.

For example, suppose that a hedge fund holds a portfolio consisting of 500 stocks. The standard deviation is 20 percent. If you choose a sample of 10 stocks and determine the sample mean to be 8 percent, you construct a 90 percent confidence interval by following these steps:

1. **Figure $\alpha/2$.**

    $100(1 - \alpha) = 90$ percent

    $\alpha = 0.10$

    $\alpha/2 = 0.05$

2. **Use the standard normal table (Table 11-2) to find the critical value:** $Z_{\alpha/2} = 1.645.$

3. Compute the confidence interval.

sample size: $n = 10$

population standard deviation: $\sigma = 0.20$

sample mean: $\bar{X} = 0.08$

Therefore, the appropriate confidence interval is

$$\bar{X} \pm Z_{\alpha/2}\frac{\sigma}{\sqrt{n}} = 0.08 \pm 1.645\frac{0.20}{\sqrt{10}}$$

$$= 0.08 \pm 0.104$$

$$= (-0.024,\ 0.184)$$

$$= (-2.4\%,\ 18.4\%)$$

For a 95 percent confidence interval, the only change you need to make is to the critical value, which you determine as follows:

$100(1 - \alpha) = 95$ percent

$\alpha = 0.05$

$\alpha/2 = 0.025$

$Z_{\alpha/2} = Z_{0.025} = 1.96$

The 95 percent confidence interval is

$$\bar{X} \pm Z_{\alpha/2}\frac{\sigma}{\sqrt{n}} = 0.08 \pm 1.96\frac{0.20}{\sqrt{10}}$$

$$= 0.08 \pm 0.124$$

$$= (-0.044,\ 0.204)$$

$$= (-4.4\%,\ 20.4\%)$$

Finally, you determine a 99 percent confidence interval with these adjustments:

$100(1 - \alpha) = 99$ percent

$\alpha = 0.01$

$\alpha/2 = 0.005$

$Z_{\alpha/2} = Z_{0.025} = 2.576$

The 99 percent confidence interval is

$$\bar{X} \pm Z_{\alpha/2}\frac{\sigma}{\sqrt{n}} = 0.08 \pm 2.576\frac{0.20}{\sqrt{10}}$$

$$= 0.08 \pm 0.163$$

$$= (-0.083,\ 0.243)$$

$$= (-8.3\%,\ 24.3\%)$$

TIP

As the level of confidence increases so does the *width* of the confidence interval because the only way to have more confidence that the interval actually contains the population mean is to include more values.

Unknown population standard deviation

If the population standard deviation is *not* known, then you compute an interval estimate for the population mean as follows:

$$\bar{X} \pm t_{\alpha/2}^{n-1} \frac{s}{\sqrt{n}}$$

where:

$t_{\alpha/2}^{n-1}$ is a quantile (critical value) which represents the location of the right tail of the t-distribution with $n-1$ degrees of freedom with an area of $\alpha/2$

s is the sample standard deviation

In this case, you make the following changes to the formula:

✔ You use the *sample* standard deviation (*s*) rather than the population standard deviation.

✔ You use the t-distribution rather than the standard normal distribution because of the greater uncertainty associated with the sample standard deviation. $t_{\alpha/2}^{n-1}$ is a quantile or critical value taken from the t-distribution and represents the location of the right tail of the t-distribution with $n-1$ degrees of freedom whose area equals $\alpha/2$.

As an example, suppose that $\alpha = 0.05$ so that $\alpha/2 = 0.025$. Also assume that the appropriate number of degrees of freedom is 9. You can get the value of $t_{\alpha/2}^{n-1}$ from a t-table, as in Table 11-1.

The appropriate column heading is $t_{0.025}$; with nine degrees of freedom, the value of $t_{\alpha/2}^{n-1}$ is 2.262.

For example, a university has 10,000 students and wants to estimate the average GPA of the entire student body. It picks a sample of ten students, and the sample mean GPA is 3.10. The sample standard deviation is 0.25. You construct confidence intervals for the population mean as follows:

✔ For a 90 percent confidence interval, the value of $\alpha/2$ is 0.05:

$100(1 - \alpha) = 90$ percent

$\alpha = 0.10$

$\alpha/2 = 0.05$

With $n - 1 = 9$ degrees of freedom, based on the t-table (Table 11-1), $t_{\alpha/2}^{n-1} = 1.833$.

The sample size is $n = 10$, the population standard deviation is $s = 0.25$, and the sample mean is $\bar{X} = 3.10$. Therefore, the appropriate confidence interval is

$$\bar{X} \pm t_{\alpha/2}^{n-1} \frac{s}{\sqrt{n}} = 3.10 + 1.833 \frac{0.25}{\sqrt{10}}$$

$$= 3.10 \pm 0.1449$$

$$= (2.955, \ 3.2449)$$

✔ For a 95 percent confidence interval, you follow similar calculations but change the critical value:

$100(1 - \alpha) = 95$ percent

$\alpha = 0.05$

$\alpha/2 = 0.025$

With $n - 1 = 9$ degrees of freedom, based on the t-table (Table 11-1), $t_{\alpha/2}^{n-1} = 2.262$. Therefore, the appropriate confidence interval is

$$\bar{X} \pm t_{\alpha/2}^{n-1} \frac{s}{\sqrt{n}} = 3.10 + 2.262 \frac{0.25}{\sqrt{10}}$$

$$= 3.10 \pm 0.1788$$

$$= (2.9212, \ 3.2788)$$

✔ For a 99 percent confidence interval, you again change the critical value to

$100(1 - \alpha) = 99$ percent

$\alpha = 0.01$

$\alpha/2 = 0.005$

With $n - 1 = 9$ degrees of freedom, based on the t-table (Table 11-1), $t_{\alpha/2}^{n-1} = 3.250$. Therefore, the appropriate confidence interval is

$$\bar{X} \pm t_{\alpha/2}^{n-1} \frac{s}{\sqrt{n}} = 3.10 + 3.250 \frac{0.25}{\sqrt{10}}$$

$$= 3.10 \pm 0.2569$$

$$= (2.8431, \ 3.3569)$$

In each case, the confidence interval is wider than it would be when using the standard normal distribution.

Chapter 12

Testing Hypotheses about the Population Mean

*H*ypothesis testing is a multi-step statistical process which is used to test claims about a population measure, such as the mean. For example, you can use hypothesis testing on the following statements to determine whether they're true:

✔ Mean income in the United States has risen over the past 25 years.

✔ The average age of the population of Egypt is above 30.

✔ The average return to the stocks in a portfolio is 10 percent.

✔ The United States and Canada have average work weeks identical in length.

✔ The average lifetime of brandy drinkers is 90.

You test hypotheses with a series of steps designed to show whether you can justify a claim. These steps apply to a lot of situations; for example, you can test claims about a population's mean, a population's variance, whether a population is normally distributed, and so forth.

This chapter focuses on testing hypotheses about the mean value of a single population and the equality of the means of two different populations.

Applying the Key Steps in Hypothesis Testing for a Single Population Mean

Hypothesis testing requires sample data to draw conclusions about the characteristics of the underlying population. The necessary steps for any type of hypothesis test are outlined in the following sections.

Writing the null hypothesis

The *null hypothesis* is a statement that's assumed to be true unless strong contrary evidence exists. The null hypothesis can take several forms. You can use it to test statements about population measures, such as means and standard deviations, and to test statements about the relationship between two populations. An example of a null hypothesis is the mean IQ of Star Trek fans is higher than the mean IQ of Star Wars fans.

You write the null hypothesis for testing the value of a single population mean as

$$H_0: \mu = \mu_0$$

where H_0 stands for the null hypotheses, μ is the true population mean (whose value we do not know,) and μ_0 is the hypothesized value of the population, or the value that you *think* is true.

For example, if you want to test the hypothesis that the mean number of runs scored per game in the American League is 4; you write the null hypothesis as $H_0: \mu = 4.0$.

If actual data shows that this is false, you *reject* the null hypothesis; otherwise, you *don't* reject the null hypothesis. (You never *accept* the null hypothesis; instead, you fail to reject it if there is not enough evidence against it.)

Coming up with an alternative hypothesis

Suppose that the null hypothesis is false. For example, you are testing the null hypothesis that the mean number of runs scored per game in the American League is 4. If data taken from actual games shows that this is false, it must be true that:

The number of runs scored is *more than* 4

The number of runs scored is *less than* 4

Prior to testing the null hypothesis, you must specify what alternative you accept if the null hypothesis is false. It turns out that there are actually three ways to express the alternative hypothesis:

The number of runs scored is *more than* 4

The number of runs scored is *less than* 4

The number of runs is *different from* 4

The alternative that you choose depends on what type of action is taken as a result of the hypothesis test. For example, suppose that the commissioner decides that if the number of runs scored is *less than* 4, the league encourages teams to shorten the distance to their outfield fences (which encourages more home runs.) You therefore use "the number of runs scored is *less than* 4" as your alternative hypothesis. This ensures that no action is taken unless it's extremely clear that the number of runs is less than 4.

There are special names associated with the three types of alternative hypotheses:

✔ Right-tailed test

✔ Left-tailed test

✔ Two-tailed test

A right-tailed test indicates that the actual population mean is *greater than* the hypothesized mean. A left-tailed test indicates that the actual population mean is *less than* the hypothesized population mean. A two-tailed test is a combination of the right-tailed and left-tailed tests; it indicates that the actual population mean is *different than* the hypothesized mean. (This combines the two alternative hypotheses that the actual population mean is *greater than* the hypothesized mean and the actual population mean is *less than* the hypothesized mean.)

Right-tailed test

A *right-tailed test* is a test to determine if the actual value of the population mean is *greater than* the hypothesized value.

Suppose you're testing a hypothesis about the mean of a population, and you're interested in only strong evidence that the mean is *greater than* a specified value. In this case, you set up a right-tailed test. ("Right tail" refers to the largest values in a probability distribution.)

As an example of a right-tailed test, suppose that a department store wants to know whether the mean length of time its merchandise remains in inventory is 30 days. If the mean time is greater than 30 days, the store will overhaul its ordering procedures; if the mean is equal to or less than 30 days, the store will do nothing.

In this case, it's extremely important for the store to know whether the mean exceeds 30 days because a key decision depends on this information. The store doesn't want to spend time overhauling its procedures unless strong evidence shows that it's necessary; therefore, the most appropriate choice is a right-tailed test that shows the mean is greater than 30 days.

In general, you write the alternative hypothesis with a right-tailed test as

$H_1: \mu > \mu_0$

Here, H_1 represents the alternative hypothesis. In this example, you'd write the alternative hypothesis as $H_1: \mu > 30$.

Left-tailed test

A *left-tailed test* is a test to determine if the actual value of the population mean is *less than* the hypothesized value. ("Left tail" refers to the smallest values in a probability distribution.)

Suppose that you're testing a hypothesis about the mean of a population, and you're interested only in strong evidence that the mean is *less than* a specified value. In this case, you set up a left-tailed test.

For example, a pension fund wants to know whether any of its portfolio managers are earning an average return that falls short of the return to the Standard & Poor's 500 (S&P) stock index. (Assume this return is currently 8 percent.) If so, these managers won't receive the company's annual Christmas bonus.

The S&P is an index that represents the values of the 500 largest publicly traded U.S. stocks; it's often used as a benchmark for comparing the returns of portfolio managers.

In this situation, the fund is interested in knowing only which managers don't qualify for the Christmas bonus. As a result, the most appropriate choice for the alternative hypothesis a left-tailed test that shows the mean return is less than 8 percent.

In general, you write the alternative hypothesis for a left-tailed test as:

$H_1: \mu < \mu_0$

In this example, you'd write the alternative hypothesis as $H_1: \mu < 0.08$.

Two-tailed test

Building on the right-tailed test and the left-tailed test, consider the *two-tailed test,* which is used to determine if the actual value of the population mean is *different than* the hypothesized value; for example, greater than or less than. (A two-tailed test uses both the right tail and left tail of a probability distribution.)

Suppose you're testing a hypothesis about the mean of a population, and you need to know whether the mean is different from a specified value.

For example, a bottling company wants to be sure that the mean volume of its 1-liter bottles is actually 1 liter. Any value less than or more than this measurement could lead to significant problems. So the most appropriate choice is a two-tailed test that shows the mean volume is *not equal to* 1.

In general, you express the alternative hypothesis for a two-tailed test as

$$H_1: \mu \neq \mu_0$$

In this example, you'd write the alternative hypothesis as $H_1: \mu \neq 1$. This expression indicates that if the null hypothesis is false then either $H_1: \mu > 1$ or $H_1: \mu < 1$ will be accepted in its place, depending on the value of the test statistic relative to the critical values.

In this case, a two-tailed test was conducted due to the extreme importance of determining immediately if the mean content of the bottles is *either* less than 1 or greater than 1. If overfilled bottles are a problem, but not underfilled bottles, you would use a right-tailed test. If underfilled bottles are a problem, but not overfilled bottles, you would use a left-tailed test.

Choosing a level of significance

To test a hypothesis, you must specify a *level of significance* — the probability of rejecting the null hypothesis when it's actually true.

Rejecting the null hypothesis when it is actually true is is known as a *Type I error.* By contrast, a *Type II error* occurs when you fail to reject the null hypothesis when it's actually false. The level of significance of a hypothesis test equals the probability of committing a Type I error. A Type I error is sometimes known as a "false positive"; a Type II error is sometimes known as a "false negative."

In the process of testing a hypothesis, the following four results can take place. The two possible correct decisions are:

- Rejecting the null hypothesis when it's false
- Failing to reject the null hypothesis when it's true

The two possible incorrect decisions are:

- ✔ Rejecting the null hypothesis when it's true
- ✔ Failing to reject the null hypothesis when it's false

The probability of committing a Type I error is often designated with the letter α ("alpha"), and the probability of committing a Type II error is often designated with the letter β ("beta").

The larger is the probability of a Type I error that you choose for a hypothesis test, the smaller will be the probability of a Type II error, and vice versa. (One way to reduce both is to increase the sample size used for the hypothesis test.)

Note: The probabilities of Type I and Type II errors do *not* add up to 1; they are *not* complementary events. (Complementary events are discussed in Chapter 6.)

When you're conducting a hypothesis test, you choose the value of α to find the right balance between avoiding Type I and Type II errors. In some types of applications, avoiding Type I errors is critically important; in other cases, Type I errors may not be as serious.

In many hypothesis tests of a population value (such as the mean), the level of significance is often 0.01, 0.05, or 0.10, with 0.05 being most common.

Although both Type I and Type II errors represent serious mistakes, in some situations, one mistake is far more important to avoid than the other. For example, in a jury trial, the null hypothesis is "the defendant is innocent," which is assumed to be true unless strong contrary evidence suggests otherwise. The alternative hypothesis is that "the defendant is guilty."

In this situation, four outcomes can occur:

- ✔ The jury reaches a correct decision by acquitting an innocent defendant.
- ✔ The jury reaches a correct decision by convicting a guilty defendant.
- ✔ The jury commits a Type I error by wrongly convicting an innocent defendant. (In this situation, the null hypothesis of innocence has been incorrectly rejected.)
- ✔ The jury commits a Type II error by acquitting a guilty defendant (because the null hypothesis of innocence hasn't been rejected when it's actually false).

For a jury trial, avoiding a Type I error is far more important than avoiding a Type II error; as such, you set α equal to a very small value, which would imply a much larger value for β. (α would never be set equal to 0 because that would ensure that no one is ever convicted!)

Because a Type I error in this case indicates that an innocent person has been convicted, and a Type II error indicates that a guilty person walks free, it's clearly imperative to avoid Type I errors even if it means more Type II errors.

Sir William Blackstone (1723–1780), the famous English judge and politician, once wrote that "It is better that ten guilty persons escape than that one innocent suffer." A statistician might rephrase this in slightly less elegant terms: "It is extremely important to avoid Type I errors in a jury trial."

Computing the test statistic

A *test statistic* is a numerical measure you construct to determine whether you should reject the null hypothesis. It shows how far the sample mean is from the hypothesized value of the population mean in terms of standard deviations. You calculate this value from a sample drawn from the underlying population.

For example, say you're testing a hypothesis about the mean age of the residents in a city. The city government wants to know whether the mean age is 40. You choose a sample of city residents, and you compute the mean age of the sample members. If the sample mean age is substantially different from 40, the null hypothesis will likely be rejected.

If you conduct a hypothesis test of the value of a single population mean, the form of the test statistic depends on two key details: the size of the sample chosen from the population and whether the population standard deviation is known.

When you're testing hypotheses about the population mean, the cutoff point between a small sample and a large sample is 30. Any sample size less than 30 is small; a sample size of 30 or more is large.

When you're conducting hypothesis tests of the mean with a small sample, the test statistic follows the Student's t-distribution. With a large sample, the test statistic follows the standard normal distribution. (See Chapters 9 and 11 for discussions on the normal distribution and Student's t-distribution.)

For a small sample (less than 30), the test statistic is

$$t = \frac{\bar{X} - \mu_0}{s / \sqrt{n}}$$

In this formula,

- t indicates that this test statistic follows the Student's t-distribution
- $\bar{X}$ is the sample mean
- s is the sample standard deviation
- n is the sample size
- $\dfrac{s}{\sqrt{n}}$ is the *standard error* of the sample mean

For a large sample (30 or more), two possibilities exist:

- In the unlikely case that you don't know the population mean but do know the population standard deviation (σ), the appropriate test statistic is

$$Z = \frac{\bar{X} - \mu_0}{\sigma / \sqrt{n}}$$

- If the population standard deviation is unknown, the appropriate test statistic is

$$Z = \frac{\bar{X} - \mu_0}{s / \sqrt{n}}$$

The letter Z indicates that these test statistics follow the standard normal distribution. The standard normal distribution (see Chapter 9) is the special case of the normal distribution with mean (μ) of 0 and a standard deviation (σ) of 1.

Comparing the critical value (s)

After you calculate a test statistic, you compare it to one or two *critical values,* depending on the alternative hypothesis, to determine whether you should reject the null hypothesis.

A critical value shows the number of standard deviations away from the mean of a distribution where a specified percentage of the distribution is above the critical value and the remainder of the distribution is below the critical value.

For example, based on the standard normal table (see Chapter 9), the probability that a standard normal random variable Z is less than 1.645 equals 0.95 or 95 percent. As a result, the probability that Z is greater than 1.645 is 0.05 or 5 percent. 1.645 is the critical value that divides the lower 95 percent of the distribution from the upper 5 percent of the distribution. Due to the symmetry of the standard normal distribution, –1.645 is the critical value that divides the lower 5 percent of the distribution from the upper 95 percent of the distribution.

This is shown in Figure 12-1. The shaded region is the upper 5 percent of the standard normal distribution, and the unshaded region is the lower 95 percent of the distribution.

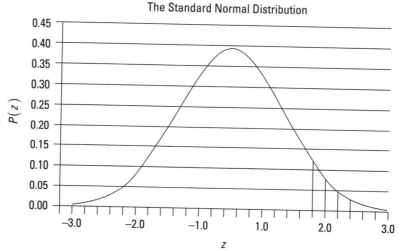

Figure 12-1: Critical value taken from the standard normal distribution.

The appropriate critical value depends on whether you are conducting a right-tailed test, a left-tailed test, or a two-tailed test, as follows:

- A right-tailed test has one positive critical value.
- A left-tailed test has one negative critical value.
- A two-tailed test has two critical values, one positive and one negative.

The appropriate critical value also depends on the sample size and whether or not the population standard deviation is known. In the following sections, I show you how to determine the critical values for a hypothesis test for the value of the population mean, for both small and large samples.

Small sample (n < 30)

As I mention earlier, a small sample is less than 30. When you use a small sample to test a hypothesis about the population mean, you take the resulting critical value or values from the Student's t-distribution, as follows:

- Right-tailed test: critical value = t_α^{n-1}
- Left-tailed test: critical value = $-t_\alpha^{n-1}$
- Two-tailed test: critical value = $\pm t_{\alpha/2}^{n-1}$

Note: α is the level of significance, and n represents the sample size.

You draw these critical values from the Student's t-distribution with $n - 1$ *degrees of freedom* (*df*). (See the Student's t-table in Chapter 11.)

The number of degrees of freedom refers to the number of *independent* elements in a sample. When testing hypotheses about a single population mean, the degrees of freedom equals the sample size (n) minus 1. This is because the sample data is used to estimate one value: the sample mean. For any given set of $n - 1$ sample elements and the sample mean, the remaining sample element is a known value. For example, if a sample contains the elements 1, 2, 3 and 4, the sample mean equals $(1 + 2 + 3 + 4) / 4 = 2.5$. If the sample elements 1, 2, 3 are chosen, the sample mean of 2.5 implies that the missing element is 4. (In other words, the sample mean of 2.5 indicates that the sum of the sample elements is 10. Because the sample elements 1, 2, and 3 sum to 6, the remaining element must be 4.) Therefore, one sample element is uniquely determined, while the remaining $n - 1$ sample elements are completely variable. As a result, the degrees of freedom equal $n - 1$.

The number of degrees of freedom used with the t-distribution depends on the particular application. For testing hypotheses about the population mean, the appropriate number of degrees of freedom is one less than the sample size (that is, $n - 1$). (See Chapter 11 for details on the Student's t-distribution.)

The critical value or values are used to locate the areas under the curve of a distribution that are too extreme to be consistent with the null hypothesis. For a right-tailed test, these are the large positive values, which are collectively known as the right tail of the distribution. For a left-tailed test, these are the large negative values, which are collectively known as the left tail of the distribution. In either case, the area in the tail equals the level of significance of the hypothesis test. For a two-tailed test, the value of the level of significance (α) is split in half; the area in the right tail equals $\alpha/2$, and the area in left tail equals $\alpha/2$, for a total of α.

Right-tailed test with a small sample

As an example of a right-tailed test, suppose the level of significance is 0.05 and the sample size is 10; then you get a single positive critical value:

$$t_{\alpha}^{n-1} = t_{0.05}^{9}$$

Refer to Table 12-1 to find the intersection of the row representing 9 degrees of freedom and the column headed $t_{0.05}$.

Table 12-1		The Student's t-distribution			
Degrees of Freedom (df)	$t_{0.10}$	$t_{0.05}$	$t_{0.025}$	$t_{0.01}$	$t_{0.005}$
6	1.440	1.943	2.447	3.143	3.707
7	1.415	1.895	2.365	2.998	3.499
8	1.397	1.860	2.306	2.896	3.355
9	1.383	1.833	2.262	2.821	3.250
10	1.372	1.812	2.228	2.764	3.169
11	1.363	1.796	2.201	2.718	3.106
12	1.356	1.782	2.179	2.681	3.055
13	1.350	1.771	2.160	2.650	3.012
14	1.345	1.761	2.145	2.624	2.977
15	1.341	1.753	2.131	2.602	2.947

The critical value is 1.833, or $t_{\alpha}^{n-1} = t_{0.05}^{9} = 1.833$, as shown in Figure 12-2.

The shaded region in the right tail represents the *rejection region*; if the test statistic falls in this area, the null hypothesis will be rejected.

Left-tailed test with a small sample

As an example of a left-tailed test, suppose the level of significance is 0.05 and the sample size is 10; then you get a single negative critical value:

$$-t_{\alpha}^{n-1} = -t_{0.05}^{9}$$

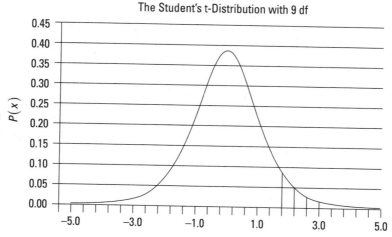

Figure 12-2: Critical value taken from the t-distribution: right-tailed test.

You get this number from the t-table (Table 12-1) at the intersection of the row representing 9 degrees of freedom and the $t_{0.05}$ column; the critical value is –1.833, or $-t_\alpha^{n-1} = -t_{0.05}^9 = -1.833$, as shown in Figure 12-3.

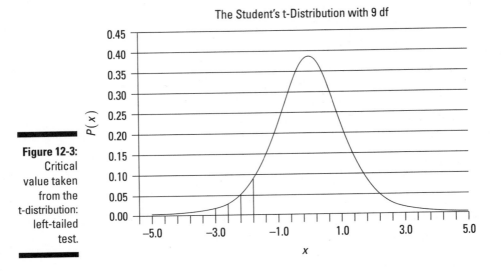

The Student's t-Distribution with 9 df

Figure 12-3:
Critical
value taken
from the
t-distribution:
left-tailed
test.

The shaded region in the left tail represents the *rejection region*; if the test statistic falls in this area, the null hypothesis will be rejected.

Two-tailed test with a small sample

As an example of a two-tailed test, suppose the level of significance is 0.05 and the sample size is 10; then you get a positive and a negative critical value:

$$\pm t_{\alpha/2}^{n-1} = \pm t_{0.025}^9$$

You can find the value of the positive critical value $\pm t_{0.025}^9$ directly from Table 12-1.

In this case, you find the positive critical value $t_{0.025}^9$ at the intersection of the row representing 9 degrees in the *Degrees of Freedom (df)* column and the $t_{0.025}$ column. The positive critical value is 2.262; therefore, the negative critical value is –2.262. You represent these two values like so (as Figure 12-4 illustrates):

$$\pm t_{\alpha/2}^{n-1} = \pm 2.262$$

The shaded region in the two tails represents the *rejection region*; if the test statistic falls in either tail, the null hypothesis will be rejected.

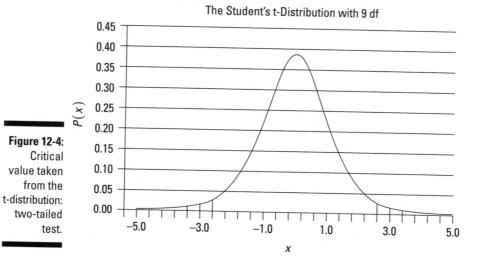

The Student's t-Distribution with 9 df

Figure 12-4:
Critical
value taken
from the
t-distribution:
two-tailed
test.

Large sample (n ≥ 30)

A large sample has a size greater than or equal to 30. When you use a large sample to test a hypothesis about the population mean, you take the resulting critical value or values from the standard normal distribution, as follows:

✔ Right-tailed test: critical value = Z_α

✔ Left-tailed test: critical value = $-Z_\alpha$

✔ Two-tailed test: critical values = $\pm Z_{\alpha/2}$

Because you draw these critical values from the standard normal distribution, you don't have to calculate degrees of freedom. Unlike the Student's t-distribution, the standard normal distribution isn't based on degrees of freedom. I walk you through how to find these critical values in the following sections.

For hypothesis testing applications, the critical values listed in Table 12-2 are used frequently; you may want to memorize them.

Table 12-2	Common Critical Values of the Standard Normal Distribution		
α	*Right-Tailed Test*	*Left-Tailed Test*	*Two-Tailed Test*
0.01	2.328	−2.328	±2.576
0.05	1.645	−1.645	±1.960
0.10	1.282	−1.282	±1.645

Right-tailed test with a large sample

A *right-tailed* hypothesis test of the population mean with a level of significance of 0.05 has a single positive critical value: $Z_\alpha = Z_{0.05}$. You find the value by checking the body of Table 12-3 for a probability of $1 - \alpha$, which is 0.9500.

Table 12-3	Standard Normal Table — Positive Values			
Z	0.04	0.05	0.06	0.07
1.5	0.9382	0.9394	0.9406	0.9418
1.6	0.9495	0.9505	0.9515	0.9525
1.7	0.9591	0.9599	0.9608	0.9616
1.8	0.9671	0.9678	0.9686	0.9693
1.9	0.9738	0.9744	0.9750	0.9756
2.0	0.9793	0.9798	0.9803	0.9808

Unfortunately, this exact value isn't in the table. The two closest values are 0.9495 and 0.9505, which you can find at the intersections of row *1.6* under the Z column and the *0.04* and *0.05* columns.. The critical value is, therefore, halfway between 1.64 and 1.65; average it out to get 1.645, or $Z_\alpha = 1.645$, and see Figure 12-5 for a graphical depiction.

A left-tailed hypothesis test with a level of significance of 0.05 has a single negative critical value $-Z_\alpha = -Z_{0.05}$, or simply -1.645: $-Z_\alpha = -1.645$. Figure 12-6 represents this critical value graphically.

The Standard Normal Distribution

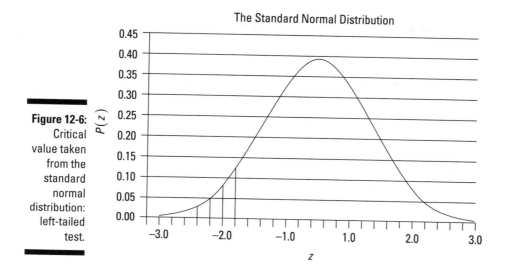

Figure 12-6:
Critical
value taken
from the
standard
normal
distribution:
left-tailed
test.

Two-tailed test with a large sample

For a two-tailed hypothesis test of the population mean with a level of significance of 0.05, the two critical values are $\pm Z_{\alpha/2} = \pm Z_{0.025}$.

You can find the positive critical value in a standard normal table, like Table 12-3.

Finding critical values in a standard normal table is more complicated than finding critical values in a t-table. The body of the standard normal table contains probabilities, unlike in the t-table where the probabilities are contained in the column headings.

In this example, you find the positive critical value $Z_{\alpha/2} = Z_{0.025}$ by checking the body of the table for a probability of

$$(1-\alpha/2) = (1-0.05/2) = (1-0.025) = 0.9750.$$

In other words, the positive critical value represents the number of standard deviations above the mean at which

✔ 2.5 percent of the area under the standard normal curve is to the right of this point.

✔ 97.5 percent of the area under the standard normal curve is to the left of this point.

Because the standard normal table shows areas to the left of specified values, you can find the positive critical value by locating the probability 0.9750, not 0.0250, in the body of the table (Table 12-3). You find this probability by following the row 1.9 under the Z column to the *0.06* column. Therefore, the critical value $Z_{\alpha/2} = Z_{0.025} = 1.96$. The corresponding negative critical value is -1.96. You can write these critical values as $\pm Z_{\alpha/2} = \pm 1.96$. Figure 12-7 shows these values graphically.

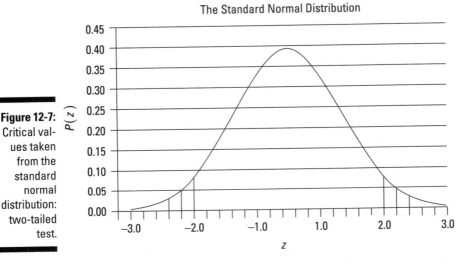

The Standard Normal Distribution

Figure 12-7: Critical values taken from the standard normal distribution: two-tailed test.

Using the decision rule

You make the decision to reject the null hypothesis by looking at the relationship between the test statistic and the critical value(s), as follows:

- **Right-tailed test:** If the test statistic is *greater than* the critical value, reject the null hypothesis H_0: $\mu = \mu_0$ in favor of the alternative hypothesis H_1: $\mu > \mu_0$; otherwise, don't reject the null hypothesis. There is insufficient evidence to show that the null hypothesis is false.

- **Left-tailed test:** If the test statistic is *less than* the critical value, reject the null hypothesis H_0: $\mu = \mu_0$ in favor of the alternative hypothesis H_1: $\mu < \mu_0$; otherwise, don't reject the null hypothesis. There is insufficient evidence to show that the null hypothesis is false.

- **Two-tailed test;** If the test statistic is *less than* the negative critical value, reject the null hypothesis H_0: $\mu = \mu_0$ in favor of the alternative hypothesis H_1: $\mu < \mu_0$. If the test statistic is *greater than* the positive critical value, reject the null hypothesis H_0: $\mu = \mu_0$ in favor of the alternative hypothesis H_1: $\mu > \mu_0$. Otherwise, don't reject the null hypothesis. There is insufficient evidence to show that the null hypothesis is false.

As an example, suppose that the government of a small country is interested in studying the characteristics of household incomes in the country. The government wants to know whether the mean household income is greater than $25,000 per year. If so, the government will propose new types of taxes; otherwise, no new taxes will occur. The appropriate steps for testing the null hypothesis that the mean household income equals $25,000 at the 5 percent level of significance are given as follows:.

The null and alternative hypotheses are

H_0: μ = 25,000

H_1: μ > 25,000

In this example, the government uses a right-tailed test because it's looking for strong evidence that the mean household incomes are *greater than* $25,000 per year. If true, the government will take an important action.

Assume that the level of significance is 0.05. The government's chief statistician selects a sample of 100 households and computes the sample mean household income to be $27,200 per year. The population standard deviation is unknown; instead, the government statistician computes the sample standard deviation, and it turns out to be $8,400.

Because the government statistician chose a large sample (greater than or equal to 30), he uses the standard normal distribution to test this hypothesis. Because the population standard deviation is unknown, the appropriate test statistic is

$$Z = \frac{\bar{X} - \mu_0}{s / \sqrt{n}}$$

The value of the test statistic is, therefore,

$$
\begin{aligned}
Z &= \frac{\bar{X} - \mu_0}{s / \sqrt{n}} \\
&= \frac{27,200 - 25,000}{8,400 / \sqrt{100}} \\
&= \frac{2,200}{840} \\
&= 2.62
\end{aligned}
$$

The critical value is $Z\alpha = Z_{0.05}$ = 1.645 (see Table 12-3).

Because the test statistic of 2.62 exceeds the critical value of 1.645, the government statistician rejects the null hypothesis in favor of the alternative hypothesis that the population mean exceeds $25,000. As a result, there are new taxes. Figure 12-8 shows this result graphically.

As another example, say the same government wants to study the average crop yields of its wheat farmers. The government wants to know whether the mean yield is equal to 10,000 bushels per year.

If the mean yield is below 10,000, the government will provide cash assistance to the farmers. If the mean yield is above 10,000, the government will export some of the surplus wheat to foreign countries. The government's chief statistician can test the null hypothesis that the mean crop yield equals 10,000 bushels. (Assume that he chooses a 5 percent level of significance.)

The null and alternative hypotheses are

$$H_0: \mu = 10,000$$
$$H_1: \mu \neq 10,000$$

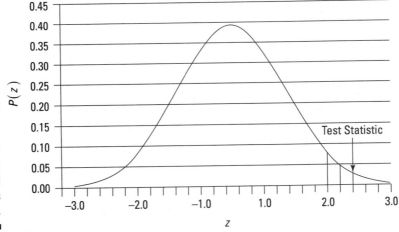

The Standard Normal Distribution

Figure 12-8:
Standard normal distribution: The null hypothesis is rejected.

This example requires a two-tailed test, because the government is looking for strong evidence that mean crop yields are either *less than* or *greater than* 10,000 bushels per year. The government will undertake an important action in either case.

Assume that the level of significance is 0.05. The government statistician selects a sample of eight farms, and estimates the sample mean and standard deviation. The mean crop yield turns out to be 9,400 bushels. The sample standard deviation is 420 bushels.

Due to the small number of farms in the country, the government statistician chose a small sample (less than 30); therefore, the hypothesis test is based on the Student's t-distribution. The appropriate test statistic is, therefore,

$$t = \frac{\bar{X} - \mu_0}{s / \sqrt{n}}$$

If the population standard deviation (σ) is known, you use the standard normal distribution, regardless of the sample size. (See Chapter 11 for details.)

The value of the test statistic is

$$t = \frac{\bar{X} - \mu_0}{s / \sqrt{n}}$$
$$= \frac{10,200 - 10,000}{420 / \sqrt{8}}$$
$$= \frac{200}{148.49}$$
$$= 1.35$$

The critical values are $\pm t_{\alpha/2}^{n-1}$.

With a sample size of $n = 8$, the appropriate number of degrees of freedom is $n - 1 = 7$. With a level of significance of 0.05, the value of $\alpha/2$ is 0.025. Therefore, you find the critical values in the t-table (Table 12-1) as follows:

$$\pm t_{\alpha/2}^{n-1} = \pm t_{0.025}^{7} = \pm 2.365$$

With a two-tailed test, the decision rule is to

✔ Reject the null hypothesis $H_0: \mu = \mu_0$ in favor of the alternative hypothesis $H_1: \mu < \mu_0$ if the test statistic is less than the negative critical value (–2.365).

✔ Reject the null hypothesis $H_0: \mu = \mu_0$ in favor of the alternative hypothesis $H_1: \mu > \mu_0$ if the test statistic is greater than the positive critical value (2.365).

✔ Not reject the null hypothesis if the test statistic is between the negative and positive critical values (–2.365 and 2.365).

Because the test statistic is 1.35, it's *greater than* the negative critical value of –2.365, and *less than* the positive critical value of 2.365. In other words, the test statistic is *not* in the rejection region, as shown in Figure 12-9.

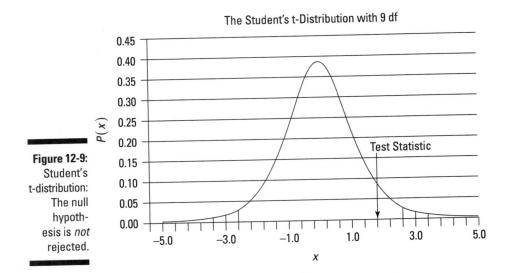

Figure 12-9:
Student's
t-distribution:
The null
hypoth-
esis is *not*
rejected.

In this example, you do *not* reject the null hypothesis H_0: $\mu = \mu_0$. As a result, the government takes no action.

Testing Hypotheses About Two Population Means

In addition to testing claims about the mean of a population, hypothesis testing can be used to compare the equality of two different population means. For example, you can use hypothesis testing on the following statements to determine whether they're true:

- The mean price of gasoline per gallon is equal in New York and New Jersey.

- The average life expectancy of men is the same in the United States and Canada.

- The mean annual rainfall is equal in Washington and Oregon.

- The length of the average flight delay is the same at Kennedy Airport and LaGuardia Airport.

The basic procedure for testing hypotheses about two population means is similar to the procedure for a single population mean (which I discuss in the section "Applying the Key Steps in Hypothesis Testing for a Single Population Mean"). The most important differences are the form of the test statistics you use for two population means and the calculation of the critical values. I outline the differences in the following sections.

Writing the null hypothesis for two population means

To test the equality of two population means, you write the null hypothesis as

H_0: $\mu_1 = \mu_2$

In this formula, H_0 is the null hypothesis, μ_1 is the mean of population 1, and μ_2 is the mean of population 2.

Note that when testing hypotheses about two population means, one population is arbitrarily chosen to be "population 1" and the other becomes "population 2."

Defining the alternative hypotheses for two population means

Just as you have an alternative hypothesis for testing a single population mean, when you test two population means, you also need an alternative hypothesis. If the null hypothesis is rejected, you must specify what other result will be accepted instead. This is the role of the alternative hypothesis.

The alternative hypothesis can take one of three forms:

- ✔ **Right-tailed test:** H_1: $\mu_1 > \mu_2$
- ✔ **Left-tailed test:** H_1: $\mu_1 < \mu_2$
- ✔ **Two-tailed test:** H_1: $\mu_1 \neq \mu_2$

A right-tailed test is used to indicate if the mean of population 1 is *greater than* the mean of population 2. Similarly, a left-tailed test is used to show if the mean if population 1 is *less than* the mean of population 2. A two-tailed test is used to show if the mean of population 1 is *different than* the mean of population 2.

Determining the test statistics for two population means

When you're testing hypotheses about two population means, you can choose from several test statistics. The choice depends on:

- ✔ whether the samples drawn from the two populations are independent of each other
- ✔ whether the variances of the two populations are equal
- ✔ whether the samples chosen from the two populations are large (at least 30) or small (less than 30)

Samples are *independent* if they're not related to each other. For example, samples of GPAs at two universities are independent samples, because none of the students in these samples attend both universities.

If you choose independent samples from two populations, you choose the test statistic and critical values based on the following questions:

- ✔ Are the variances of the two populations equal?
- ✔ If the variances are unequal, are the sample sizes large (at least 30)?

If the samples are *dependent,* the choice for test statistics and critical values are different. For example, suppose that medical researchers are conducting a study to determine whether a new cholesterol drug is effective in reducing LDL (bad cholesterol) in patients. If you chose a sample of LDL readings chosen from a set of patients prior to taking the drug and a sample of LDL readings among the same patients after taking the drug, these two samples would be closely related and, therefore, *dependent.* This type of hypothesis test requires a different procedure for constructing the test statistic and critical values than for independent samples. I explore using independent and dependent, or *paired,* samples in the following sections.

Using independent samples

When using independent samples, you first have to decide whether the populations being tested have equal variances (or if you have reason to believe that they're equal).

With equal population variances, the test statistic requires the calculation of a pooled variance — this is the variance that the two populations have in common. You use the Student's t-distribution to find the test statistic and critical values.

With unequal population variances, there are two possibilities.

✔ You use the standard normal distribution for the test statistic and critical values if the samples are large (at least 30).

✔ You use the t-distribution if at least one of the samples is small (less than 30).

The choice of distribution for the hypothesis test based on independent samples is summarized in Table 12-4:

Table 12-4	Choice of Probability Distribution for Independent Samples	
Condition	*Distribution*	
Equal variances	Student's t	
Unequal variances: large samples	Standard Normal (Z)	
Unequal variances: at least one small sample	Student's t	

Equal population variances

If the variances of two populations are equal (or are assumed to be equal) the appropriate test statistic is based on the Student's t-distribution:

$$t = \frac{(\bar{x}_1 - \bar{x}_2) - (\mu_1 - \mu_2)_0}{\sqrt{s_p^2 \left(\frac{1}{n_1} + \frac{1}{n_2} \right)}}$$

Here's what each term means:

✔ $\bar{x}_1$ is the mean of the sample chosen from population 1.

✔ $\bar{x}_2$ is the mean of the sample chosen from population 2.

✔ μ_1 is the mean of population 1.

✔ μ_2 is the mean of population 2.

✔ $(\mu_1 - \mu_2)_0$ is the hypothesized difference between populations 1 and 2, which is 0 when the population means are hypothesized to be equal.

✔ n_1 is the size of the sample chosen from population 1.

✔ n_2 is the size of the sample chosen from population 2.

✔ s^2_1 is the variance of the sample chosen from population 1.

> ✔ s^2_2 is the variance of the sample chosen from population 2.
>
> ✔ s^2_p is the estimated common pooled variance of the two populations, or in mathematical terms:

$$s^2_p = \frac{(n_1 - 1)s^2_1 + (n_2 - 1)s^2_2}{n_1 + n_2 - 2}$$

If you are conducting a hypothesis test of two population means with equal population variances, you take the critical values from the Student's t-distribution with $n_1 + n_2 - 2$ degrees of freedom, which gives you the following critical values:

> ✔ Right-tailed test: $t_\alpha^{n_1 + n_2 - 2}$
>
> ✔ Left-tailed test: $-t_\alpha^{n_1 + n_2 - 2}$
>
> ✔ Two-tailed test: $\pm t_{\alpha/2}^{n_1 + n_2 - 2}$

As an example, say a marketing company is interested in determining whether men and women are equally likely to buy a new product. The company randomly chooses samples of men and women and asks them to assign a numerical value to their likelihood of buying the product (1 being the least likely, and 10 being the most likely).

Based on past experience, the population variances are assumed to be equal. The first step is to assign one group to be the first population ("population 1") and the other group to be the second population ("population 2"). The company designates men as population 1 and women as population 2.

The next step is to choose samples from both populations. (The sizes of these samples do not have to be equal.) Suppose that the company chooses samples of 21 men and 21 women. These samples are used to compute the sample mean and sample standard deviation for both men and women. (Sample means are covered in Chapter 3; sample standard deviations are covered in Chapter 4.)

Assume that the sample mean score of the men is 7.2; the sample mean score of the women is 6.7. Also assume that the sample standard deviation of the men is 0.4, and the sample standard deviation of the women is 0.3. With this data in place, the null hypothesis that the population mean scores are equal is tested by the marketing company at the 5 percent level of significance.

You can summarize the sample data like so:

$\bar{x}_1 = 7.2$ and $\bar{x}_2 = 6.7$

$s_1 = 0.4$ and $s_2 = 0.3$

$n_1 = 21$ and $n_2 = 21$

The null hypothesis is H_0: $\mu_1 = \mu_2$. The alternative hypothesis is H_1: $\mu_1 \neq \mu_2$.

To compute the test statistic, you first calculate the pooled variance:

$$s_p^2 = \frac{(n_1-1)s_1^2 + (n_2-1)s_2^2}{n_1+n_2-2}$$

$$= \frac{(21-1)(0.4)^2 + (21-1)(0.3)^2}{21+21-2}$$

$$= \frac{32+18}{40}$$

$$= 0.125$$

You then substitute this result into the test statistic formula:

$$t = \frac{(\bar{x}_1 - \bar{x}_2) - (\mu_1 - \mu_2)_0}{\sqrt{s_p^2\left(\frac{1}{n_1}+\frac{1}{n_2}\right)}}$$

$$= \frac{(7.2-6.7)-0}{\sqrt{0.125\left(\frac{1}{21}+\frac{1}{21}\right)}}$$

$$= \frac{0.5}{0.109}$$

$$= 4.587$$

You can find the appropriate critical values from Table 12-5 (which is an excerpt from the Student's t-table, covered in Chapter 11). These are found as follows. The top row of the Student's t-table lists different values of tα, where the right tail of the Student's t-distribution has a probability (area) equal to α ("alpha").

In this case, alpha (α) is 0.05; using a tail area of 0.025 (α/2) and 40 degrees of freedom, you find that the critical values are:

$$\pm t_{\alpha/2}^{n_1+n_2-2} = \pm t_{0.05/2}^{21+21-2} = \pm t_{0.025}^{40} = \pm 2.021$$

Table 12-5	**The Student's t-Distribution with a Large Number of Degrees of Freedom**				
Degrees of Freedom (df)	$t_{0.10}$	$t_{0.05}$	$t_{0.025}$	$t_{0.01}$	$t_{0.005}$
30	1.310	1.697	2.042	2.457	2.750
40	1.303	1.684	2.021	2.423	2.704
60	1.296	1.671	2.000	2.390	2.660

Note that with a large number of degrees of freedom, the Student's t-distribution closely resembles the standard normal distribution (see Chapter 9 for more discussion of the normal distribution). For example, if you perform a two-tailed hypothesis test with $\alpha = 0.05$, the critical values drawn from the standard normal distribution are ± 1.96, compared with ± 2.000 for the Student's t-distribution with 60 degrees of freedom.

Because the test statistic (4.587) exceeds the positive critical value (2.021), the null hypothesis H_0: $\mu_1 = \mu_2$ is rejected.

With a two-tailed test, there are actually two alternatives available to the null hypothesis: H_1: $\mu_1 > \mu_2$ (that is, the mean rating among men is greater than the mean rating among women) or H_1: $\mu_1 < \mu_2$ (that is, the mean rating among men is less than the mean rating among women). In this case, the test statistic is large and positive, which suggests that the mean for men is greater than the mean for women. A large and positive test statistic indicates that the sample mean for men is significantly greater than the sample mean for women. In other words, men are more likely to buy the new product than women.

Unequal population variances: At least one sample is small

If the variances of two populations *aren't* equal (or you don't have any reason to believe that they're equal) and at least one sample is small (less than 30), the appropriate test statistic is

$$t = \frac{(\bar{x}_1 - \bar{x}_2) - (\mu_1 - \mu_2)_0}{\sqrt{\left(\dfrac{s_1^2}{n_1} + \dfrac{s_2^2}{n_2}\right)}}$$

In this case, you get the critical values from the t-distribution with degrees of freedom equal to

$$df = \frac{\left[\left(s_1^2 / n_1\right) + \left(s_2^2 / n_2\right)\right]^2}{\left[\dfrac{\left(s_1^2 / n_1\right)^2}{\left(n_1 - 1\right)} + \dfrac{\left(s_2^2 / n_2\right)^2}{\left(n_2 - 1\right)}\right]}$$

This value isn't necessarily equal to a whole number; if the resulting value contains a fractional part, you must round it to the next closest whole number.

For example, assume that Major League Baseball (MLB) is interested in determining whether the mean number of runs scored per game is higher in the American League (AL) than in the National League (NL). The population variances are assumed to be unequal.

The first step is to assign one group to represent the first population ("population 1") and the other group to represent the second population ("population 2"). MLB designates the American League as population 1 and the National League as population 2.

The next step is to choose samples from both populations. Suppose that MLB choose a sample of 10 American League and 12 National League teams. The results are used to compute the sample mean and sample standard deviation for both leagues. Assume that the sample mean for runs scored among the AL games is 8.1, whereas the sample mean for the NL games is 7.9. The sample standard deviation is 0.5 for AL games and 0.3 for NL games.

MLB tests the null hypothesis that the population mean scores are equal at the 5 percent level of significance.

Here's a summary of the sample data:

$$\bar{x}_1 = 8.1 \text{ and } \bar{x}_2 = 7.9$$

$$s_1 = 0.5 \text{ and } s_2 = 0.3$$

$$n_1 = 10 \text{ and } n_2 = 12$$

The null hypothesis is

$$H_0: \mu_1 = \mu_2$$

Because MLB is interested in determining whether the mean number of runs scored per game is higher in the American League than in the National League, you use a right-tailed test. The alternative hypothesis is $H_1: \mu_1 > \mu_2$.

In other words, the test is designed to find strong evidence that the mean of population 1 is *greater than* the mean of population 2. You then solve the test statistic as follows:

$$t = \frac{(\bar{x}_1 - \bar{x}_2) - (\mu_1 - \mu_2)_0}{\sqrt{\left(\frac{s_1^2}{n_1} + \frac{s_2^2}{n_2}\right)}}$$

$$= \frac{(8.1 - 7.9) - 0}{\sqrt{\left(\frac{0.5^2}{10}\right) + \left(\frac{0.3^2}{12}\right)}}$$

$$= \frac{0.2}{0.1803}$$

$$= 1.109$$

And you find the degrees of freedom like so:

$$df = \frac{\left[\left[\left(s_1^2 / n_1\right) + \left(s_2^2 / n_2\right)\right]\right]^2}{\dfrac{\left(s_1^2 / n_1\right)^2}{\left(n_1 - 1\right)} + \dfrac{\left(s_2^2 / n_2\right)^2}{\left(n_2 - 1\right)}}$$

$$= \frac{\left[\left(0.5^2 / 10\right) + \left(0.3^2 / 1\right)\right]^2}{\dfrac{\left(0.5^2 / 10\right)^2}{\left(10 - 1\right)} + \dfrac{\left(0.3^2 / 12\right)^2}{\left(12 - 1\right)}}$$

$$= \frac{\left[0.025 + 0.0075\right]^2}{0.00006944 + 0.0000051136}$$

$$= \frac{0.00105625}{0.00007455536}$$

$$= 14.167$$

You round down the value of 14.167 to 14 because the degrees of freedom must be a whole number (or *integer*). With 14 degrees of freedom and a 5 percent level of significance, the critical value is $t_{0.05}^{14} = 1.761$.

This result is obtained from Table 12-1 by finding the column headed $t_{0.05}$ and the row corresponding to 14 degrees of freedom.

Because the test statistic (1.109) is below the critical value (1.761), the null hypothesis that $H_0: \mu_1 = \mu_2$ fails to be rejected. There's insufficient evidence to conclude that more runs are scored during American League games than National League games.

Unequal population variances: Both sample sizes are large

If the variances of two populations *aren't* equal, and the size of both samples is 30 or greater, the appropriate test statistic is

$$Z = \frac{\left(\bar{x}_1 - \bar{x}_2\right) - \left(\mu_1 - \mu_2\right)_0}{\sqrt{\left(\dfrac{s_1^2}{n_1} + \dfrac{s_2^2}{n_2}\right)}}$$

This test statistic is based on the standard normal distribution.

As an example, say that a restaurant chain is interested in finding out whether the average sale per customer is the same in its domestic and foreign restaurants. The population variances are assumed to be unequal. The restaurant chooses a random sample of 40 domestic and 50 foreign restaurants, designating domestic restaurants as population 1 and foreign restaurants as population 2.

The sample mean spending per customer is $5.14 in the domestic market and $4.59 in the foreign market. The sample standard deviation is $0.54 in the domestic market and $0.38 in the foreign market. The null hypothesis that the population mean spending is equal in the two markets is tested at the 5 percent level of significance.

Here's a summary of this data:

$$\bar{x}_1 = 5.14 \text{ and } \bar{x}_2 = 4.59$$

$$s_1 = 0.54 \text{ and } s_2 = 0.38$$

$$n_1 = 40 \text{ and } n_2 = 50$$

The null hypothesis is $H_0: \mu_1 = \mu_2$.

Because example requires a two-tailed test, the alternative hypothesis is H_1: $\mu_1 \neq \mu_2$.

You find the test statistic like so:

$$Z = \frac{(\bar{x}_1 - \bar{x}_2) - (\mu_1 - \mu_2)_0}{\sqrt{\left(\dfrac{s_1^2}{n_1} + \dfrac{s_2^2}{n_2}\right)}}$$

$$= \frac{(5.14 - 4.59) - 0}{\sqrt{\left(\dfrac{0.54^2}{40}\right) + \left(\dfrac{0.38^2}{50}\right)}}$$

$$= \frac{0.055}{\sqrt{0.00729 + 0.002888}}$$

$$= 5.452$$

The critical values are then $\pm Z_{\alpha/2} = \pm Z_{0.025} = \pm 1.96$ (see Table 12-3).

Because the test statistic (5.452) is greater than the positive critical value (1.96), the null hypothesis $H_0: \mu_1 = \mu_2$ is rejected.

Because this is a two-tailed test, you may reject the null hypothesis in favor of the alternative $H_1: \mu_1 > \mu_2$ (that is, mean spending per customer is greater in the domestic market than the foreign market) or $H_1: \mu_1 < \mu_2$ (that is, mean spending per customer is lower in the domestic market than the foreign market.) Because the test statistic is large and positive, the alternative $H_1: \mu_1 > \mu_2$ is chosen. In other words, mean spending per customer in the domestic market is greater than in the foreign market.

Working with dependent samples

You can choose samples to compare the mean of a population before and after a given event. In this case, the samples aren't independent; instead, they're dependent, or *paired* samples. Examples of paired samples include:

The cholesterol readings of randomly selected patients before taking a new drug and the cholesterol readings of the same patients after taking the drug

The grade point averages of randomly chosen students before being tutored and the grade point averages of the same students after being tutored

The productivity of a randomly selected group of employees prior to taking a new training course and the productivity of the same employees after taking the training course

With paired samples, the null hypothesis is based on the *differences* between the sample elements. Instead of stating that the population means are equal, the null hypothesis is that the difference between the population means equals 0.

When you're testing hypotheses about the equality of two population means with paired samples, you write the null hypothesis as

$$H_0: \mu_d = 0$$

where μ_d represents the mean difference between the two populations; it equals $\mu_d = \mu_1 - \mu_2$.

The three possible alternative hypotheses are

- **Right-tailed test:** $H_1: \mu_d > 0$. In this case, the alternative hypothesis is that the mean of population 1 is *greater than* the mean of population 2.

- **Left-tailed test:** $H_1: \mu_d < 0$. In this case, the alternative hypothesis is that the mean of population 1 is *less than* the mean of population 2.

- **Two-tailed test:** $H_1: \mu_d \neq 0$. In this case, the alternative hypothesis is that the means of populations 1 and 2 *aren't* equal.

For paired samples, the test statistic is always based on the Student's t-distribution:

$$t = \frac{\bar{d}}{s_d / \sqrt{n}}$$

Here, $\bar{d}$ is the average difference between paired samples, and s_d is the standard deviation of the sample differences.

Compute the mean of the differences like this:

$$\bar{d} = \frac{\sum\limits_{i=1}^{n} d_i}{n}$$

This formula indicates that you calculate the average difference between the paired samples by adding up all the individual differences and then dividing by the total number of elements in each sample..

Compute the standard deviation of the differences like this:

$$s_d = \sqrt{\frac{\sum\limits_{i=1}^{n} \left(d_i - \bar{d}\right)^2}{n-1}}$$

Note that this is the sample standard deviation formula (covered in Chapter 4.)

With paired samples, you take the critical values from the Student's t-distribution with $n - 1$ degrees of freedom, where n is the number of paired observations.

For example, say a pharmaceutical company is testing a new diet pill to determine whether taking it leads to weight loss. The company chooses a sample of eight volunteers. Table 12-6 shows the mean weights of these individuals before and after using the diet pill, along with the necessary calculations for computing the sample standard deviation:

Table 12-6   Paired Differences Between Two Samples

Subject	Weight Prior to Taking Diet Pill (x_1)	Weight After Taking Diet Pill (x_2)	$d_i = x_1 - x_2$	$\left(d_i - \bar{d}\right)^2$
1	192	190	2	1.891
2	189	185	4	0.391
3	204	199	5	2.641
4	177	177	0	11.391
5	156	151	5	2.641
6	228	224	4	0.391
7	244	239	5	2.641
8	201	199	2	1.891
		Sum	**27**	**23.875**
		Mean	**3.375**	

The company tests the null hypothesis that weight remains unchanged after taking the diet pill at the 5 percent level of significance. The null hypothesis is H_0: $\mu_1 = \mu_2$.

Because the pharmaceutical company is looking for strong evidence that the weights of the volunteers *dropped* after taking the pill, it uses a right-tailed test. (In other words, the mean weights of the volunteers before taking the pill is *greater than* the mean weights of the volunteers after taking the pill.)

The alternative hypothesis is H_1: $\mu_1 > \mu_2$.

You work through the test statistic as follows:

1. The first step is to compute the mean of the differences:

$$\bar{d} = \frac{27}{8} = 3.375$$

2. The next step is to compute the sample standard deviation of the differences:

$$s_d = \sqrt{\frac{\sum_{i=1}^{n}\left(d_i - \bar{d}\right)^2}{n-1}}$$

$$= \sqrt{\frac{23.875}{8-1}}$$

$$= 1.847$$

3. These results are used to compute the test statistic:

$$t = \frac{\bar{d}}{s_d / \sqrt{n}}$$

$$= \frac{3.375}{1.847 / \sqrt{8}}$$

$$= \frac{3.375}{0.653}$$

$$= 5.168$$

The critical value is found in Table 12-1: $t_\alpha^{n-1} = t_{0.05}^{7} = 1.895$

Because the test statistic (5.168) exceeds the critical value (1.895), the null hypothesis is rejected in favor of the alternative hypothesis, which states that the difference between the weights prior to taking the pill and after taking the pill is positive. The results show that the pills are contributing to weight loss.

Chapter 13

Testing Hypotheses about Multiple Population Means

. . . .

In This Chapter

▶ Understanding the properties of the F-distribution

▶ Implementing the ANOVA methodology

▶ Testing hypotheses about the equality of multiple population means

. . . .

*T*he *analysis of variance* (ANOVA) methodology allows you to directly compare the means of two or more populations. In Chapter 12, I show you how to test hypotheses about the equality of two population means, but with ANOVA, you can test hypotheses about the equality of any number of population means. You can use ANOVA for a wide variety of applications, such as evaluating claims about the effectiveness of competing products, determining whether a new production process reduces costs, identifying the most profitable products to produce, and so forth.

The ANOVA methodology is based on a continuous distribution known as the *F-distribution.* I cover the properties of the F-distribution in depth in this chapter, as well as techniques for computing probabilities under this distribution. I also show you how to calculate the moments of the F-distribution. The F-distribution reappears in later chapters, including Chapters 14 and 16.

Getting to Know the F-Distribution

The F-distribution is a *continuous* probability distribution, which means that it is defined for an *infinite* number of different values. (Continuous probability distributions, such as the normal distribution, are introduced in Chapter 9.)

The F-distribution (named after the statistician Sir Ronald Fisher) can be used for several types of applications, including testing hypotheses about the equality of two population variances and testing the validity of a multiple regression equation. (Testing hypotheses about the equality of two population variances is covered in Chapter 14; multiple regression analysis is covered in Chapter 16.)

The F-distribution shares one important property with the Student's t-distribution (introduced in Chapter 11): Probabilities are determined by a concept known as *degrees of freedom*. Unlike the Student's t-distribution, the F-distribution is characterized by *two* different types of degrees of freedom — *numerator* and *denominator* degrees of freedom.

The F-distribution has two extremely important properties:

- ✔ It's defined only for positive values.
- ✔ It's *not* symmetrical about its mean; instead, it's *positively skewed*.

A distribution is positively skewed if the mean is greater than the median. (The mean and the median are introduced in Chapter 3. The mean is the average value of a distribution, and the median is the midpoint; half of the values in the distribution are below the median, and half are above.)

A good example of a positively skewed distribution is household incomes. Suppose that half of the households in a country have incomes below $50,000 and half have incomes above $50,000; this indicates that the median household income is $50,000. Among households with incomes below $50,000, the smallest possible value is $0. Among households with incomes above $50,000, there may be incomes of several million dollars per year. This imbalance between incomes below the median and above the median causes the mean to be substantially higher than the median. Suppose for example that the mean income in this case is $120,000. This shows that the distribution of household incomes is positively skewed.

Another key property of the F-distribution is that it's uniquely characterized by two values, or parameters, known as *degrees of freedom (df)*. These are known as numerator degrees of freedom and denominator degrees of freedom.

Figure 13-1 shows a graph of the F-distribution for different combinations of numerator and denominator degrees of freedom. In each case, numerator degrees of freedom are listed first, and denominator degrees of freedom are listed second (for example, *1,5* indicates 1 numerator degree of freedom, and 5 denominator degrees of freedom). The *level of significance* in each case is 0.05.

A level of significance is used to test a *hypothesis*. (Hypothesis testing is covered in detail in Chapter 12.) A hypothesis test begins with a *null hypothesis;*

this is a statement that's assumed to be true unless there is *strong* contrary evidence. There is also an *alternative* hypothesis; this is a statement that is accepted in place of the null hypothesis if there's sufficient evidence to reject the null hypothesis.

The level of significance, designated α (alpha), refers to the probability of incorrectly rejecting the null hypothesis when it is actually true. This is known as a *Type I error*. By contrast, a *Type II error* occurs when you fail to reject the null hypothesis when it's actually false. Therefore, with a level of significance of 0.05, there is a 5 percent chance of committing a Type I error.

Figure 13-1 shows that the distribution isn't defined for negative values (as you can see, no negative values appear along the horizontal axis). Additionally, as the number of degrees of freedom increases, the shape of the distribution shifts to the right. The distribution has a long right tail (more formally, it's *skewed to the right,* or *positively skewed*).

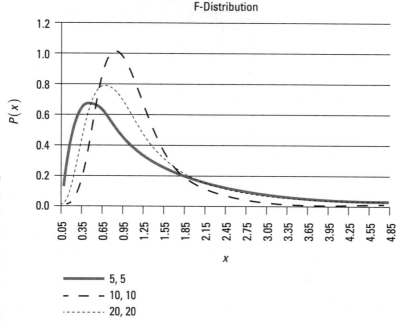

Figure 13-1: The shape of the F-distribution varies with its degrees of freedom (df).

In the following sections, I go into even more detail about the F-distribution, such as the properties of the F random variable and show you how to compute the moments of the F-distribution.

Defining an F random variable

The F-distribution is defined in terms of the chi-square (χ^2) distribution (see Chapter 14 for details). The chi-square distribution is a continuous distribution that is characterized by its *degrees of freedom*. Like the F-distribution, the chi-square distribution is only defined for positive values and is positively skewed.

The chi-square distribution has several different applications, including testing hypotheses about the variance of a population and testing hypotheses about the probability distribution followed by a population.

The following equation shows that an F random variable is the ratio of two *independent* chi-square random variables (χ_1^2 and χ_2^2) and their respective degrees of freedom (v_1 and v_2):

$$F^{v_1,v_2} = \frac{\chi_1^2 / v_1}{\chi_2^2 / v_2}$$

F^{v_1,v_2} is a random variable that follows the F-distribution and has v_1 numerator degrees of freedom and v_2 denominator degrees of freedom.

Measuring the moments of the F-distribution

Moments are summary measures of a probability distribution and include the following:

- ✔ The *expected value* is known as the first moment of a probability distribution and represents the mean or average value of a distribution.

- ✔ The *variance* is the second central moment and shows how spread out or scattered the values of a distribution are around the expected value.

- ✔ The *standard deviation* isn't a separate moment but is the square root of the variance.

For most applications, the standard deviation is more useful than the variance (because the standard deviation is measured in the same units as the expected value whereas the variance is not). For the F-distribution, you use this formula to determine the expected value:

$$E(X) = \frac{v_2}{v_2 - 2}$$

$E(X)$ represents the expected value, and v_2 represents the denominator degrees of freedom (defined in the previous section).

The expected value formula requires the denominator degrees of freedom to be greater than 2. Otherwise, the expected value becomes negative or undefined.

The expected value represents the *average* value of the F-distribution. For example, Figure 13-1 shows a graph of the F-distribution with 5 numerator degrees of freedom and 5 denominator degrees of freedom. The expected value equals:

$$E(X) = \frac{v_2}{v_2 - 2}$$

$$= \frac{5}{5-2}$$

$$= \frac{5}{3}$$

$$= 1.67$$

Figure 13-1 also shows a graph of the F-distribution with 20 numerator degrees of freedom and 20 denominator degrees of freedom. The expected value equals:

$$E(X) = \frac{v_2}{v_2 - 2}$$

$$= \frac{20}{20 - 2}$$

$$= \frac{20}{18}$$

$$= 1.11$$

This shows that the average value of the F-distribution with 20 numerator degrees of freedom and 20 denominator degrees of freedom is *less than* the average value of the F-distribution with 5 numerator degrees of freedom and 5 denominator degrees of freedom.

To compute the variance, you use this formula:

$$\sigma^2 = \frac{2v_2^2(v_1 + v_2 - 2)}{v_1(v_2 - 2)^2(v_2 - 4)}$$

The variance formula requires the denominator degrees of freedom to be greater than 4; otherwise, the variance becomes negative or undefined.

The standard deviation is the *square root* of the variance:

$$\sigma = \sqrt{\frac{2v_2^2(v_1 + v_2 - 2)}{v_1(v_2 - 2)^2(v_2 - 4)}}$$

The variance and the standard deviation are used as measures of how spread out the values of the F-distribution are compared with the expected value.

For example, for the F-distribution with 5 numerator degrees of freedom and 5 denominator degrees of freedom, the variance equals

$$\begin{aligned}
\sigma^2 &= \frac{2v_2^2(v_1 + v_2 - 2)}{v_1(v_2 - 2)^2(v_2 - 4)} \\
&= \frac{2(5^2)(5 + 5 - 2)}{5(5 - 2)^2(5 - 4)} \\
&= \frac{2(25)(8)}{5(9)(1)} \\
&= \frac{400}{45} \\
&= 8.89
\end{aligned}$$

The standard deviation equals the square root of 8.89, or 2.98.

For the F-distribution with 20 numerator degrees of freedom and 20 denominator degrees of freedom, the variance equals

$$\begin{aligned}
\sigma^2 &= \frac{2v_2^2(v_1 + v_2 - 2)}{v_1(v_2 - 2)^2(v_2 - 4)} \\
&= \frac{2(20^2)(20 + 20 - 2)}{20(20 - 2)^2(20 - 4)} \\
&= \frac{2(400)(38)}{20(324)(16)} \\
&= \frac{30,400}{103,680} \\
&= 0.29
\end{aligned}$$

The standard deviation equals the square root of 0.29, or 0.54.

In Figure 13-1, the F-distribution with 20 numerator degrees of freedom and 20 denominator degrees of freedom has a tail that falls off very rapidly (so that the distribution is less spread out) compared with the F-distribution with 5 numerator degrees of freedom and 5 denominator degrees of freedom;

therefore, the distribution with 20 numerator and denominator degrees of freedom has a lower variance and standard deviation.

Using ANOVA to Test Hypotheses

You use analysis of variance (ANOVA) to test hypotheses about the equality of two or more population means. ANOVA is based on experiments performed on subjects that are *independent* of each other; in other words, they are not related to each other. For example, suppose that a department store chain wants to compare the mean sales of household appliances at its stores in New York, Boston, and Philadelphia. Because these stores are in different geographical locations, the sales at one store don't influence sales at the other stores (they're independent of each other.) And because the sales at these stores are independent, ANOVA can be used to test the hypothesis that mean sales are equal at all three stores.

As an example of the ANOVA process, suppose a manufacturer is considering releasing one of three new types of batteries and wants to determine whether one of these batteries has a longer mean lifetime than the others. If so, it will manufacture this battery exclusively. Otherwise, it will randomly pick one of the three to be manufactured. The proposed names for the three battery types are Electrica, Readyforever, and Voltagenow.

In this experiment, battery lifetime is referred to as the *dependent variable*. The hypothesis tested is that the mean battery lifetime is the same for Electrica, Readyforever, and Voltagenow. The three battery types are *treatments*.

If the mean lifetimes of the Electrica, Readyforever, and Voltagenow batteries are different, this may be due to two different sources. These are known as variation *between* groups (battery types) and variation *within* groups (variation among batteries of the same type).

The process used to test whether the mean battery lifetimes are equal for each type is known as *one-way* ANOVA. If the manufacturer wants to compare the mean lifetimes according to type *and* determine if there can be substantial differences within each type, a more complex version of ANOVA is used. This is known as *two-way* ANOVA.

In the following sections, I walk you through the necessary steps for testing the hypothesis that multiple population means are equal. First, the null and alternative hypotheses are explained, followed by a discussion of a concept known as the level of significance. I show you how to construct a test statistic from the F-distribution and how to find the critical values that the test statistic is compared with. I also explain how the final conclusion is reached.

The following procedure is based on the assumptions that

✔ The samples chosen are independent of each other

✔ The underlying populations have equal variances

✔ The populations are normally distributed

Writing the null and alternative hypotheses

The null hypothesis is a statement that's assumed to be true unless you find strong contrary evidence. For testing the hypothesis that three population means are equal, you write:

$$H_0 : \mu_1 = \mu_2 = \mu_3$$

In this expression,

H_0 represents the null hypothesis

μ_1, μ_2, μ_3 represent the means of population 1, 2 and 3

The alternative hypothesis is a statement that you accept in the event that the null hypothesis is rejected (for example, there's strong evidence against it). When testing the hypothesis that three population means are equal, the alternative hypothesis is simply that the three population means are *not* equal.

This alternative hypothesis can be expressed in different ways, such as:

H_1: The three means are *not* all equal

H_1: At least one of the three means is different from the others

In these examples, H_1 represents the alternative hypothesis.

Choosing the level of significance

To test a hypothesis, you have to choose a *level of significance*. The level of significance, designated with α, equals the probability of incorrectly rejecting the null hypothesis when it's actually true. This is called a *Type I error*. A Type II error occurs when you fail to reject the null hypothesis when it's not true. (Check out Chapter 12 for details on Type I and Type II errors in hypothesis testing.)

For many business applications, the level of significance is chosen as 0.05 (5 percent). Other frequent choices include 0.001, 0.01, and 0.10.

Computing the test statistic

The test statistic is a numerical value that is used to determine if the null hypothesis should be rejected. The form of the test statistic depends on the type of hypothesis being tested. If the test statistic has an extremely large positive or negative value, this may be a sign that the null hypothesis is incorrect and should be rejected.

Constructing the test statistic for ANOVA is quite complex, compared with other types of hypothesis tests (see Chapter 12 for a discussion of the steps required for hypothesis testing).

Referring to the battery example, assume that the manufacturer randomly chooses a sample of four Electrica batteries, four Readyforever batteries, and four Voltagenow batteries and then tests their lifetimes. Table 13-1 lists the results (in hundreds of hours).

Table 13-1	**Battery Lifetimes (in Hundreds of Hours)**		
	Electrica	*Readyforever*	*Voltagenow*
Battery 1	2.4	1.9	2.0
Battery 2	1.7	2.1	2.3
Battery 3	3.2	1.8	2.1
Battery 4	1.9	1.6	2.2

Each element in this table can be represented as a variable with two *indexes*, one for the row and one for the column. In general, this is written as X_{ij}. The *subscript i* represents the row index and *j*, represents the column index. For example, X_{23} represents the element found in the second row and third column. (In Table 13-1, this is 2.3.) X_{31} represents the element found in the third row and the first column. (In Table 13-1, this is 3.2.) Table 13-2 shows the appropriate indexes for all the elements in Table 13-1.

Table 13-2	Battery Lifetimes Shown with Subscripts		
	Electrica	Readyforever	Voltagenow
Battery 1	X_{11}	X_{12}	X_{13}
Battery 2	X_{21}	X_{22}	X_{23}
Battery 3	X_{31}	X_{32}	X_{33}
Battery 4	X_{41}	X_{42}	X_{43}

The data in Table 13-1 is used to construct the test statistic. The first step in constructing the test statistic is to calculate the following three measures:

Error sum of squares (SSE)

Treatment sum of squares (SSTR)

Total sum of squares (SST)

The calculations are detailed in the following sections.

Finding the error sum of squares (SSE)

The error sum of squares (abbreviated SSE) is obtained by first computing the mean lifetime of each battery type. For each battery of a specified type, the mean is subtracted from each individual battery's lifetime and then squared. The sum of these squared terms for all battery types equals the SSE.

SSE is a measure of *sampling error*. This refers to the fact that the values computed from a sample will be somewhat different from one sample to the next.

To compute the SSE for this example, the first step is to find the mean for each column. So, for example, you find the mean of column 1, with this formula:

$$\bar{X}_{\bullet 1} = \frac{\sum_{i=1}^{n} X_{i1}}{n_1}$$

Here's what each term means:

- $\bar{X}_{\bullet 1}$ is the mean of column 1 (the bar indicates that this is a mean). The subscripts indicate that this average is computed from all elements within column 1.

- X_{i1} is the value of X in row i and column 1.

- n_1 is the number of elements in column 1.

So, using the values in Table 13-1, you find the mean of column 1 like so:

$$
\begin{aligned}
\bar{X}_{\bullet 1} &= \frac{\sum_{i=1}^{n} X_{i1}}{n_1} \\
&= \frac{2.4 + 1.7 + 3.2 + 1.9}{4} \\
&= \frac{9.2}{4} \\
&= 2.3
\end{aligned}
$$

In other words, you sum the lifetimes of the four Electrica batteries and divide by 4. The mean lifetime of the Electrica batteries in this sample is 2.3.

Similarly, you find the mean of column 2 (the Readyforever batteries) as

$$
\begin{aligned}
\bar{X}_{\bullet 2} &= \frac{\sum_{i=1}^{n} X_{i2}}{n_2} \\
&= \frac{1.9 + 2.1 + 1.8 + 1.6}{4} \\
&= \frac{7.4}{4} \\
&= 1.85
\end{aligned}
$$

And column 3 (the Voltagenow batteries) as

$$
\begin{aligned}
\bar{X}_{\bullet 3} &= \frac{\sum_{i=1}^{n} X_{i3}}{n_3} \\
&= \frac{2.0 + 2.3 + 2.1 + 2.2}{4} \\
&= \frac{8.6}{4} \\
&= 2.15
\end{aligned}
$$

The next step is to subtract the mean of each column from each element within that column, then square the result. I set up the calculations in Table 13-3.

Table 13-3	Battery Lifetimes: Squared Differences from the Column Means		
	Electrica	*Readyforever*	*Voltagenow*
Battery 1	$(2.4 - 2.3)^2 = 0.01$	$(1.9 - 1.85)^2 = 0.0025$	$(2.0 - 2.15)^2 = 0.0225$
Battery 2	$(1.7 - 2.3)^2 = 0.36$	$(2.1 - 1.85)^2 = 0.0625$	$(2.3 - 2.15)^2 = 0.0225$
Battery 3	$(3.2 - 2.3)^2 = 0.81$	$(1.8 - 1.85)^2 = 0.0025$	$(2.1 - 2.15)^2 = 0.0025$
Battery 4	$(1.9 - 2.3)^2 = 0.16$	$(1.6 - 1.85)^2 = 0.0625$	$(2.2 - 2.15)^2 = 0.0025$
Sum	**1.34**	**0.13**	**0.05**

For example, because 2.3 is the mean of column 1, you subtract 2.3 from each element in column 1. You square the result in each row, and the sum of these squared values is 1.34. Repeat the process for columns 2 and 3 to get sums of 0.13 and 0.05, respectively. Add up the sums to get the error sum of squares (SSE): 1.34 + 0.13 + 0.05 = 1.52.

The error sum of squares shows how much variation there is among the lifetimes of the batteries of a given type. The smaller the SSE, the more uniform the lifetimes of the different battery types.

Calculating the treatment sum of squares (SSTR)

After you find the SSE, your next step is to compute the *treatment sum of squares (SSTR)*. This is a measure of how much variation there is among the mean lifetimes of the battery types. With a low SSTR, the mean lifetimes of the different battery types are similar to each other.

First, you need to calculate the overall average for the sample, known as the *overall mean* or *grand mean*. In the battery example from the previous sections, you have 12 total observations (four batteries chosen from each of three battery types; the data are in Table 13-1). You may obtain the overall mean by adding up the 12 sample values and dividing by 12:

$$\frac{2.4 + 1.7 + 3.2 + 1.9 + 1.9 + 2.1 + 1.8 + 1.6 + 2.0 + 2.3 + 2.1 + 2.2}{12} = \frac{25.2}{12} = 2.1$$

You then compute the SSTR with the following steps for each column:

1. **Compute the squared difference between the column mean and the overall mean.**

2. **Multiply the result by the number of elements in the column.**

So in this example, SSTR equals

$$SSTR = 4(2.3 - 2.1)^2 + 4(1.85 - 2.1)^2 + 4(2.15 - 2.1)^2 = 0.42.$$

The calculations are based on the following results obtained in previous sections:

✔ There are four observations in each column.

✔ The overall mean is 2.1.

✔ The column means are 2.3 for column 1, 1.85 for column 2 and 2.15 for column 3.

After you compute SSE and SSTR, the sum of these terms is calculated, giving the total sum of squares (SST). This is shown in the next section.

Computing the total sum of squares (SST)

The *total sum of squares (SST)* equals the sum of the SSTR and the SSE (see the preceding sections). So using the battery example, you get

$$SST = SSTR + SSE$$
$$= 0.42 + 1.52$$
$$= 1.94$$

When you compute SSE, SSTR, and SST, you're ready to proceed to the next step in computing the test statistic. The test statistic is computed from the mean (average) of SSE and SSTR; these are known as:

Error mean square (MSE)

Treatment mean square (MSTR)

The calculations are detailed in the following sections.

Getting the error mean square (MSE)

After you find the sums of squares (see sections "Calculating the treatment sum of squares (SSTR)" and "Computing the total sum of squares (SST)"), you compute the means of the SSE and SSTR. These are known as *error mean square (MSE)* and *treatment mean square (MSTR)*.

You find the MSE by dividing the SSE by N (total number of observations) minus t (total number of treatments) as shown in this formula:

$$MSE = \frac{SSE}{N - t}$$

In the battery lifetimes example (based on Table 13-1), there are a total of 12 observations or elements in the sample data, so N = 12; there are also three battery types, so the number of treatments is t = 3. Therefore, the MSE is

$$MSE = \frac{SSE}{N - t}$$
$$= \frac{1.52}{12 - 3} = 0.1689$$

MSE measures the average variation *within* the treatments; for example, how different the battery means are within the same type.

Getting the treatment mean square (MSTR)

The MSTR equals the SSTR divided by the number of treatments, minus 1 (t – 1), which you can write mathematically as:

$$MSTR = \frac{SSTR}{t - 1}$$

So you find the MSTR for the battery example, (here, *t* is the number of battery types) as follows:

$$MSTR = \frac{SSTR}{t - 1}$$
$$= \frac{0.42}{3 - 1} = 0.21$$

MSTR measures the average variation *among* the treatment means, such as how different the means of the battery types are from each other.

Solving for the F-statistic

The test statistic for the ANOVA process follows the F-distribution, and it's often called the *F-statistic*. The test statistic is computed as follows:

$$F = \frac{MSTR}{MSE}$$
$$= \frac{0.21}{0.1689} = 1.24$$

The test statistic shows the ratio of the treatment mean square (MSTR) to the error mean square (MSE). The greater is this value, the more unlikely it is that the means of the three batteries are equal to each other. As a result, a sufficiently large value of this test statistic results in the null hypothesis being rejected.

Finding the critical values using the F-table

Because the F-distribution is based on two types of degrees of freedom, there's one table for each possible value of α (the level of significance). Table 13-4 shows the different values of the F-distribution corresponding to a 0.05 (5 percent) level of significance.

Table 13-4	The F-Distribution with $\alpha = 0.05$							
v2\v1	2	3	4	5	6	7	8	9
2	19.00	19.16	19.25	19.30	19.33	19.35	19.37	19.38
3	9.55	9.28	9.12	9.01	8.94	8.89	8.85	8.81
4	6.94	6.59	6.39	6.26	6.16	6.09	6.04	6.00
5	5.79	5.41	5.19	5.05	4.95	4.88	4.82	4.77
6	5.14	4.76	4.53	4.39	4.28	4.21	4.15	4.10
7	4.74	4.35	4.12	3.97	3.87	3.79	3.73	3.68
8	4.46	4.07	3.84	3.69	3.58	3.50	3.44	3.39
9	4.26	3.86	3.63	3.48	3.37	3.29	3.23	3.18

The numbers across the top row of the table represent the numerator degrees of freedom (v_1). You read across this top row to find the appropriate numerator degrees of freedom. The first column represents the denominator degrees of freedom (v_2); you read down this column to find the appropriate denominator degrees of freedom. The critical value is found at the intersection of the row and column you choose. For example, suppose that the numerator degrees of freedom is 5 and the denominator degrees of freedom is 7. The appropriate test statistic is 3.97.

For the one-way ANOVA process, you compute the numerator and denominator degrees of freedom as follows:

Numerator degrees of freedom = treatments $- 1 = t - 1 = 3 - 1 = 2$

Denominator degrees of freedom = total observations minus treatments = $N - t = 12 - 3 = 9$

In this example, you're looking for a right-tail area of 5 percent under the F-distribution with numerator degrees of freedom = $v_1 = t - 1 = 2$ and denominator degrees of freedom = $v_2 = N - t = 9$. You find this critical value at the intersection of the *2 degrees of freedom* column and the *9 degrees of freedom* row. The critical value equals 4.26, which you can write as

$$F_\alpha^{v_1, v_2} = F_{0.05}^{2,9} = 4.26$$

The superscripts represent the numerator and denominator degrees of freedom, respectively. The subscript represents the level of significance.

Coming to the decision

The one-way ANOVA hypothesis test is a right-tailed test. This type of test leads to the rejection of the null hypothesis if the value of the test statistic is *too large* to be consistent with the null hypothesis; in other words, if the test statistic is *greater than* the critical value, the null hypothesis is rejected. (Otherwise, the null hypothesis is *not* rejected; there is not enough evidence against it.)

In the battery lifetime example introduced in the section "Using ANOVA to Test Hypotheses," the test statistic equals 1.24, whereas the critical value equals 4.26. Because the test statistic does *not* exceed the critical value, the null hypothesis that the three population means are equal is *not* rejected. This indicates that there is not enough evidence against the hypothesis of equal means to reject it.

Figure 13-2 shows the F-distribution with 2 numerator degrees of freedom and 9 denominator degrees of freedom and a level of significance of 0.05. The test statistic is 1.24 and the critical value is 4.26.

The area to the right of the critical value is the *rejection region*. This is the area under the F-distribution, which is too far away from the critical value to be consistent with the null hypothesis. Because the test statistic doesn't fall within the rejection region, the null hypothesis fails to be rejected. The result indicates that there is not enough evidence against the assumed equality of the mean lifetimes of Electrica, Readyforever, and Voltagenow. Because the manufacturer wants to produce the battery with the longest mean lifetime, it can choose any of the three.

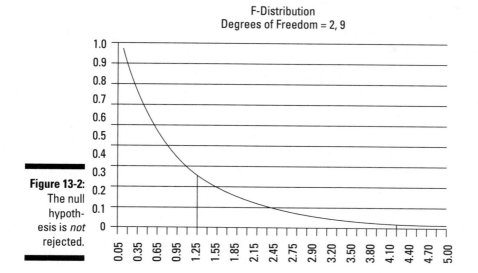

Figure 13-2:
The null hypoth-esis is *not* rejected.

Using a spreadsheet

As an alternative to computing the test statistic and the critical value, you can use a spreadsheet program, such as Excel, to test the null hypothesis that the three population means are equal. If you choose to use a spread-sheet, you'd skip the steps in the sections "Computing the test statistic" and "Finding the critical values using the F-table."

The output of the spreadsheet program is obtained as follows. The first step is to enter the sample data:

	Electrica	*ReadyForever*	*Voltagenow*
Battery 1	2.4	1.9	2.0
Battery 2	1.7	2.1	2.3
Battery 3	3.2	1.8	2.1
Battery 4	1.9	1.6	2.2

If you are using Excel, the next step is to choose the Data tab, then select Data Analysis. This opens up a dialog box containing several statistical pro-cedures that may be performed. The appropriate choice for this example is ANOVA: Single Factor. Click this choice to open a new dialog box; enter the range of cells containing the data into the box Input Range. Be sure to check the box Labels in First Row. Click the OK button to produce the output shown in Figure 13-3.

Anova: Single Factor

SUMMARY

Groups	Count	Sum	Average	Variance
Electrica	4	9.2	2.3	0.446667
Readyforever	4	7.4	1.85	0.043333
Voltagenow	4	8.6	2.15	0.016667

ANOVA

Source of Variation	SS	df	MS	F	P-value	F crit
Between Groups	0.45	2	0.21	1.243421	0.333571	4.256495
Within Groups	1.52	9	0.168889			
Total	1.94	11				

Figure 13-3:
The results of a one-way ANOVA test.

Figure 13-3 shows the following key results:

✔ The column means in the *Average* column of the *Summary* section (2.3, 1.85 and 2.15)

✔ The error sum of squares (SSE) in the *Within Groups* row of the *ANOVA: Source of Variation* section (1.52)

✔ The treatment sum of squares (SSTR) in the *Between Groups* row of the *ANOVA: Source of Variation* section (0.42)

✔ The total sum of squares (SST) or *Total* (1.94)

✔ The treatment mean square (MSTR) at the intersection *Between Groups* and the *MS* column under the *ANOVA: Source of Variation* section (0.21)

✔ The error mean square (MSE) at the intersection of *Within Groups* and *MS* under the *ANOVA: Source of Variation* section (0.168889)

✔ The F-statistic at the intersection of *Between Groups* and the *F* column (1.243421)

✔ The critical value at the intersection of *Between Groups* and *F crit* Column (4.256495)

The printout confirms the results of the previous sections. Because the test statistic is less than the critical value, the null hypothesis that the mean battery lifetimes are equal should *not* be rejected.

Chapter 14

Testing Hypotheses about the Population Mean

*T*his chapter covers two types of hypothesis tests: tests about the population variance, and *goodness of fit* tests. Goodness of fit tests determine whether a population follows a specified distribution, such as the normal distribution (for a thorough introduction to the normal distribution, see Chapter 9). Because many business applications rely on the assumption of normality, goodness of fit tests are particularly valuable.

To implement a goodness of fit test, you use a continuous distribution known as the *chi-square distribution.* This distribution has many interesting features, which I explain in detail and illustrate throughout this chapter; its properties are quite different from the normal distribution.

I also explain how to use a chi-square table to compute probabilities under the chi-square distribution, and I show you how to compute moments for the chi-square distribution. (*Moments* are summary measures of a probability distribution that provide a great deal of useful information in a very compact form.)

You can use the chi-square distribution to test hypotheses about the variance of a population. For example, you can use the chi-square distribution to determine the level of risk contained in a stock portfolio. (The process of testing a hypothesis about a population variance is closely related to other types of hypothesis tests, which I cover in Chapter 12.)

What about two populations, you ask? Testing hypotheses about the equality of two population variances requires yet another continuous distribution: the F-distribution. (I provide an overview of the F-distribution in Chapter 13.) The F-distribution also plays a key role in multiple regression analysis (see Chapter 16).

Staying Positive with the Chi-Square Distribution

The chi-square distribution (χ^2) is a *continuous* probability distribution, which means that it's defined for an infinite number of values. I introduce continuous probability distributions, including the normal, Student's t-, and F-distributions, in Chapters 9, 11, and 13. (To read about discrete probability distributions, check out Chapter 8.)

The chi-square distribution has several different applications. This section shows you how to use the chi-square distribution to:

- Test hypotheses about the variance of a population
- Carry out "goodness of fit" tests

Portfolio managers, financial analysts, traders, and so on regularly use continuous distributions in business applications to analyze the properties of financial variables. Two of the more widely used continuous distributions are the normal and Student's t-distributions (see Chapters 9 and 11, respectively). Many business situations can be described with the normal distribution, such as returns to stocks, corporate profits, and so on. The normal and Student's t-distribution can also be used to construct confidence intervals (described in Chapter 11) and test hypotheses about population means (described in Chapter 12.)

As with the Student's t-distribution, the chi-square distribution is uniquely characterized by a value known as *degrees of freedom (df)*. The number of degrees of freedom is based on the sizes of samples used to estimate population parameters, such as the mean or the variance.

Here are two important features of the chi-square distribution:

- It's defined only for positive values.
- It's *not* symmetrical about its mean; instead, it's positively skewed.

A distribution may be symmetrical about its mean, in which case the area below the mean is a mirror image of the area above the mean. For a symmetric distribution, the mean equals the median. (I discuss symmetry in Chapter 3.) A distribution may also be negatively skewed, where the mean is less than the median, or positively skewed, where the mean is greater than the median.

The chi-square distribution is positively skewed; graphically, it has a long right tail. The next section shows several graphs of the chi-square distribution with different numbers of degrees of freedom. The smaller the degrees of freedom, the more skewed the distribution is; with a larger number of degrees of freedom, the distribution becomes more symmetrical and begins to resemble the normal distribution.

Following the graphs of the chi-square distribution is a discussion of how to compute the moments of the chi-square distribution.

Representing the chi-square distribution graphically

Figures 14-1, 14-2, and 14-3 show the chi-square distribution with 5, 10, and 30 degrees of freedom. In each case, the horizontal axis represents different possible values of the chi-square distribution; the vertical axis represents the corresponding probabilities. With a continuous distribution such as the chi-square, probabilities correspond to areas under the curve.

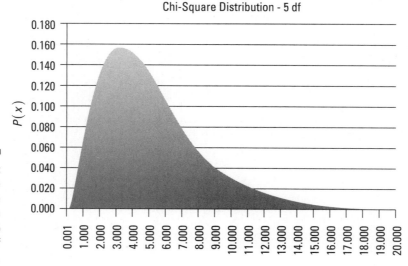

Figure 14-1: The chi-square distribution with 5 degrees of freedom.

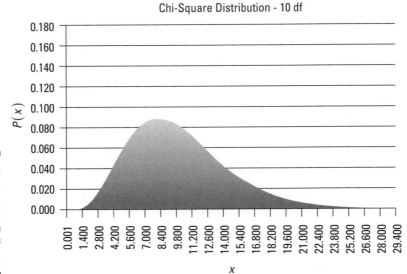

Figure 14-2:
The chi-square distribution with 10 degrees of freedom.

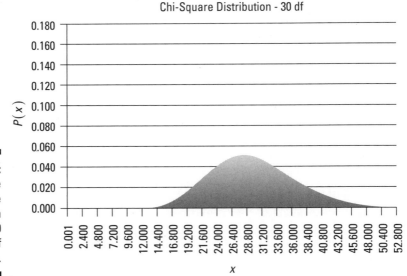

Figure 14-3:
The chi-square distribution with 30 degrees of freedom.

As you can see in each figure, the distribution isn't defined for negative values — that is, no negative values appear along the horizontal axis. Additionally, as the number of degrees of freedom increases, the distribution shifts to the right and begins to resemble the normal distribution (it has a long right tail and is skewed to the right).

Defining a chi-square random variable

A *chi-square random variable* is composed of a sum of independent, squared standard normal random variables (Z^2) (see Chapter 7 for details). The standard normal distribution is the special case of the normal distribution where the mean (μ) equals 0 and the standard deviation (σ) equals 1. You can write the definition of a chi-square random variable mathematically as

$$\chi_v^2 = Z_1^2 + Z_2^2 + Z_3^2 + \ldots + Z_v^2$$

Because each standard normal random variable is squared, the sum of these terms is guaranteed to be positive (which is why the chi-square distribution isn't defined for negative values).

The letter v (or "nu") represents the number of terms in this expression; here, v is the number of degrees of freedom of the distribution. For example, the chi-square distribution with 5 degrees of freedom is defined as follows:

$$\chi_5^2 = Z_1^2 + Z_2^2 + Z_3^2 + Z_4^2 + Z_5^2$$

Checking out the moments of the chi-square distribution

Moments are summary measures of a probability distribution (see Chapter 8 for details) and include the *expected value* (or mean) and the *variance* (how spread out the values are). The *standard deviation* is the square root of the variance.

Each probability distribution has its own unique set of formulas for computing the expected value, variance, and standard deviation. For the chi-square distribution, these are given as follows:

- ✔ The expected value equals the number of degrees of freedom (v) of the distribution:

  $$E(X) = v$$

  For example, in a chi-square distribution with 5 degrees of freedom, the expected value is 5.

- ✔ The variance equals two times the number of degrees of freedom:

  $$\sigma^2 = 2v$$

  For example, for the chi-square distribution with 5 degrees of freedom, the variance is $2 \times 5 = 10$.

✔ The standard deviation is the square root of the variance:

$$\sigma = \sqrt{2v}$$

For example, for the chi-square distribution with 5 degrees of freedom, the standard deviation is the square root of 10, which is approximately 3.16.

Moments capture the key properties of a probability distribution. The expected value is another name for the average; the variance and standard deviation show how "spread out" the values of the distribution are relative to the expected value.

Testing Hypotheses about the Population Variance

In business, one of the most widely used applications of the chi-square distribution is to determine whether the variance of a population equals a specified value. The basic approach to testing a hypothesis about the population variance exactly mirrors the approach used for the population mean (which I cover in Chapter 12). The most important changes take place in the test statistic and critical values you use.

In the following sections, I walk you through the steps to testing hypotheses about the population variance.

Defining what you assume to be true: The null hypothesis

The first step in the hypothesis testing procedure is writing the *null hypothesis,* which is a statement that's assumed to be true unless strong contrary evidence exists against it. For example, suppose that a manufacturer is concerned that the variance of the computer chips that it produces exceeds 0.001, which would indicate that there's a problem with the production process. The manufacturer could test this hypothesis by selecting a sample of computer chips and computing their sample variance.

The manufacturer may not want to make any changes to the production process unless clear evidence shows that it's necessary. Therefore, it uses the null hypothesis that the variance equals 0.001. If this hypothesis is rejected, the alternative that the variance exceeds 0.001 is accepted instead. Unless the null hypothesis can be disproved with strong evidence, no changes are made to the production process. (Hypothesis testing is introduced in Chapter 12.)

For testing hypotheses about the population variance, the null hypothesis statement is based on the assumption that the population variance equals the *hypothesized value* of the population (σ_0^2). This assumption isn't abandoned without strong contradictory evidence.

Mathematically, you write the null hypothesis as

$$H_0 : \sigma^2 = \sigma_0^2$$

The variance with a subscript of 0 (σ_0^2) is the hypothesized value of the variance. This is the value that you believe the population variance is equal to. The hypothesis test shows whether this belief is backed up by actual data.

For example, suppose that an economist wants to determine whether the variance of the inflation rate over the past 20 years equals 0.0001, in which case, you write the null hypothesis as $H_0 : \sigma^2 = 0.0001$. The economist continues to assume that this is the correct variance unless the hypothesis test provides strong evidence against this claim.

Stating the alternative hypothesis

Your second step in a hypothesis test is to specify the *alternative hypothesis*. If the statistical evidence against the null hypothesis is strong enough to reject it, you need an alternative statement to accept in its place.

The alternative hypothesis is a statement of what you accept to be true if the null hypothesis is rejected. For example, the economist in the previous section may want to know whether the actual variance is less than 0.0001, greater than 0.0001, or simply different from 0.0001 if the null hypothesis is rejected.

You can express the alternative hypothesis in three ways: as right-tailed, left-tailed, and two-tailed tests.

- ✔ With a right-tailed test, you look for evidence that the actual population variance is *greater than* the hypothesized value.
- ✔ With a left-tailed test, you look for evidence that the population variance is *less than* the hypothesized value.
- ✔ With a two-tailed test, you look for evidence that the population variance is *either* less than or greater than the hypothesized value.

I explore each option in the following sections. (Right-tailed tests, left-tailed tests, and two-tailed tests are introduced in Chapter 12.)

Right-tailed test: Determining whether the hypothesized variance is too low

If you're interested in knowing only whether the population variance is greater than the hypothesized value, you use a right-tailed test. In this case, you express the alternative hypothesis (H_1) as

$$H_1 : \sigma^2 > \sigma_0^2$$

For example, suppose that a manufacturing company wants to keep the weights of its computer chips as uniform as possible. It determined from experience that the maximum variance the chips can tolerate is 0.0006 milligrams squared. (Variances are measured in terms of squared units, as I discuss in Chapter 4.) The manufacturing company can test the variance by choosing a sample off of the assembly line and computing the sample variance. In this case, the company can test the hypothesis that the variance equals 0.0006 ($H_0 : \sigma^2 = 0.0006$); the alternative hypothesis is that the variance exceeds (or is greater than) 0.0006 ($H_1 : \sigma^2 > 0.0006$).

The results of this test show whether the manufacturing process is working correctly or whether it needs to be adjusted.

Left-tailed test: Determining whether the hypothesized variance is too high

If you're interested in knowing only whether the population variance is less than the hypothesized value, you use a left-tailed test. In this case, you express the alternative hypothesis as

$$H_1 : \sigma^2 < \sigma_0^2$$

For example, suppose that an equity analyst is studying the pattern of returns to U.S. stocks since the outbreak of the last financial crisis. The analyst wants to determine whether markets have begun to stabilize since the crisis began, which is indicated by a drop in the variances of the returns to U.S. stocks. The analyst believes that one stock is particularly representative of the performance of the overall economy. He wants to see whether the variance of its returns has remained at 0.0004 or whether it's fallen below this level. In this case, the analyst can test the null hypothesis that the variance equals 0.0004 ($H_0 : \sigma^2 = 0.0004$); the alternative hypothesis is that the variance is less than 0.0004 ($H_1 : \sigma^2 < 0.0004$).

The results of this test show whether the variance of this stock has fallen below 0.0004. If so, the markets have stabilized since the outbreak of the financial crisis.

Two-tailed test: Determining whether the hypothesized variance is too low or too high

In some situations, it's extremely important for you to know whether the population variance is greater than or less than the hypothesized value. In this case, you use the two-tailed test, and write the alternative hypothesis as

$$H_1 : \sigma^2 \neq \sigma_0^2$$

For example, suppose that the variance of the returns to an investor's portfolio has historically been 0.0009; the investor wants to determine whether this number has increased or decreased over the past year. In this case, the investor can use a two-tailed hypothesis test. The null hypothesis is that the variance equals 0.0009 ($H_0 : \sigma^2 = 0.0009$), and the alternative hypothesis is that the variance doesn't equal 0.0009 ($H_1 : \sigma^2 \neq 0.0009$).

Choosing the level of significance

To test a hypothesis, you have to choose a *level of significance*. The level of significance, designated with α, refers to the probability of rejecting the null hypothesis when it's actually true, called a *Type I error*. (Chapter 12 provides details on Type I and Type II errors in hypothesis testing.)

You must choose the level of significance carefully. The greater the level of significance, the greater the likelihood of rejecting the null hypothesis when it's true — and the lower the likelihood of failing to reject the null hypothesis when it's false.

You choose the level of significance based on the relative importance of avoiding these errors. For many business applications, the level of significance is set to 0.05 (or 5 percent.) Other commonly used values are 0.01 and 0.10.

Calculating the test statistic

To test hypotheses about the population variance, you must draw a sample from the underlying population so you can compute the sample variance. The sample variance is required to compute the test statistic:

$$\chi^2 = \frac{(n-1)s^2}{\sigma_0^2}$$

This equation shows that the test statistic follows the chi-square distribution, with $n - 1$ degrees of freedom (n is the sample size); s^2 is the sample variance, and σ_0^2 is the hypothesized value of the population variance.

This expression is used as a test statistic because it can be shown to follow the chi-square distribution with $n - 1$ degrees of freedom.

The purpose of the test statistic is to determine how extreme a sample statistic is (in this case, the sample variance) compared with the hypothesized value of the corresponding population parameter (here, the population variance.) If the test statistic is too extreme (the value is an extremely large positive or negative number), it's highly unlikely that the null hypothesis is true, and it will be rejected. Otherwise, the null hypothesis won't be rejected.

To determine how extreme the test statistic is, you compare its value to one or two numbers known as *critical values,* depending on the alternative hypothesis. When testing hypotheses about the population variance, critical values are taken from the chi-square distribution. They represent the cutoff point between a specified area under the chi-square distribution.

For example, for the chi-square distribution with 10 degrees of freedom, a critical value of 18.30 is the cutoff point between the upper 5 percent of the chi-square distribution and the lower 95 percent of the chi-square distribution.

In other words, for a chi-square random variable X,

$$P(X \geq 18.30) = 0.05$$
$$P(X \leq 18.30) = 0.95$$

Determining the critical value (s)

To test a hypothesis about the variance of a population, the critical value(s) depends on the alternative hypothesis. Unlike critical values drawn from the standard normal distribution or the Student's t-distribution, the chi-square distribution has no negative critical values. Instead, you determine the critical values with the alternative hypothesis tests as explained in the following sections.

Right-tailed test: Testing hypotheses about the population variance

A right-tailed test has a single critical value because you're looking only for evidence that the test statistic is *too large* to be consistent with the null hypothesis. If you don't find this evidence, you won't reject the null hypothesis. The form of the critical value is

$$\chi^2_{\alpha, n-1}$$

In this expression,

χ^2 = a value chosen from the chi-square distribution

α = the level of significance of the hypothesis test (for example, 0.01, 0.05, 0.10, and so on)

n = the sample size

The values of α and n uniquely identify the appropriate test statistic drawn from the chi-square distribution. This value represents the threshold of the right tail of the chi-square distribution with area α and $n - 1$ degrees of freedom. The area in the right tail is α. You can find this critical value in a chi-square table, such as Table 14-1.

Table 14-1			The Chi-Square Table					
df\Right-Rail Area	0.99	0.975	0.95	0.90	0.10	0.05	0.025	0.01
1	0.00	0.00	0.00	0.016	2.706	3.841	5.024	6.635
2	0.020	0.051	0.103	0.211	4.605	5.991	7.378	9.210
3	0.115	0.216	0.352	0.584	6.251	7.815	9.348	11.345
4	0.297	0.484	0.711	1.064	7.779	9.488	11.143	13.277
5	0.554	0.831	1.145	1.610	9.236	11.070	12.833	15.086
6	0.872	1.237	1.635	2.204	10.645	12.592	14.449	16.812
7	1.239	1.690	2.167	2.833	12.017	14.067	16.013	18.475
8	1.646	2.180	2.733	3.490	13.362	15.507	17.535	20.090
9	2.088	2.700	3.325	4.168	14.684	16.919	19.023	21.666
10	2.558	3.247	3.940	4.865	15.987	18.307	20.483	23.209

For example, suppose you conduct a right-tailed test with a level of significance of 0.05 (5 percent). You draw a sample of size 10. Plugging those numbers into the critical value, you get

$$\chi^2_{\alpha,\, n-1} = \chi^2_{0.05,\, 9}$$

You then look at the chi-square table (Table 14-1). The top row represents areas in the right tail of the chi-square distribution. The first column represents the number of degrees of freedom.

In this example, you're looking for a right-tail area of 0.05 with 9 degrees of freedom ($n - 1 = 10 - 1 = 9$). By looking in the row corresponding to 9 degrees of freedom and the column corresponding to a right-tail area of 0.05, you see that the critical value is 16.919. Therefore,

$$\chi^2_{\alpha,\, n-1} = \chi^2_{0.05,\, 9} = 16.919$$

As a result, if the test statistic is greater than 16.919, you reject the null hypothesis; otherwise, you don't reject the null hypothesis.

Left-tailed test: Testing hypotheses about the population variance

A left-tailed test has a single critical value because you're looking only for evidence that the test statistic is *too small* to be consistent with the null hypothesis. If you don't find this evidence, you won't reject the null hypothesis. The form of the test statistic is

$$\chi^2_{(1-\alpha),\, n-1}$$

This value represents the threshold of the left tail of the chi-square distribution with area α and $n - 1$ degrees of freedom. The area in the right tail is, therefore, $1 - \alpha$.

Using the example in the previous section and referring to Table 14-1, if you do a left-tailed test with a level of significance of 0.05 and a sample of size 10, you find the appropriate critical value in the row with 9 degrees of freedom but a right-tail area of 0.95, which is

$$\chi^2_{(1-\alpha),\, n-1} = \chi^2_{0.95,\, 9} = 3.325$$

As a result, if the test statistic is less than 3.325, you reject the null hypothesis; otherwise, you don't reject the null hypothesis.

Two-tailed test: Testing hypotheses about the population variance

A two-tailed test has two critical values. You're looking for evidence that the test statistic is too large *or* too small to be consistent with the null hypothesis. If you don't find this evidence, you won't reject the null hypothesis. The form of the critical values are

$$\chi^2_{(1-\alpha/2),\, n-1}$$

$$\chi^2_{(\alpha/2),\, n-1}$$

The two-tailed test has a right tail and a left tail. Each has an area equal to $\alpha/2$. So, for example, if you do a two-tailed test with a level of significance of 0.05 and a sample of size 10, the appropriate critical values are 2.700 and 19.023 (see Table 14-1).

$$\chi^2_{(1-\alpha/2),\, n-1} = \chi^2_{0.975,\, 9} = 2.700$$

$$\chi^2_{(\alpha/2),\, n-1} = \chi^2_{0.025,\, 9} = 19.023$$

The boundary of the left 2.5 percent tail of the chi-square distribution is 2.700, and the boundary of the right 2.5 percent tail of the chi-square distribution is 19.023. Note that with the right-tailed test, the right tail has an area of 5 percent; with a left-tailed test, the left tail has an area of 5 percent. With a two-tailed test, the 5 percent area is split between the left and right tails; therefore, each has an area of 2.5 percent.

As a result, if the test statistic is less than 2.700 or greater than 19.023, you reject the null hypothesis; otherwise, you don't reject the null hypothesis.

Making the decision

You decide whether to reject the null hypothesis by looking at the relationship between the test statistic and the critical value(s). There are three possible cases: a right-tailed test, a left-tailed test, and a two-tailed test.

- ✔ **Right-tailed test:** If the test statistic is greater than the critical value $\chi^2_{\alpha, n-1}$, you reject the null hypothesis H_0: $\sigma^2 = \sigma_0^2$ in favor of the alternative hypothesis H_1: $\sigma^2 > \sigma_0^2$. Otherwise, you don't reject the null hypothesis.

- ✔ **Left-tailed test:** If the test statistic is less than the critical value $\chi^2_{(1-\alpha), n-1}$, you reject the null hypothesis H_0: $\sigma^2 = \sigma_0^2$ in favor of the alternative hypothesis H_1: $\sigma^2 < \sigma_0^2$. Otherwise, you don't reject the null hypothesis.

- ✔ **Two-tailed test:** If the test statistic is less than the critical value $\chi^2_{(1-\alpha/2), n-1}$, you reject the null hypothesis H_0: $\sigma^2 = \sigma_0^2$ in favor of the alternative hypothesis H_1: $\sigma^2 < \sigma_0^2$.

  If the test statistic is greater than the critical value $\chi^2_{(\alpha/2), n-1}$, you reject the null hypothesis H_0: $\sigma^2 = \sigma_0^2$ in favor of the alternative hypothesis H_1: $\sigma^2 > \sigma_0^2$. Otherwise, you don't reject the null hypothesis.

As an example of the complete process used to test hypotheses about the population variance, suppose that an investor chooses a sample of 30 stocks from her portfolio. She calculates the standard deviation of the returns on these stocks (that is, their *volatility*) to be 23 percent on an annual basis. The investor wants to know whether the volatility of the entire portfolio is less than 25 percent on an annual basis at the 5 percent level of significance. (A volatility of 25 percent [0.25] translates into a variance of $0.25^2 = 0.0625$.) So the null hypothesis is $H_0 : \sigma^2 = 0.0625$, and alternative hypotheses is $H_1 : \sigma^2 < 0.0625$.

Because the investor wants to know only whether the variance is less than 0.0625, you use a left-tailed test. The level of significance is $\alpha = 0.05$.

With a sample size of 30 and a sample variance of 0.23, the test statistic is

$$\chi^2 = \frac{(n-1)s^2}{\sigma_0^2}$$

$$= \frac{(30-1)(0.23)^2}{(0.25)^2}$$

$$= 24.546$$

Because this is a left-tailed test with $\alpha = 0.05$ and sample size = 30, the number of degrees of freedom = 29 (30 − 1). The critical value is, therefore, $\chi^2_{(1-\alpha),\,n-1} = \chi^2_{0.95,\,29}$.

You can find the result in a chi-square table, such as Table 14-2.

Table 14-2	The Chi-Square Table with Larger Numbers of Degrees of Freedom							
df\Right-Tail Area	*0.99*	*0.975*	*0.95*	*0.90*	*0.10*	*0.05*	*0.025*	*0.01*
28	13.565	15.308	16.928	18.939	37.916	41.337	44.461	48.278
29	14.256	16.047	17.708	19.768	39.087	42.557	45.722	49.588
30	14.953	16.791	18.493	20.599	40.256	43.773	46.979	50.892

You find the critical value in the row corresponding to 29 degrees of freedom ($n − 1 = 30 − 1 = 29$) and the column with a right-tail area of 0.095 ($[1 − \alpha] = [1 − 0.05] = 0.095$). The result is 17.708.

To reject this hypothesis, the test statistic must be less than the critical value. In this case, the critical value is 24.55, and the test statistic is 17.708; therefore, the null hypothesis isn't rejected. There isn't enough evidence to conclude that the portfolio volatility is less than 25 percent.

Practicing the Goodness of Fit Tests

One of the most important applications of the chi-square distribution is to test whether a population conforms to a specific probability distribution. This type of test is called a *goodness of fit test*.

In this section, I show you examples of how to use sample data from a population to determine whether the population follows the Poisson distribution (covered in Chapter 8) or the normal distribution (discussed in Chapter 9). Note that these aren't the only possible applications of goodness of fit tests; in principle, you can compare any population to any probability distribution.

Comparing a population to the Poisson distribution

You use the Poisson distribution to describe the distribution of events occurring over a given interval of time. To test the hypothesis that a population follows the Poisson distribution, you express the null and alternative hypotheses as follows:

✔ H_0: The population follows the Poisson distribution.

✔ H_1: The population doesn't follow the Poisson distribution.

Alternatively, the null and alternative hypotheses may include an assumption about the parameter λ, which represents the expected number of events that occur during a given time frame.

For example, the null and alternative hypotheses could be

✔ H_0: The population follows the Poisson distribution with $\lambda = 1$.

✔ H_1: The population doesn't follow the Poisson distribution with $\lambda = 1$.

Use this approach if you have reason to believe that the value of $\lambda = 1$. In this case, the interpretation of the results is slightly different. If the null hypothesis that the population follows the Poisson distribution is rejected, the population actually follows a different distribution. If the null hypothesis that the population follows the Poisson distribution with $\lambda = 1$ is rejected, the population either doesn't follow the Poisson distribution or it follows the Poisson distribution but with a different value of λ.

One of the unusual features of a goodness of fit test is that you always implement the alternative hypothesis as a right-tailed test. Based on the construction of the test statistic, the null hypothesis that a population follows a specified distribution is rejected only if the test statistic is *too large;* therefore, a goodness of fit test is always right-tailed.

And you construct the test statistic in such a way as to see how closely the elements in a sample match up with the assumed probability distribution. To construct the test statistic, you choose sample data and arrange them into categories.

For example, suppose that a bank manager wants to determine whether the distribution of customers that enters the bank during lunch hour (12 noon to 1 p.m.) follows the Poisson distribution. This information helps the manager determine the optimal number of tellers to use during this time period.

In this case, the population consists of the number of customers that enter the bank during lunch hour. Suppose that the manager chooses a random sample of 100 lunch hours from the past year and counts the number of customer that enters during each of those 100 hours. He then organizes the results as shown here:

Number of Customers per Hour	*Number of Hours*
0	9
1	12
2	15
3	20
4	27
5	12
6	5

According to these results, during each hour in the sample, the number of customers ranged from 0 to 6, so the manager organizes the data into a total of seven categories. The number of customers in each category is known as the *observed frequency* of the category. You must compare these numbers with the *expected frequencies* — the number of customers expected if the distribution of customers per hour really does follow the Poisson distribution.

In this example, you can find the expected frequencies for each category by computing the Poisson probabilities for each category and multiplying the result by the sample size. For example, suppose that the probability of three customers entering the bank each hour under the Poisson distribution is 0.2240, indicating that in a sample of 100 hours, the expected number of customers (or the expected frequency) is $0.2240 \times 100 = 22.40$ customers. (Of course, it's impossible for 22.40 customers to show up during lunch hour! This is simply an average.)

After you determine the expected frequency of each category, you compute the test statistic with this formula:

$$\chi^2 = \sum_{j=1}^{k} \frac{\left(O_j - E_j\right)^2}{E_j}$$

Here, j is an index for the category being tested, k is the number of total categories, O_j is the observed frequency in category j, and E_j is the expected frequency in category j.

The closer the observed frequencies are to the expected frequencies, the smaller the value of the test statistic. A small value for this statistic indicates that the null hypothesis (which states that the population follows the Poisson distribution) should *not* be rejected.

Because the goodness of fit test is always right-tailed, it has a single critical value:

$$\chi^2_{\alpha,\, k-1-m}$$

Note that m is a parameter whose value equals 0 if the null hypothesis specifies a value of λ and 1 if the null hypothesis doesn't specify a value of λ.

Unlike hypothesis tests of the population variance, where the appropriate number of degrees of freedom is $n - 1$, with a goodness of fit test, the appropriate number of degrees of freedom is $k - 1 - m$.

When you determine the values of the test statistic and the critical value, the decision rule is to reject the null hypothesis if the test statistic exceeds the critical value; otherwise, don't reject the null hypothesis.

To test the hypothesis that the distribution of customers that enters the bank during lunch hour follows the Poisson distribution, the first step is to specify the null and alternative hypotheses:

- H_0: The population follows the Poisson distribution.
- H_1: The population doesn't follow the Poisson distribution.

Assume that the level of significance is 0.05 (5 percent).

Before you construct the table of observed and expected frequencies, you must estimate the value of λ from the sample data, because it isn't specified in the null hypothesis. In this case, λ represents the average number of bank customers per hour.

Because each possible number of bank customers is repeated many times in the sample, the average number of bank customers per hour can be computed as a weighted average (see Chapter 3). The formula is

$$\bar{X} = \frac{\sum\limits_{i=1}^{n} w_i X_i}{\sum\limits_{i=1}^{n} w_i}$$

In this formula,

$\bar{X}$ is the sample mean

X_i is a single sample element

w_i is the *weight* associated with element X_i, which equals the number of times that the element appears in the sample

To compute the numerator of this formula, you multiply each number of customers per hour in the sample by the actual number of hours in which this number occurred. This is shown as follows:

Number of Customers per Hour	Number of Hours	Customers per Hour × Number of Hours
0	9	(0)(9) = 0
1	12	(1)(12) = 12
2	15	(2)(15) = 30
3	20	(3)(20) = 60
4	27	(4)(27) = 108
5	12	(5)(12) = 60
6	5	(6)(5) = 30
SUM		300

This results in a sum of 300. The denominator is the sum of the weights:

$$9 + 12 + 15 + 20 + 27 + 12 + 5 = 100$$

The average number of customers is

$$\bar{X} = \frac{\sum_{i=1}^{n} w_i X_i}{\sum_{i=1}^{n} w_i} = \frac{300}{100} = 3$$

You use this result as the value of lambda: $\lambda = 3$.

The next step is to compute the expected frequencies for each category. You find the probability of no customers entering the bank during the next hour when $\lambda = 3$ from the Poisson distribution with this formula:

$$P(X = x) = e^{-\lambda} \frac{\lambda^x}{x!}$$

The key terms in this formula are

X = a Poisson random variable

x = number of events (phone calls) that occur

λ = the average number of events that occur per time (hour)

e = a constant equal to approximately 2.71828

! = the "factorial" operator (introduced in Chapter 8)

The factorial operator can only be applied to positive whole numbers and zero. So 0! equals 1, as does 1!, and 2! equals (2)(1) = 2; in other words, 2! equals itself times all smaller positive whole numbers. Based on this pattern,

3! equals (3)(2)(1) = 6, and 4! equals (4)(3)(2)(1) = 24. All remaining factorials are computed in the same way. The factorial operator may be used for several applications; one of these is to count the number of *arrangements* that may be formed from a collection of objects. For example, if three paintings are hung next to each other in the reading room of a library, the number of ways the paintings may be arranged equals 3! = 6.

For the bank customer case, the probability of no customers entering the bank during the lunch hour is computed with the Poisson formula as follows:

$$P(X=0) = e^{-\lambda} \frac{\lambda^x}{x!}$$
$$= e^{-3} \frac{3^0}{0!}$$
$$= 0.0498$$

You do the same calculations with the probabilities for X = 1, X = 2 all the way up to X = 6. The probability that X = 1 is computed as follows:

$$P(X=1) = e^{-\lambda} \frac{\lambda^x}{x!}$$
$$= e^{-3} \frac{3^1}{1!}$$
$$= 0.1494$$

The probability that X = 2 is computed as follows:

$$P(X=2) = e^{-\lambda} \frac{\lambda^x}{x!}$$
$$= e^{-3} \frac{3^2}{2!}$$
$$= 0.2240$$

The probabilities for X = 3, 4, 5, and 6 are computed in a similar manner:

$P(X = 3) = 0.2240$

$P(X = 4) = 0.1680$

$P(X = 5) = 0.1008$

$P(X = 6) = 0.0504$

Because the sample size is 100, you multiply the probabilities by 100 to get the expected frequencies, as shown here:

$X = 0$: expected frequency = 0.0498(100) = 4.98

$X = 1$: expected frequency = 0.1494(100) = 14.94

$X = 2$: expected frequency = 02240(100) = 22.40

$X = 3$: expected frequency = 0.2240(100) = 22.40

$X = 4$: expected frequency = $0.1680(100) = 16.80$

$X = 5$: expected frequency = $0.1008(100) = 10.08$

$X = 6$: expected frequency = $0.0504(100) = 5.04$

Substitute these values into the test statistic formula:

$$\chi^2 = \sum_{j=1}^{k} \frac{\left(O_j - E_j\right)^2}{E_j}$$

$$= \frac{(0-4.98)^2}{4.98} + \frac{(12-14.94)^2}{14.94} + \frac{(30-22.40)^2}{22.40} + \frac{(60-22.40)^2}{22.40} +$$

$$\frac{(108-16.80)^2}{16.80} + \frac{(60-10.08)^2}{10.08} + \frac{(30-5.04)^2}{5.04}$$

$$= 71.22$$

Then, you determine the critical value as follows:

$$\chi^2_{\alpha,\, k-1-m}$$

The first step is to identify the values of α, k, and m:

- ✔ $\alpha = 0.05$ because you're using a level of significance of 0.05 (5 percent).
- ✔ $k = 7$ because there are seven categories (the number of customers that enter the bank during lunch hour is 0, 1, 2, 3, 4, 5, or 6, for a total of 7 possibilities).
- ✔ $m = 1$ because the null hypothesis doesn't specify a value of λ. (In other words, you computed the value of λ from the sample data.)

Therefore, $k - 1 - m = 7 - 1 - 1 = 5$.

You can find the critical value in Table 14-1 by finding the intersection of the 0.05 right-tail area column and the 5 df row:

$$\chi^2_{\alpha,\, k-1-m} = \chi^2_{0.05,\, 7-1-1} = \chi^2_{0.05,\, 5} = 11.070$$

The test statistic doesn't exceed the critical value. Because this is a right-tailed test, the correct conclusion is that the null hypothesis can't be rejected. In other words, the number of cellphone calls per hour does follow the Poisson distribution.

Comparing a population to the normal distribution

Testing the hypothesis that a population follows the normal distribution is similar to testing the hypothesis that a population follows the Poisson distribution (see the previous section). The two most important differences are that you compute the expected frequencies from the normal distribution, and the definition of m is slightly different for the critical value. In this case, m is defined as follows:

- ✔ $m = 0$ if the value of the mean (μ) and standard deviation (σ) are both specified in the null hypothesis.

- ✔ $m = 1$ if the value of the mean or the standard deviation (but not both) is specified in the null hypothesis.

- ✔ $m = 2$ if the value of neither the mean nor the standard deviation are specified in the null hypothesis.

As an example, suppose that a portfolio manager wants to determine whether the returns to a portfolio are normally distributed, with a mean of 5 percent and a standard deviation of 10 percent.

The observed frequencies are 22 for –15 to –5 percent returns, 29 for –5 to 5 percent returns, 37 for 5 to 15 percent returns, and 12 for 15 to 25 percent returns. The null and alternative hypotheses are

- ✔ H_0: The population is normally distributed with a mean of 5 percent and standard deviation of 10 percent.

- ✔ H_1: The population isn't normally distributed with mean of 5 percent and standard deviation of 10 percent.

Assume that the level of significance is 0.05 (5 percent).

You determine the expected frequencies from the standard normal distribution by following these steps:

1. **Define X to be the return to a portfolio.**

   The mean return is 5 percent and the standard deviation of the return is 10 percent.

2. **Assume that X is normally distributed.**

   To compute probabilities for X using the normal table, you must first convert it into a standard normal random variable (I show you how to do so in Chapter 9).

In this example, the returns are normally distributed with a mean of 5 percent and a standard deviation of 10 percent. Next, you compute the probability that X is between –15 percent and –5 percent.

Because X is a normal random variable but not *standard normal,* you must convert X into the equivalent standard normal form. (Recall that the standard normal distribution has a mean of 0 and a standard deviation of 1, as discussed in Chapter 9.) The appropriate formula is

$$Z = \frac{X - \mu}{\sigma}$$

In this formula,

μ is the mean of X.

σ is the standard deviation of X.

By converting X into a standard normal random variable, it is now possible to compute probabilities for X, using the standard normal tables.

$$P(-15 \leq X \leq -5) = P\left(\frac{-15-5}{10} \leq Z \leq \frac{-5-5}{10}\right) = P(-2.00 \leq Z \leq -1.00)$$

The standard normal tables are set up to compute *cumulative* probabilities; in other words, the probability that Z is less than or equal to a specified value.

In this example, you're looking for the probability that Z is between –2.00 and –1.00. This can be computed from the standard normal tables by rewriting the expression in the equivalent form:

$$P(Z \leq -1.00) - P(Z \leq -2.00)$$

You can get these probabilities from the standard normal table. See Table 14-3 for a selection of probabilities associated with negative Z values.

Table 14-3	Selected Standard Normal Probabilities for Negative Z Values			
Z	*0.00*	*0.01*	*0.02*	*0.03*
–2.0	0.0228	0.0222	0.0217	0.0212
–1.5	0.0668	0.0655	0.0643	0.0630
–1.0	0.1587	0.1562	0.1539	0.1515

You find the probability that Z is less than or equal to –1.00 at the intersection of the row for –1.0 under the Z column and the *0.00* column, which is 0.1587.

Likewise, you find the probability that Z is less than or equal to –2.00 at the intersection of the –2.0 row and the *0.00* column, which is 0.0228.

Combining these values gives you $P(Z \leq -1.00) - P(Z \leq -2.00) = 0.1587 - 0.0228 = 0.1359$.

You determine the probability that X is between –5 percent and +5 percent as follows.

$$P(-5 \leq X \leq 5) = P\left(\frac{-5-5}{10} \leq Z \leq \frac{5-5}{10}\right) = P(-1.00 \leq Z \leq 0.00)$$

Algebraically, this is equivalent to

$$P(Z \leq 0.00) - P(Z \leq -1.00)$$

One of the properties of the standard normal distribution is that the probability that Z is less than or equal to 0 is 0.5 because the entire area under the standard normal curve equals 1 and because the distribution is symmetrical about the mean of 0. These statements imply the following:

$$P(Z \leq 0.00) = 0.5$$

$$P(Z \geq 0.00) = 0.5$$

Based on Table 14-3, the probability that Z is less than or equal to –1.00 = 0.1587. Therefore, $P(Z \leq 0.00) - P(Z \leq -1.00) = 0.5 - 0.1587 = 0.3413$.

You compute the probability that X is between +5 percent and +15 percent as follows:

$$P(5 \leq X \leq 15) = P\left(\frac{5-5}{10} \leq Z \leq \frac{15-5}{10}\right) = P(0.00 \leq Z \leq 1.00)$$

You can rewrite this as $P(Z \leq 1.00) - P(Z \leq 0.00)$.

You can find the probability that Z is less than or equal to 1.00 in the standard normal table. Take a look at Table 14-4 to see a section of this table for positive Z values.

Table 14-4	Selected Standard Normal Probabilities for Positive Z Values			
Z	*0.00*	*0.01*	*0.02*	*0.03*
1.0	0.8413	0.8438	0.8461	0.8485
1.5	0.9332	0.9345	0.9357	0.9370
2.0	0.9772	0.9778	0.9783	0.9788

You have already determined that the probability that Z is less than or equal to 0 equals 0.5. You can see the probability that Z is less than or equal to 1.00 by intersecting the row for *1.0* and the *0.00* column, which is 0.8413. Therefore, $P(Z \leq 1.00) - P(Z \leq 0.00) = 0.8413 - 0.5000 = 0.3413$.

You determine the probability that X is between +15 percent and +25 percent in a similar manner:

$$P(15 \leq X \leq 25) = P\left(\frac{15-5}{10} \leq Z \leq \frac{25-5}{10}\right) = P(1.00 \leq Z \leq 2.00) \text{ or}$$
$$P(Z \leq 2.00) - P(Z \leq 1.00) = 0.9772 - 0.8413 = 0.1359$$

Because the sample size equals 100, the expected frequency of each category equals the probability of each category times 100.

$P(-15\% \leq X \leq -5\%)$: $0.1359(100) = 13.59$

$P(-5\% \leq X \leq 5\%)$: $0.3413(100) = 34.13$

$P(5\% \leq X \leq 15\%)$: $0.3413(100) = 34.13$

$P(15\% \leq X \leq 25\%)$: $0.1359(100) = 13.59$

You can then combine the observed and expected returns into a single table, as Table 14-5 shows.

Table 14-5	Observed and Expected Frequencies			
Returns	*−15% to −5%*	*−5% to 5%*	*5% to 15%*	*15% to 25%*
Observed frequency	22	29	37	12
Expected frequency	13.59	34.13	34.13	13.59

Based on this table, the test statistic is computed as follows:

$$\chi^2 = \sum_{j=1}^{k} \frac{(O_j - E_j)^2}{E_j}$$
$$= \frac{(22-13.59)^2}{13.59} + \frac{(29-34.13)^2}{34.13} + \frac{(37-34.13)^2}{34.13} + \frac{(12-13.59)^2}{13.59}$$
$$= 6.40$$

The critical value is determined as follows:

$$\chi^2_{\alpha, k-1-m}$$

The first step is to identify the values of α, λ, and μ.

✔ $\alpha = 0.05$ because you're using a level of significance of 0.05 (5 percent).

✔ $\lambda = 4$ because there are four categories of returns: –15 percent to –5 percent, –5 percent to +5 percent, +5 percent to +15 percent, and +15 percent to +25 percent.

✔ $m = 0$, because the value of the mean (μ) and standard deviation (σ) are both specified in the null hypothesis.

Therefore, $\lambda - 1 - \mu = 3$.

You can find the critical value in Table 14-1 by finding the intersection of the 0.05 right-tail area column and the 3 df row:

$$\chi^2_{\alpha, k-1-m} = \chi_{0.05, 3} = 7.815$$

Because this is a right-tailed test, the test statistic must exceed the critical value to reject the null hypothesis that the population is normal with a mean of 5 percent and a standard deviation of 10 percent. Because the test statistic is 6.40 and the critical value is 7.815, you don't reject the null hypothesis. This indicates that the population is, in fact, normally distributed with a mean of 5 percent and a standard deviation of 10 percent.

Testing Hypotheses about the Equality of Two Population Variances

Hypothesis testing for the equality of two population variances is based on the F-distribution (covered in Chapter 13). One of the unique features of the F-distribution is that it's characterized by two types of degrees of freedom, known as *numerator* degrees of freedom and *denominator* degrees of freedom.

The degrees of freedom are called numerator and denominator because an F random variable is actually the ratio of two chi-square random variables, each of which has its own number of degrees of freedom. This is shown in the following equation:

$$F = \frac{\chi^2_1 / \upsilon_1}{\chi^2_2 / \upsilon_2}$$

In this expression,

χ_1^2, χ_2^2 = two chi-square random variables

υ_1, υ_2, = the degrees of freedom corresponding to χ_1^2 and χ_2^2

υ_1 = the *numerator* degrees of freedom of F

υ_2 = the *denominator* degrees of freedom of F

Just like the chi-square distribution, discussed earlier in this chapter, the F-distribution isn't defined for negative values and is skewed to the right.

The basic six-step process you use to test hypotheses about the equality of two population variances is the same as for testing hypotheses about a single population variance (which I explain in detail in the section "Testing Hypotheses about the Population Variance"). The main differences are the form of the null and alternative hypotheses and the calculation of the test statistic and critical values, which are based on the F-distribution instead of the chi-square distribution.

In the following sections, I walk you through testing hypotheses for two population variances.

The null hypothesis: Equal variances

The first step in the hypothesis testing procedure is writing the *null hypothesis,* which is a statement that's assumed to be true unless strong contrary evidence exists against it.

In this case, the null hypothesis is written as follows:

$$H_0 : \sigma_1^2 = \sigma_2^2$$

σ_1^2 is the variance of population 1, and σ_2^2 is the variance of population 2.

The null hypothesis is that the two population variances are equal. This is accepted unless strong evidence indicates otherwise.

The alternative hypothesis: Unequal variances

The alternative hypothesis is a statement of what you will accept to be true if the null hypothesis is rejected. The alternative hypothesis can take one of three forms:

✔ **Right-tailed test:** You use a right-tailed test if you're interested only in knowing whether the variance of population 1 is greater than the variance of population 2. In this case, the alternative hypothesis is

$$H_1 : \sigma_1^2 > \sigma_2^2$$

✔ **Left-tailed test:** You use a left-tailed test if you're interested only in knowing whether the variance of population 1 is less than the variance of population 2. In this case, the alternative hypothesis is

$$H_1 : \sigma_1^2 < \sigma_2^2$$

✔ **Two-tailed test:** You use a two-tailed test to determine whether the variances of population 1 and 2 are different. In this case, the alternative hypothesis is

$$H_1 : \sigma_1^2 \neq \sigma_2^2$$

The test statistic

For testing hypotheses about the equality of two population variances, the appropriate test statistic is

$$F = \frac{s_1^2}{s_2^2}$$

Here, F indicates that the test statistic follows the F-distribution, s_1^2 is the variance of the sample drawn from population 1, and s_2^2 is the variance of the sample drawn from population 2. Note that the test statistic requires that s_1^2 be greater than or equal to s_2^2.

The critical value (s)

To test a hypothesis, you have to choose a *level of significance.* The level of significance, designated with α, refers to the probability of rejecting the null hypothesis when it's actually true.

To test a hypothesis about the equality of two population variances, you use the following critical values.

Right-tailed test for the F-distribution

A right-tailed test has a single critical value:

$$F_\alpha^{\upsilon_1, \upsilon_2}$$

υ_1 is the numerator degrees of freedom of the F-distribution and equals $n_1 - 1$, where n_1 is the size of the sample drawn from population 1. υ_2 is the denominator degrees of freedom of the F-distribution and equals $n_2 - 1$, where n_2 is the size of the sample drawn from population 2.

This critical value represents the threshold of the right tail of the F-distribution with υ_{21} and υ_{22} degrees of freedom; the area in the right tail is

α. You can find this critical value in an F-table. Because each critical F-value requires two types of degrees of freedom, it's impossible to show both degrees of freedom and the level of significance together in the same table. Instead, you must dedicate an entire table to a single value of the level of significance. (You can see an excerpt of the F-table for a value of α equal to 0.05 in Table 14-6.)

For example, say you conduct a right-tail test with a level of significance of 0.05 (5 percent). You draw a sample size of 5 from the first population and a sample size of 4 from the second population.

You compute the numerator degrees of freedom by subtracting 1 from the size of the sample drawn from population 1:

$$v_1 = n_1 - 1 = 5 - 1 = 4$$

You find the denominator degrees of freedom by subtracting 1 from the size of the sample drawn from population 2:

$$v_2 = n_2 - 1 = 4 - 1 = 3$$

You can find the appropriate critical value in Table 14-6.

Table 14-6	A Section of the F-Table with $\alpha = 0.05$						
$v_2 \backslash v_1$	3	4	5	6	7	8	9
3	9.28	9.12	9.01	8.94	8.89	8.85	8.81
4	6.59	6.39	6.26	6.16	6.09	6.04	6.00
5	5.41	5.19	5.05	4.95	4.88	4.82	4.77
6	4.76	4.53	4.39	4.28	4.21	4.15	4.10
7	4.35	4.12	3.97	3.87	3.79	3.73	3.68
8	4.07	3.84	3.69	3.58	3.50	3.44	3.39
9	3.86	3.63	3.48	3.37	3.29	3.23	3.18

The top row represents the numerator degrees of freedom (v_1). The first column represents the denominator degrees of freedom (v_2). In this example, you're looking for a right-tail area of 5 percent with $v_1 = n_1 - 1 = 5 - 1$, which is 4 numerator degrees of freedom, and $v_2 = n_2 - 1 = 4 - 1$, which is 3 denominator degrees of freedom.

You find this critical value at the intersection of the *4* column and the row labeled *3* under the v_2/v_1 heading; it equals 9.12.

Left-tailed test for the F-distribution

A left-tailed test also has a single critical value, represented as

$$F_\alpha^{\upsilon_1, \upsilon_2}$$

This is a very unusual result. The critical value is the same for a right-tailed or a left-tailed test because the F-distribution is undefined for negative values. Also, the test statistic is set up with the larger sample variance in the numerator. The null hypothesis is rejected when the ratio of the sample variances is substantially greater than 1. The test statistic can't be negative.

Two-tailed test for the F-distribution

A two-tailed test has a *single* critical value:

$$F_{\alpha/2}^{\upsilon_1, \upsilon_2}$$

The decision about the equality of two population variances

You make the decision whether to reject the null hypothesis by looking at the relationship between the test statistic and the critical value(s). Here, I break down the results of the three alternative hypothesis tests:

- ✔ **Right-tailed test:** If the test statistic is greater than the critical value $F_\alpha^{\upsilon_1, \upsilon_2}$, you reject the null hypothesis $H_0 : \sigma_1^2 = \sigma_2^2$ in favor of the alternative hypothesis $H_1 : \sigma_1^2 > \sigma_2^2$; otherwise, you don't reject the null hypothesis.

- ✔ **Left-tailed test:** If the test statistic is greater than the critical value $F_\alpha^{\upsilon_1, \upsilon_2}$, you reject the null hypothesis $H_0 : \sigma_1^2 = \sigma_2^2$ in favor of the alternative hypothesis $H_1 : \sigma_1^2 < \sigma_2^2$; otherwise, you don't reject the null hypothesis.

- ✔ **Two-tailed test:** If the test statistic is greater than the critical value $F_{\alpha/2}^{\upsilon_1, \upsilon_2}$, you reject the null hypothesis $H_0 : \sigma_1^2 = \sigma_2^2$ in favor of the alternative hypothesis $H_1 : \sigma_1^2 \neq \sigma_2^2$; otherwise, you don't reject the null hypothesis.

As an example, suppose that an investor wants to determine whether two portfolios have the same volatility (that is, standard deviation.) She takes a sample of ten stocks from each portfolio. The sample standard deviation of portfolio 1 is 26 percent, and the sample standard deviation of portfolio 2 is 24 percent.

The null hypothesis is $H_0 : \sigma_1^2 = \sigma_2^2$, and the alternative hypothesis is $H_1 : \sigma_1^2 \neq \sigma_2^2$.

Assume that the level of significance is $\alpha = 0.05$ (5 percent).

The test statistic is

$$F = \frac{s_1^2}{s_2^2}$$

with s_1^2 greater than or equal to s_2^2.

Plugging in the numbers, you get the following result:

$$F = \frac{s_1^2}{s_2^2}$$
$$= \frac{(0.26)^2}{(0.24)^2}$$
$$= 1.174$$

Because this is a two-tailed test with a 5 percent level of significance, with both samples having size 10, the numerator and denominator degrees of freedom both equal 9. The critical value is $= F^{9,9}_{(0.025)}$ (that is, 4.03), as you find from the F-table with $\alpha = 0.025$ (see Table 14-7).

Table 14-7	A Section of the F Table with $\alpha = 0.025$.			
$\upsilon_2 \backslash \upsilon_1$	**7**	**8**	**9**	**10**
7	4.99	4.90	4.82	4.76
8	4.53	4.43	4.36	4.30
9	4.20	4.10	4.03	3.96
100	3.95	3.85	3.78	3.72

Because the test statistic is 1.174, which is well below the critical value of 4.03, you don't reject the null hypothesis. The investor concludes that the volatilities of the two portfolios are equal.

Part IV
More Advanced Techniques: Regression Analysis and Forecasting

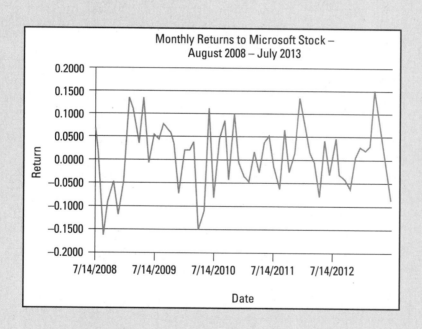

Monthly Returns to Microsoft Stock –
August 2008 – July 2013

Learn about more forecasting and regression analysis at www.dummies.com/
extras/businessstatistics.

In this part...

- ✔ Use the powerful technique of regression analysis to estimate the relationship between two variables, and take an in-depth look at multiple regression where a single dependent variable depends on two or more independent variables.

- ✔ Understand the effects of seasonal variation on sales of everything from gasoline prices to retail items. Use a scatterplot to see if a time series exhibits seasonal variation and, if so, what type.

- ✔ Predict the future values of economic variables, including stock prices, interest rates, and more.

Chapter 15

Simple Regression Analysis

· ·

· ·

*R*egression analysis is a statistical methodology that helps you estimate the strength and direction of the relationship between two or more variables. The two types of regression analysis are *simple regression analysis* (which I discuss in this chapter) and *multiple regression analysis* (which I cover in Chapter 16). Simple regression analysis allows you to estimate the relationship between a dependent variable (Y) and an independent variable (X). Multiple regression analysis allows you to estimate the relationship between a dependent variable (Y) and two or more independent variables (Xs).

For example, suppose a researcher is interested in analyzing the relationship between the annual returns to the Standard & Poor's 500 (S&P 500) and the annual returns to Apple stock.

The Standard and Poor's 500 (S&P 500) is a broad-based stock market index; it contains the 500 largest U.S. stocks, based on *market capitalization*. (The market capitalization of a stock equals the market price of the stock times the number of outstanding shares.) The returns to the S&P 500 are often used to represent the performance of the U.S. stock market.

The researcher assumes that the returns to Apple stock are at least partially explained by the returns to the S&P 500 because the S&P reflects overall activity in the economy. In other words, the researcher assumes that the return on Apple stock depends on the returns to the S&P 500.

To analyze this relationship with simple regression analysis, you treat the returns on Apple stock as a dependent variable (Y) and the returns to the S&P 500 as an independent variable (X). Regression analysis makes it possible to determine *how much* the returns on Apple stock are affected by the returns to the S&P 500. (In other words, how strong is the relationship between Apple stock and the S&P 500.)

This chapter introduces the basic regression analysis framework, including the underlying assumptions and the formulas you need to estimate the relationships between different variables. I also cover techniques for testing the validity of the results in great detail.

The Fundamental Assumption: Variables Have a Linear Relationship

Simple regression analysis is based on the assumption that a linear relationship exists between X and Y. Intuitively, if two variables have a linear relationship between them, a graph of the two variables is a straight line. (For a more formal discussion of linear relationships, see the following section "Defining a linear relationship.")

For example, suppose that an equity analyst at a prestigious investment bank wants to determine the relationship between a corporation's sales and profits to help him estimate the proper value of the corporation's stock. He has reason to believe that the relationship between sales and profits is linear. Further, he assumes that profits are the dependent variable in this relationship, while sales are the independent variable. Specifically, he believes that each $1,000 increase in sales triggers an increase in profits by $200, while each $1,000 decrease in sales has the opposite effect.

The analyst may use regression analysis to determine the actual relationship between these variables by looking at the corporation's sales and profits over the past several years. The regression results show whether this relationship is valid. In addition to sales, other factors may also determine the corporation's profits, or it may turn out that sales don't explain profits at all. The regression results also show the estimated amount that the profits change when sales change by $1,000.

In the following sections, I dig deeper into the linear relationship between the dependent and independent variables and show you how to represent this relationship graphically.

Defining a linear relationship

In terms of geometry, you can graph a linear relationship with a straight line. Algebraically, the general expression for a linear relationship is

$$Y = mX + b$$

X is the independent variable, Y is the dependent variable whose value is determined by the value of X, m is the slope coefficient (how much Y changes in response to a change in X), and b is the intercept (the value of Y if X equals 0).

You calculate the slope of a line (m) with this formula:

$$m = \frac{\Delta Y}{\Delta X}$$

Here, ΔY ("delta Y") represents the change in Y, and ΔX ("delta X") represents the change in X.

Think of the slope as a measure of how much Y changes due to a given change in X, or how *sensitive* the value of Y is to changes in X. A linear relationship is one in which the slope is a *constant*.

You see a linear relationship graphed as a straight line, with the dependent variable (Y) on the vertical axis and the independent variable (X) on the horizontal axis. See Figure 15-1 for the relationship between X and Y in the equation $Y = 2X + 3$.

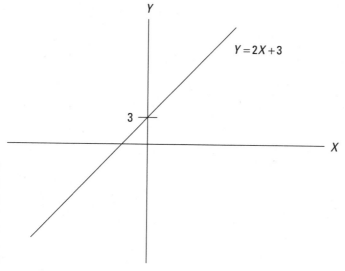

Figure 15-1:
Graph of a
linear
relationship:
$Y = 2X + 3$.

The equation of the line, $Y = 2X + 3$, tells you two important things:

- The *slope* of the line is 2 (this is the constant that's multiplied by X), which shows that

    - For each increase in X by 1, Y increases by 2.

    - For each decrease in X by 1, Y decreases by 2.

- The *intercept* of the line is 3, so if $X = 0$, the value of Y is 3. (In Figure 15-1, you see that 3 is the point where the line crosses the Y axis.)

Using scatter plots to identify linear relationships

A *scatter plot* is a special type of graph designed to show the relationship between two variables. (See Chapter 5 for an introduction to scatter plots.)

With regression analysis, you can use a scatter plot to visually inspect the data to see whether X and Y are linearly related. The following are some examples.

Figure 15-2 shows a scatter plot for two variables that have a *nonlinear* relationship between them.

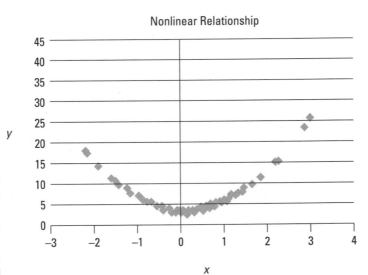

Figure 15-2:
Scatter plot of a nonlinear relationship.

Each point on the graph represents a single (*X*, *Y*) pair. Because the graph isn't a straight line, the relationship between *X* and *Y* is nonlinear. Notice that starting with negative values of X, as *X* increases, *Y* at first decreases; then as X continues to increase, *Y* increases. The graph clearly shows that the slope is continually changing; it isn't a constant. With a linear relationship, the slope never changes.

In this example, one of the fundamental assumptions of simple regression analysis is violated, and you need another approach to estimate the relationship between *X* and *Y*. One possibility is to transform the variables; for example, you could run a simple regression between ln(X) and ln(Y). ("ln" stands for the natural logarithm.) This often helps eliminate nonlinearities in the relationship between X and Y. Another possibility is to use a more advanced type of regression analysis, which can incorporate nonlinear relationships.

One regression technique that may be used with nonlinear data is known as *nonlinear least squares* (details may be found at `https://en.wikipedia.org/wiki/Non-linear_least_squares`).

Figure 15-3 shows a scatter plot for two variables that have a strongly positive linear relationship between them. The correlation between *X* and *Y* equals 0.9. (See Chapter 5 for an overview on correlation.)

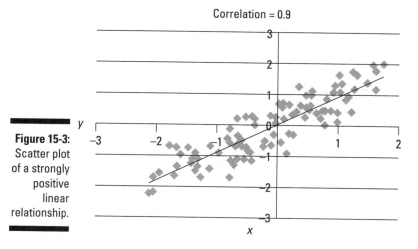

Figure 15-3: Scatter plot of a strongly positive linear relationship.

Figure 15-3 shows a very strong tendency for *X* and *Y* to both rise above their means or fall below their means at the same time. The straight line is a *trend line,* designed to come as close as possible to all the data points. The trend line has a positive slope, which shows a positive relationship between X and Y. The points in the graph are tightly clustered about the trend line due to the strength of the relationship between X and Y. (*Note:* The slope of the line is *not* 0.9; 0.9 is the correlation between X and Y.)

Figure 15-4 shows a scatter plot for two variables that have a weakly positive linear relationship between them; the correlation between X and Y equals 0.2

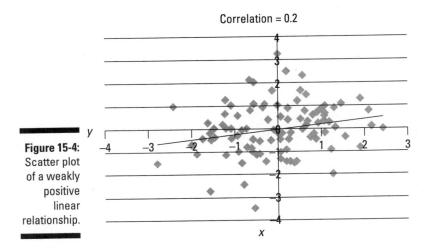

Figure 15-4: Scatter plot of a weakly positive linear relationship.

Figure 15-4 shows a weaker connection between X and Y. Note that the points on the graph are more scattered about the trend line than in Figure 15-3, due to the weaker relationship between X and Y.

Figure 15-5 is a scatter plot for two variables that have a strongly negative linear relationship between them; the correlation between X and Y equals -0.9.

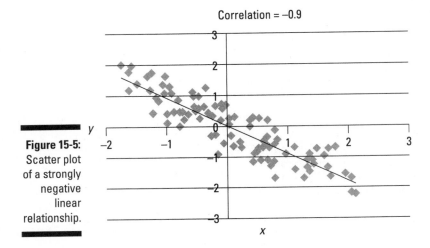

Figure 15-5: Scatter plot of a strongly negative linear relationship.

Figure 15-5 shows a very strong tendency for X and Y to move in opposite directions; for example, rise above or fall below their means at opposite times. The trend line has a negative slope, which shows a negative relationship between X and Y. The points in the graph are tightly clustered about the trend line due to the strength of the relationship between X and Y.

Figure 15-6 is a scatter plot for two variables that have a weakly negative linear relationship between them. The correlation between X and Y equals –0.2.

Correlation = –0.2

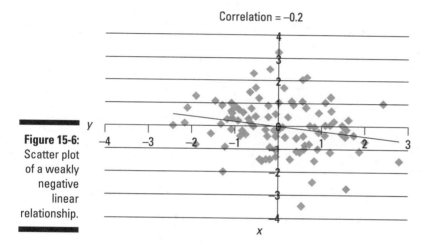

Figure 15-6:
Scatter plot
of a weakly
negative
linear
relationship.

Figure 15-6 shows a very weak connection between X and Y. Note that the points on the graph are more scattered about the trend line than in Figure 15-5 due to the weaker relationship between X and Y.

Defining the Population Regression Equation

With regression analysis, you typically draw a sample of data from a population to estimate the relationship between X and Y. The equation that best explains the population data is known as the *population regression equation,* or *population regression line:*

$$Y_i = \beta_0 + \beta_1 X_i + \varepsilon_i$$

The symbol β is the Greek letter "beta," and the symbol ε is "epsilon." β_0 and β_1 are known as *coefficients* of the regression line. β_1 is the slope coefficient and β_0 is the intercept coefficient (or simply the intercept). A coefficient is a constant that is multiplied by a variable.

Based on the assumption that the relationship between X and Y is linear, the regression line is designed to capture this relationship as closely as possible.

Other key terms in the equation are

- ✔ i = an index used to identify the members of the population.
- ✔ Y_i = a single value of Y, indexed by i, in a population of size n, with the values of Y expressed as $Y_1, Y_2, Y_3, \ldots, Y_n$.
- ✔ X_i = a single value of X, indexed by i, in a population of size n, with the values of X expressed as $X_1, X_2, X_3, \ldots, X_n$.
- ✔ ε_i = an "error term," indexed by i; each observation in the population (X_i, Y_i) has an error term associated with it.

Using the example of the equity analyst from the earlier section, "The Fundamental Assumption: Variables Have a Linear Relationship," suppose that the corporation has been in business for the past ten years (2003 to 2012). X_1 represents sales in 2003, and Y_1 represents profits in 2003. X_2 represents sales in 2004, and Y_2 represents profits in 2004. The analyst continues through 2012, where X_{10} is 2012 sales, and Y_{10} is 2012 profits. Each (X_i, Y_i) pair is a single observation chosen from the population.

The population regression equation has a slope and an intercept and one other term that you don't normally find in the equation for a straight line — the *error term*. The error term is included because the population regression equation doesn't perfectly capture the relationship between X and Y. For example, suppose that in the population regression line, β_0 = 10 and β_1 = 2. Assume that actual year 2003 sales were $100 million. The population regression line indicates that profits in 2003 should be

$$Y_1 = \beta_0 + \beta_1(X_1)$$
$$Y_1 = 10 + (2)(100)$$
$$= \$210 \text{ million}$$

Suppose that 2003 profits were actually $200 million. The population regression line *overstates* actual 2003 sales by $10 million. As a result, you compute the error term for 2003 (ε_1) as follows:

$$Y_1 = 10 + 2X_1 + \varepsilon_1$$
$$\varepsilon_1 = Y_1 - 10 - 2X_1$$
$$\varepsilon_1 = 200 - 10 - 2(100)$$
$$\varepsilon_1 = 200 - 10 - 200$$
$$\varepsilon_1 = -10$$

Estimating the Population Regression Equation

In most situations, estimating the population regression line with the entire population is impractical because collecting the amount of required data can be expensive and time-consuming. Instead, you draw a sample from the underlying population that reflects the underlying population as closely as possible). You use the sample data to construct a *sample regression equation,* or *sample regression line,* which you then use as an estimate of the actual population regression equation. (Sampling techniques and sampling distributions are discussed in Chapter 10.)

The sample regression equation is expressed as

$$\widehat{Y}_i = \widehat{\beta}_0 + \widehat{\beta}_1 X_i$$

Here, $\widehat{Y}_i$ is the estimated value of Y, associated with X_i, $\widehat{\beta}_0$ is the estimated value of β_0, and $\widehat{\beta}_1$ is the estimated value of β_1.

Note that there is no estimated error term in this equation because the estimated value of Y_i is actually the average value of a probability distribution; thus, there is no error term associated with it.

The symbol ^ often indicates an *estimated value.* The proper name for this punctuation mark is *caret.* Often, it's informally called a "hat." For example, you pronounce $\widehat{\beta}_0$ as "beta zero hat."

You determine these estimated values for $\widehat{\beta}_0$ and $\widehat{\beta}_1$ by minimizing the sum of the squared differences between the actually observed Y values contained in the sample data and those that have been *predicted* by the sample regression equation, as shown in the following equation:

$$\min \sum_{i=1}^{n} \left(Y_i - \widehat{Y}_i\right)^2$$

Note: In this formula, *min* stands for "minimize" and tells you to choose values of $\widehat{\beta}_0$ and $\widehat{\beta}_1$ so that the predicted values of Y are as close as possible to the actual values of Y. Think of each term

$$\left(Y_i - \widehat{Y}_i\right)$$

as a potential mistake or error by the regression line. If this term is *positive,* the regression line has *underestimated* the true value of Y_i. If this term is *negative*, the regression line has *underestimated* the true value of Y_i. If this term equals zero, the regression line has correctly estimated the true value of Y_i.

The objective of regression analysis is to find the equation that minimizes the sum of these errors.

Note that the value being minimized is actually the sum of the *squared* values of $(Y_i - \hat{Y}_i)$. This is because the sum of these terms always equals zero.

The difference between the actual value of Y_i and the predicted value of Y_i is known as a *residual* — an estimate of the corresponding error term in the population regression equation — and is expressed as follows:

$$\hat{\varepsilon}_i = Y_i - \hat{Y}_i$$

$\hat{\varepsilon}_i$ represents the residual associated with a single observation from the population (X_i, Y_i).

As an example, suppose the quality control manager for a manufacturing company is interested in seeing the relationship between annual costs of production and total output for a specific product. She estimates a regression equation based on production data for the years 2005 to 2012. In this case, X_i represents quantity produced during a given year, and Y_i represents total costs during the same year. X represents the quantity produced and Y represents the total costs because costs depend on output, not the other way around.

The manager assigns indexes to the years in the sample as follows: 2005 = Year 1, 2006 = Year 2, 2007 = Year 3, and so forth.

Based on the production data taken from the years 2005 to 2012, the estimated regression equation is

$$\hat{Y}_i = 3 - 1.5X_i$$

The diagram in Figure 15-7 shows the relationship between the actual value of Y, the predicted value of Y, the mean of Y, and the residual for Year 1 (2005).

The variables in this diagram are:

X_1 is total output during Year 1.

Y_1 is total cost during Year 1.

$\hat{Y}_1$ is the estimated total cost during Year 1.

$\overline{Y}$ is known as "Y bar" and is the average value of Y during the sample period.

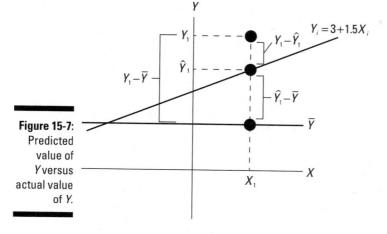

Figure 15-7:
Predicted
value of
Y versus
actual value
of Y.

Notice that the actual value of Y_1 is greater than the value estimated by the regression line. Both values are greater than the average or mean value of Y. (This information is used to construct a measure that explains how well the regression line matches the sample data in the later section "Computing the coefficient of determination.")

For each year's production data from 2005 to 2012,

- $Y_i - \hat{Y}_i$ is the difference between the actual and estimated total cost in Year i.
- $\hat{Y}_i - \overline{Y}$ is the difference between the estimated total cost in Year i and the average total cost during the sample period.
- $Y_i - \overline{Y}$ is the difference between the total cost in Year i and the average total cost during the sample period.

Note that $Y_i - \overline{Y} = \left(Y_i - \hat{Y}_i\right) + \left(\hat{Y}_i - \overline{Y}\right)$.

- $\left(Y_i - \hat{Y}_i\right)$ is the size of the incorrect prediction (error) by the regression equation. It equals the difference between the actual value of Y and the value predicted by the regression equation.
- $\left(\hat{Y}_i - \overline{Y}\right)$ shows the benefit of using this regression equation to predict the value of Y_i instead of using an alternative, such as simply assuming that each value of Y_i equals $\overline{Y}$.

You estimate the regression equation with formulas for $\hat{\beta}_0$ and $\hat{\beta}_1$ that minimize the sum of the squared residuals:

$$\min \hat{\varepsilon}\,_i^2 = \sum_{i=1}^{n}\left(Y_i - \hat{Y}_i\right)^2$$

The resulting equations for the slope of the estimated regression equation is

$$\hat{\beta}_1 = \frac{\sum_{i=1}^{n}(X_i - \overline{X})(Y_i - \overline{Y})}{\sum_{i=1}^{n}(X_i - \overline{X})^2}$$

And the equation for the intercept is

$$\hat{\beta}_0 = \overline{Y} - \hat{\beta}_1 \overline{X}$$

These formulas are known as *ordinary least squares* (OLS) estimators. OLS is a methodology for estimating regression coefficients. Some of the more advanced versions include generalized least squares (GLS) and weighted least squares (WLS).

$\overline{X}$ is the mean or average value of X; $\overline{Y}$ is the mean or average value of Y.

As an example, suppose that X represents the monthly number of hours of studying by college students, and Y represents their corresponding grade point averages (GPAs). To conduct this study, you choose a sample of eight students and list their study hours and GPAs like so:

Y (GPA)	X (Monthly Hours of Studying)
3.5	16
3.2	14
3.0	12
2.6	11
2.9	12
3.3	15
2.7	13
2.8	11

Then you can create a scatter plot like Figure 15-8 to represent the data.

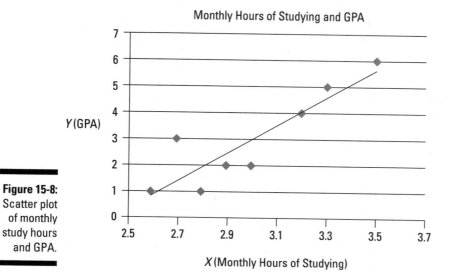

Figure 15-8:
Scatter plot
of monthly
study hours
and GPA.

Figure 15-8 shows that the relationship between these two variables is approximately linear. As a result, you can estimate the relationship between these two variables with simple regression analysis.

You compute the coefficients of the sample regression equation by following these steps:

1. Find the sample mean of X and Y:

$$
\begin{aligned}
\overline{X} &= \frac{\sum_{i=1}^{n} X_i}{n} \\
&= \frac{X_1 + X_2 + X_3 + X_4 + X_5 + X_6 + X_7 + X_8}{n} \\
&= \frac{16 + 14 + 12 + 11 + 12 + 15 + 13 + 11}{8} \\
&= 13.0
\end{aligned}
$$

In this case, you add up the monthly hours of studying for the eight students in the sample and then divide by 8. This gives a sample mean of 13.0 hours for these students.

$$\bar{Y} = \frac{\sum_{i=1}^{n} Y_i}{n}$$

$$= \frac{Y_1 + Y_2 + Y_3 + Y_4 + Y_5 + Y_6 + Y_7 + Y_8}{n}$$

$$= \frac{3.5 + 3.2 + 3.0 + 2.6 + 2.9 + 3.3 + 2.7 + 2.8}{8}$$

$$= 3.0$$

In this case, you add up the GPAs for the eight students in the sample and then divide by 8. This gives a sample mean of 3.0 for these students.

The results of the remaining steps are summarized in Table 15-1.

Table 15-1   Computing the Regression Slope and Intercept

Y (GPA)	X (Monthly Hours of Studying)	$(X_i - \bar{X})$	$(X_i - \bar{X})^2$	$(Y_i - \bar{Y})$	$(X_i - \bar{X})(Y_i - \bar{Y})$
3.5	16	3	9	0.5	1.5
3.2	14	1	1	0.2	0.2
3.0	12	−1	1	0.0	0.0
2.6	11	−2	4	−0.4	0.8
2.9	12	−1	1	−0.1	0.1
3.3	15	2	4	0.3	0.6
2.7	13	0	0	−0.3	0.0
2.8	11	−2	4	−0.2	0.4
Sum			24		3.6

2. To compute $(X_i - \bar{X})$, you subtract the mean of X from each value of X.
3. To find the value of $(X_i - \bar{X})^2$, you square the value of $(X_i - \bar{X})$ for each result you found in the previous step.
4. You calculate $(Y_i - \bar{Y})$ by subtracting the mean of Y from each value of Y.
5. You compute $(X_i - \bar{X})(Y_i - \bar{Y})$ multiplying the results in Steps 2 and 4.
   The sum in the $(X_i - \bar{X})^2$ column shows that $\sum_{i=1}^{n}(X_i - \bar{X})^2 = 24$. The sum in the $(X_i - \bar{X})(Y_i - \bar{Y})$ column shows that $\sum_{i=1}^{n}(X_i - \bar{X})(Y_i - \bar{Y}) = 3.6$.

6. Based on these results, you compute the values of the regression coefficients as follows:

$$\hat{\beta}_1 = \frac{\sum_{i=1}^{n}(X_i - \bar{X})(Y_i - \bar{Y})}{\sum_{i=1}^{n}(X_i - \bar{X})^2} = \frac{3.6}{24} = 0.15$$

$$\hat{\beta}_0 = \bar{Y} - \hat{\beta}_1\bar{X} = 3 - (0.15)(13) = 1.05$$

7. You write the estimated (sample) regression equation as

$$\hat{Y}_i = 1.05 + 0.15X_i$$

The slope of this equation shows that for students who study between 11 and 16 hours per month, each additional monthly hour of studying adds 0.15 points to a student's GPA. The intercept may be interpreted to mean that a student who doesn't study at all will have a GPA of 1.05.

You can use the sample regression equation to estimate the GPA that results from a specified number of hours of studying. For example, if a student studies for 15 hours a month, the sample regression equation predicts a GPA of $\hat{Y}_i = 1.05 + 0.15X_i = 1.05 + (0.15)(15) = 3.30$.

When using a regression line to predict the value of Y for a given value of X, don't use any values of X that aren't contained in the sample data. In this example, the regression line is based on values of X between 11 and 16; the results of using a value of X outside of this range is subject to a great deal of uncertainty.

Testing the Estimated Regression Equation

After you estimate the regression line (see the earlier section "Estimating the Population Regression Equation"), you can do several tests to check the validity of the results. It may be the case that there is no real relationship between the dependent and independent variables; simple regression generates results even if this is the case. It is, therefore, important to subject the regression results to some key tests that enable you to determine if the results are reliable.

In the following sections, I introduce a statistic that is designed to check whether a regression equation makes sense. This is known as the *coefficient of determination*, also known as R^2 (R squared). This is used as a measure of how well the regression equation actually describes the relationship between the dependent variable (Y) and the independent variable (X).

The next technique that may be used to check regression results is a hypothesis test of the coefficients of the regression equation. The steps used to carry out this hypothesis test are similar to those found in Chapter 12, where hypothesis testing is introduced for the first time. This hypothesis test is sometimes known as the "t-test" because the test statistic and critical values are derived from the Student's t-distribution (discussed in Chapter 11). In this case, if the null hypothesis fails to be rejected, this calls into question the validity of the regression results.

Using the coefficient of determination (R^2)

The coefficient of determination, also known as R^2, is a statistical measure that shows the proportion of *variation* explained by the estimated regression line. *Variation* refers to the sum of the squared differences between the values of Y and the mean value of Y, expressed mathematically as

$$\sum_{i=1}^{n}\left(Y_i - \bar{Y}\right)^2$$

R^2 always takes on a value between 0 and 1. The closer R^2 is to 1, the better the estimated regression equation fits or explains the relationship between X and Y.

The expression $\sum_{i=1}^{n}\left(Y_i - \bar{Y}\right)^2$ is also known as the *total sum of squares* (TSS).

This sum can be divided into the following two categories:

- **Explained sum of squares (ESS):** Also known as the *explained variation,* the ESS is the portion of total variation that measures how well the regression equation explains the relationship between X and Y.

  You compute the ESS with the formula

  $$ESS = \sum_{i=1}^{n}\left(\hat{Y}_i - \bar{Y}\right)^2$$

- **Residual sum of squares (RSS):** This expression is also known as *unexplained variation* and is the portion of total variation that measures discrepancies (errors) between the actual values of Y and those estimated by the regression equation.

You compute the RSS with the formula

$$RSS = \sum_{i=1}^{n} \left(Y_i - \hat{Y}_i\right)^2$$

The smaller the value of RSS relative to ESS, the better the regression line fits or explains the relationship between the dependent and independent variable.

✔ **Total sum of squares (TSS):**

The sum of RSS and ESS equals TSS.

$$\sum_{i=1}^{n} \left(Y_i - \hat{Y}_i\right)^2 + \sum_{i=1}^{n} \left(\hat{Y}_i - \bar{Y}\right)^2 = \sum_{i=1}^{n} \left(Y_i - \bar{Y}\right)^2$$

R^2 (the coefficient of determination) is the ratio of explained sum of squares (ESS) to total sum of squares (TSS):

$$R^2 = \frac{ESS}{TSS}$$

You can also use this formula:

$$R^2 = 1 - \frac{RSS}{TSS}$$

Based on the definition of R^2, its value can never be negative. Also, R^2 can't be greater than 1, so $0 \le R^2 \le 1$.

With simple regression analysis, R^2 equals the square of the correlation between X and Y.

Computing the coefficient of determination

The coefficient of determination is used as a measure of how well a regression line explains the relationship between a dependent variable (Y) and an independent variable (X). The closer the coefficient of determination is to 1, the more closely the regression line fits the sample data.

The coefficient of determination is computed from the sums of squares determined in the earlier section "Using the coefficient of determination (R^2)." These calculations are summarized in Table 15-2.

Table 15-2   Computing the Coefficient of Determination (R^2)

Yi	Xi				
3.5	16	3.45	0.0025	0.2025	0.25
3.2	14	3.15	0.0025	0.0225	0.04
3.0	12	2.85	0.0225	0.0225	0.00
2.6	11	2.70	0.0100	0.0900	0.16
2.9	12	2.85	0.0025	0.0225	0.01
3.3	15	3.30	0.0000	0.0900	0.09
2.7	13	3.00	0.0900	0.0000	0.09
2.8	11	2.70	0.0100	0.0900	0.04
Sum			**0.1400**	**0.5400**	**0.68**

To compute ESS, you subtract the mean value of Y from each of the estimated values of Y; each term is squared and then added together:

$$ESS = \sum_{i=1}^{n}\left(\hat{Y}_i - \bar{Y}\right)^2 = 0.54$$

To compute RSS, you subtract the estimated value of Y from each of the actual values of Y; each term is squared and then added together:

$$RSS = \sum_{i=1}^{n}\left(Y_i - \hat{Y}_i\right)^2 = 0.14$$

To compute TSS, you subtract the mean value of Y from each of the actual values of Y; each term is squared and then added together:

$$TSS = \sum_{i=1}^{n}\left(Y_i - \bar{Y}\right)^2 = 0.68$$

Alternatively, you can simply add ESS and RSS to obtain TSS:

$$TSS = ESS + RSS = 0.54 + 0.14 = 0.68$$

The coefficient of determination (R^2) is the ratio of ESS to TSS:

$$R^2 = \frac{ESS}{TSS} = \frac{0.54}{0.68} = 0.7941$$

This shows that 79.41 percent of the variation in Y is explained by variation in X. Because the coefficient of determination can't exceed 100 percent, a value of 79.41 indicates that the regression line closely matches the actual sample data.

The t-test

Another important test of the results of regression analysis is to determine whether the slope coefficient (β_1) is different from 0. If the slope coefficient is close to 0, X provides little or no explanatory power for the value of Y. In such a case, you should replace X with another independent variable in the regression equation.

To determine whether β_1 is different from 0, you need to conduct a *hypothesis test*. (You find more about hypothesis testing in Chapter 12.) The name of the hypothesis test used in this case is the *t-test*, because the test statistic and critical values are based on the Student's t-distribution (covered in Chapter 11). You use this test to determine whether the slope coefficient (β_1) of the estimated regression equation is significantly different from 0. If $\beta_1 = 0$, X doesn't explain the value of Y, and the regression results are then meaningless.

The t-test is conducted in several stages. These are detailed in the following sections.

Null and alternative hypotheses

The first is to specify the null hypothesis and the alternative hypothesis. A null hypothesis is a statement that is assumed to be true unless you find very strong evidence against it. An alternative hypothesis is a statement that is accepted instead of the null hypothesis if you reject the null hypothesis.

With the t-test, the null hypothesis is that the slope coefficient (β_1) equals 0: $H_0 : \beta_1 = 0$.

This hypothesis implies that the independent variable (X) doesn't explain the value of the dependent variable (Y). The t-test is a very conservative test; the burden of proof is to show that X *does* explain Y.

The alternative hypothesis is that the slope coefficient doesn't equal 0: $H_1 : \beta_1 \neq 0$.

As discussed in Chapter 12, this type of alternative hypothesis is known as a *two-tailed* test.

Level of significance

The level of significance of a hypothesis test is a measure of the likelihood of a specific type of error, known as a *Type I error*. This occurs when the null hypothesis is incorrectly rejected when it is actually true. A Type II error results when the null hypothesis is *not* rejected even though it is false. With a small level of significance, there is a very low chance of committing a Type I error, but a relatively large probability of committing a Type II error. As the level of significance is increased, the probability of a Type I error increases but the probability of a Type II error decreases.

The choice of level of significance is based on the importance of avoiding Type I errors. When you test hypotheses about regression coefficients, the level of significance (α) is often 0.05 (5 percent).

Test statistic

A test statistic is a numerical value that is used to determine if the null hypothesis should be rejected. If the test statistic has a large value (positive or negative), the likelihood that the null hypothesis is rejected is also large.

For testing hypotheses about β_1 the appropriate test statistic is

$$t = \frac{\hat{\beta}_1}{s_{\hat{\beta}_1}}$$

This expression is known as a *t-statistic* because it follows the Student's t-distribution (covered in Chapter 11).

The term $s_{\hat{\beta}_1}$ is the *standard error* of $\hat{\beta}_1$ which you can think of as the standard deviation of $\hat{\beta}_1$. (Standard errors are covered in Chapter 10.)

In other words, $s_{\hat{\beta}_1}$ is the amount of *uncertainty* associated with the use of $\hat{\beta}_1$ to estimate β_1. The larger the standard error of $\hat{\beta}_1$, the less likely you are to reject the null hypothesis that $\beta_1 = 0$.

You compute the test statistic for this hypothesis test as follows:

Also known as *standard error of the regression (SER)*, the SEE is a measure of the dispersion of the sample values above and below the estimated regression line.

$$SEE = \sqrt{\frac{RSS}{n-2}} = \sqrt{\frac{\sum_{i=1}^{n}\left(Y_i - \hat{Y}_i\right)^2}{n-2}}$$

Based on Table 15-2, SEE is computed as follows:

RSS is computed as:

$$\sum_{i=1}^{n}\left(Y_i - \hat{Y}_i\right)^2 = 0.14$$

With a sample size of 8, SEE equals:

$$SEE = \sqrt{\frac{\sum_{i=1}^{n}\left(Y_i - \hat{Y}_i\right)^2}{n-2}}$$

$$= \sqrt{\frac{0.14}{6}}$$

$$= 0.15275$$

1. Calculate the standard error of $\hat{\beta}_1$:

$$S_{\hat{\beta}_1} = \frac{SEE}{\sqrt{\sum_{i=1}^{n}X_i^2 - n\bar{X}^2}}$$

SEE equals 0.15275. $\sum_{i=1}^{n}X_i^2$ represents the sum of the squared values of X. $n\bar{X}^2$ represents the sample size times the square of the sample mean.

You can get the values of $\sum_{i=1}^{n}X_i^2$ and $n\bar{X}^2$ from Table 15-3.

Table 15-3	The Standard Error of $\hat{\beta}_1$
X_i	X_i^2
16	256
14	196
12	144
11	121
12	144
15	225
13	169
11	121

The sample mean is obtained by adding up the values in the X_i column, then dividing the sum by the sample size of 8:

$$\bar{X} = \frac{\sum_{i=1}^{n}X_i}{n} = \frac{16+14+12+11+12+15+13+11}{8} = 13$$

The sum of the squared values of X is obtained by squaring each value of X and then summing the results:

$$\sum_{i=1}^{n} X_i^2 = 256 + 196 + 144 + 121 + 144 + 225 + 169 + 121 = 1,376$$

The formula for computing the standard error of $\hat{\beta}_1$ is:

$$S_{\hat{\beta}_1} = \frac{SEE}{\sqrt{\sum_{i=1}^{n} X_i^2 - n\bar{X}^2}} = \frac{0.15275}{\sqrt{1,376 - (8)(13^2)}} = 0.03118$$

2. **Calculate the test statistic:**

$\hat{\beta}_1 = 0.15$ (see the earlier section "Estimating the Population Regression Equation"); therefore, combining this with the standard error of $\hat{\beta}_1$, the t-statistic for $\hat{\beta}_1$ is computed as

$$t = \frac{\hat{\beta}_1}{s_{\hat{\beta}_1}} = \frac{0.15}{0.03118} = 4.81$$

Critical values

A critical value shows the number of standard deviations away from the mean of a distribution where:

- ✔ a specified percentage of the distribution is above the critical value
- ✔ the remainder of the distribution is below the critical value

To test a hypothesis, the test statistic is compared with one or two critical values. If the test statistic is more *extreme* than the relevant critical value, the null hypothesis is rejected. Otherwise, the null hypothesis fails to be rejected. (It's technically incorrect to say that a null hypothesis is accepted, because you don't know every value in the population being tested.)

With simple regression analysis, the critical values are taken from the Student's t-table with $n - 2$ degrees of freedom. (These are found in Table 15-4.)

Degrees of freedom refers to the number of *independent* values in a sample. When it's necessary to estimate two measures from a sample (in this case, $\hat{\beta}_0$ and $\hat{\beta}_1$) the number of degrees of freedom equals the sample size minus 2.

The Student's t-distribution is a continuous distribution that has a mean of zero and a larger variance and standard deviation than the standard normal distribution (covered in Chapter 9). The distribution is sometimes described as having "fat tails" because it's more spread out.

The purpose of the t-distribution is to describe the statistical properties of sample means that are estimated from *small* samples; the standard normal distribution is used for *large* samples. (There's much more about the Student's t-distribution Chapter 11.)

In this case, say you choose the level of significance (α) to be 0.05. (This is a widely used value for testing hypotheses about regression coefficients.) Because the sample size (n) is 8, the appropriate critical values are

$$\pm t_{\alpha/2}^{n-2} = \pm t_{0.025}^{6}$$

You find these values in the Student's t-table, such as Table 15-4.

Table 15-4	The Student's t-Distribution				
Degrees of Freedom	**t0.10**	**t0.05**	**t0.025**	**t0.01**	**t0.005**
5	1.476	2.015	2.571	3.365	4.032
6	1.440	1.943	2.447	3.143	3.707
7	1.415	1.895	2.365	2.998	3.499
8	1.397	1.860	2.306	2.896	3.355
9	1.383	1.833	2.262	2.821	3.250
10	1.372	1.812	2.228	2.764	3.169

You find the value of the positive critical value $t_{0.025}^{6}$ at the intersection of the row for 6 degrees of freedom and the column labeled $t_{0.025}$, which is 2.447. The value of the negative critical value $-t_{0.025}^{6}$ is then –2.447.

Decision rule

A decision rule is used to determine if the null hypothesis should be rejected. Because the alternative hypothesis is $H_1 : \beta_1 \neq 0$, there are two critical values: one positive, one negative. (These are shown to be -2.447 and 2.447 in the previous section.)

If the test statistic is either greater than 2.447 or less than -2.447, the null hypothesis will be *rejected*. This indicates that there is strong evidence that the slope coefficient β_1 is not equal to zero; in other words, the regression equation *does* explain the relationship between the dependent variable (GPA) and the independent variable (monthly hours of studying).

If the test statistic falls between these two values, the null hypothesis *fails* to be rejected. In this case, there is insufficient evidence to reject the hypothesis that β_1 equals zero. This shows that the regression equation does *not* explain the relationship between the dependent variable (GPA) and the independent variable (monthly hours of studying).

In this case, the test statistic is 4.81, which is greater than 2.447. Therefore, you reject the null hypothesis in favor of the alternative hypothesis, indicating that $\hat{\beta}_1$ is different from 0 (that is, it's *statistically significant*). Therefore, strong evidence shows that X (monthly hours of studying) does explain the value of Y (GPA.)

This result does not imply that hours of studying is the *only* factor that explains GPA, but it is an important determinant of GPA.

You can also test whether the estimated intercept $(\hat{\beta}_0)$ is statistically significant, but often doing so isn't necessary. The slope coefficient is the most important value in the regression equation.

Using Statistical Software

Many spreadsheet programs (such as Excel) and specialized statistical packages (such as SPSS) allow you to generate the results you need for regression analysis. For example, you can use a spreadsheet program to get the results shown in Figure 15-9 for the GPA example from the "Estimating the Population Regression Equation" section earlier in this chapter (these results were generated using Excel).

As you can see, Figure 15-9 shows the values of $\hat{\beta}_0$ and $\hat{\beta}_1$ under the *Coefficients* column; the values of the coefficient of determination (R^2) and the standard error of the estimate, under the *Regression Statistics* column; and the standard errors of $\hat{\beta}_0$ and $\hat{\beta}_1$ and the t-statistics, under the columns *Standard Error* and *t-Stat*.

Figure 15-9 provides one additional useful measure you can use to test hypotheses about the coefficients, called *p-values* (or *probability values*). The p-value represents the likelihood of finding the given t-statistic if the null hypothesis is true. An extremely low p-value indicates that the null hypothesis of a 0 coefficient should be rejected. More formally, when testing the hypothesis $H_0 : \beta_1 = 0$, if the p-value is less than the level of significance (α), the null hypothesis is rejected; otherwise, it isn't rejected.

In this example, the p-value for $\hat{\beta}_1$ is 0.002968105; the level of significance is 0.05; therefore, because the p-value is less than the level of significance, the null hypothesis is rejected, confirming the results found when testing the hypothesis with the t-statistic.

SUMMARY OUTPUT

Regression Statistics	
Multiple R	0.891132789
R Square	0.794117647
Adjusted R Square	0.759803922
Standard Error	0.152752523
Observations	8

ANOVA

	df	SS	MS	F
Regression	1	0.54	0.54	23.14285714
Residual	6	0.14	0.023333333	
Total	7	0.68		

Figure 15-9:
GPA
regression
problem.

	Coefficients	Standard Error	t Stat	P-value
Intercept	1.05	0.408928138	2.56768831	0.042466896
X (Monthly Hours)	0.15	0.031180478	4.810702354	0.002968105

TIP

Using the t-statistic or the p-value to test the significance of a regression coefficient will always provide the same results.

Assumptions of Simple Linear Regression

The simple regression model shown in this chapter is based on several extremely important assumptions. If any of these assumptions are violated, the reliability of the regression results is questionable.

The most important assumptions include the following:

✔ The expected value of each error term is 0; that is, $E(\varepsilon_i) = 0$. So although some error terms are positive and some are negative, they add up to 0.

✔ The variances of the error terms are finite and constant for all values of x_i; this common variance is designated σ^2.

✔ The error terms are independent of each other (for example, they don't influence each other).

✔ Each error term, ε_i, is independent of the corresponding value of X_i (the value of Xi doesn't influence the value of the error term and vice versa).

✔ The error terms are *normally distributed*. Although this assumption isn't required for linear regression, it's often used and allows you to compute confidence intervals for the regression coefficients. It also allows you to test hypotheses about the coefficients.

With simple regression analysis, two of the most important violations of the assumptions include autocorrelation and heteroscedasticity:

✔ **Autocorrelation** occurs when the error terms are correlated with each other (they are related to each other). It violates the assumption of independence. Two independent variables have a correlation of 0 between them.

Autocorrelated error terms can cause the standard errors of the regression coefficients to be understated, thus increasing the risk that coefficients will be incorrectly found to be statistically significant (for example, different from zero).

✔ **Heteroscedasticity** occurs when the error terms don't have a constant variance. This problem can cause the standard errors of the regression coefficients to be understated, increasing the risk that coefficients will be incorrectly found to be statistically significant (for example, different from zero).

Formal statistical tests are available to help you determine whether these problems are present. For example, the Durbin-Watson test is used to find evidence of autocorrelation in sample data. (More details can be found at `http://en.wikipedia.org/wiki/Durbin%E2%80%93Watson_statistic`.) The White test is used to find evidence of heteroscedasticity in sample data. (More details can be found at `http://en.wikipedia.org/wiki/White_test`.)

If autocorrelation is present, you may use the Cochrane-Orcutt procedure, which adjusts the regression model for autocorrelation. (More details can be found at `https://en.wikipedia.org/wiki/Cochrane-Orcutt_procedure`.)

In the case of heteroscedasticity, you may transform the variables into natural logarithms and rerun the regression equation; for example, the dependent variable could be ln(Y) and the independent variable could be ln(X). ("ln" is standard for natural logarithm.) More formal procedures are also available to correct for heteroscedasticity, such as heteroscedasticity-consistent standard errors. (More information about this procedure is found at `http://en.wikipedia.org/wiki/Heteroscedasticity-consistent_standard_errors`.)

Chapter 16

Multiple Regression Analysis: Two or More Independent Variables

In This Chapter

▶ Getting familiar with the assumptions underlying multiple regression analysis

▶ Implementing the multiple regression model

▶ Watching for multicollinearity

*Y*ou use regression analysis to estimate the strength and direction of the relationship between two or more variables. As I explain in Chapter 15, simple regression analysis allows you to estimate the relationship between a dependent variable (Y) and an independent variable (X).

In this chapter, I explore the possibilities of multiple regression analysis, which you use to estimate the relationship between a dependent variable (Y) and two or more independent variables ($X_1, X_2, \ldots$).

The additional independent variable(s) introduces more complications into multiple regression analysis. In particular, it takes more statistical testing to validate the results of a multiple regression model. Further, additional errors may arise in multiple regression analysis that can't take place with simple regression analysis.

This chapter explains how to implement multiple regression analysis, how to test the results, and what potential pitfalls may arise.

The Fundamental Assumption: Variables Have a Linear Relationship

Just as with simple regression analysis (discussed in Chapter 15), multiple regression analysis is based on the assumption that the dependent variable and the independent variables have a *linear relationship* between them.

If two variables are linearly related, a graph of their relationship is a straight line. The equation of a straight line is:

$$Y = mX + b$$

✔ X is the independent variable

✔ Y is the dependent variable

✔ m is the slope coefficient

✔ b is the intercept

In this equation, the value of Y depends on the value of X (not the other way around). The slope tells you *how much* Y changes when X changes; the intercept tells you the value of Y when X equals 0.

For example, suppose that the equation of a straight line is:

Y = 4X – 7

The slope of 4 shows that:

✔ if X increases by 1, Y increases by 4

✔ if X decreases by 1, Y decreases by 4

The intercept of –7 shows that Y equals –7 when X equals 0.

In addition to having a linear relationship between the dependent variable and each independent variable, there must be a joint linear relationship between the dependent variable and *all* the dependent variables.

If variables don't have a linear relationship, you can still use regression analysis; however, you may have to make adjustments to the regression equation. For example, it may be that the relationship between Y and X is *nonlinear* but that the relationship between $\ln(Y)$ — the *natural logarithm* with base $e = 2.71828$ — and X_1 and X_2 is linear. In this case, you can run a regression using $\ln(Y)$ as the dependent variable and X_1 and X_2 as the independent variables. Another possibility is that the relationship between $\ln(Y)$, $\ln(X_1)$, and $\ln(X_2)$ is linear. In this case, you use $\ln(Y)$ as the dependent variable, and $\ln(X_1)$ and $\ln(X_2)$ as the independent variables. (Logarithmic transformations for regression analysis are discussed in Chapter 15.)

Estimating a Multiple Regression Equation

With multiple regression analysis, the population regression equation may contain any number of independent variables, such as

$$Y_i = \beta_0 + \beta_1 X_{1i} + \beta_2 X_{2i} + \ldots + \beta_k X_{ki} + \varepsilon_i$$

In this case, there are k independent variables, indexed from 1 to k.

For example, suppose that the Human Resources department of a major corporation wants to determine whether the salaries of its employees are related to the employees' years of work experience and their level of graduate education. To test this idea, the HR department picks a sample of eight employees randomly and records their annual salaries (measured in thousands of dollars per year), years of experience, and years of graduate education.

The following variables are defined:

✔ Y represents an employee's annual salary, measured in thousands of dollars.

✔ X_1 represents an employee's number of years of job experience. A value of 0 represents someone who has no job experience (such as a recent college graduate).

✔ X_2 represents the number of years of graduate education. A value of 0 represents a college graduate with no graduate education.

The following lists the sample data.

Y (Annual Salary, in Thousands)	X₁ (Years of Experience)	X₂ (Years of Graduate Education)
80	1	0
90	2	1
100	3	2
120	4	2
85	1	0
95	2	1
105	2	2
140	8	3

The HR department runs a regression using a spreadsheet program, such as Excel. Figure 16-1 shows the results.

SUMMARY OUTPUT

Regression Statistics	
Multiple R	0.971774936
R Square	0.944346527
Adjusted R Square	0.922085137
Standard Error	5.52943278
Observations	8

ANOVA

	df	SS	MS	F-stat	Significance F
Regression	2	2594.001866	1297.000933	42.42082621	0.000730686
Residual	5	152.8731343	30.57462687		
Total	7	2746.875			

	Coefficients	Standard Error	P-value	Lower 95%	Upper 95%
Intercept	76.47014925	3.397844048	22.50549118	3.21898E-06	85.20458544
X₁ (Years of experience)	5.320895522	1.695561146	3.13813249	0.025720437	9.679474206
X₂ (Years of graduate education)	7.350746269	3.669054725	2.003444162	0.101492144	16.7823517

Figure 16-1: Spreadsheet showing salary regression results.

Taking the intercept and slope coefficients (X_1 and X_2) from the *Coefficients* column in Figure 16-1, you can fill in the estimated regression equation as

$$\hat{Y}_i = 76.47 + 5.32X_{1i} + 7.35X_{2i}$$

(The values are rounded to two decimal places.)

This equation shows that the following is true for this firm:

- ✔ The starting salary for a new employee with no experience or graduate education is $76,470. This amount is based on the intercept of the regression equation.

- ✔ Each additional year of experience adds $5,320 to an employee's salary; this amount is based on the coefficient of X_1 (years of experience).

- ✔ Each additional year of graduate education adds $7,350 to an employee's salary, which is based on the coefficient of X_2 (years of graduate education).

In each case, you multiply the coefficients by $1,000 to get the impact on salary because these variables are measured in thousands of dollars per year.

The intercept of the equation, 76.47, shows the value of Y (the employee's annual salary) when *both* X_1 (years of experience) and X_2 (years of graduate education) equal 0 (that is, a new employee with no experience or graduate education). The intercept shows that the starting salary is $76.47 \times \$1,000 = \$76,470$.

The coefficient of X_1, 5.32, shows how much Y changes due to a one-unit change in X_1. Because X_1 represents years of experience, a one-unit change in X_1 is one additional year of experience. Therefore, each additional year of experience adds $5.32 \times \$1,000 = \$5,320$ to an employee's salary.

The coefficient of X_2, 7.35, shows how much Y changes due to a one-unit change in X_2. Because X_2 represents years of graduate education, a one-unit change in X_2 is one additional year of graduate school. Therefore, each additional year of graduate school adds $7.35 \times \$1,000 = \$7,350$ to an employee's salary.

The following sections show how you can use the results from the spreadsheet to predict the salary of an employee with a specified number of years of experience and education. A new measure is introduced to determine how well the regression equation "fits" or explains the sample data; this is known as the *adjusted coefficient of determination*.

Two types of hypothesis tests are covered. A hypothesis is tested for all the slope coefficients of the regression equation as a group; if this hypothesis fails to be rejected, then *none* of the independent variables belong in the regression equation. Hypotheses are also tested about the individual slope coefficients of the regression equation to see if any of the independent variables should be discarded from the regression equation.

Predicting the value of Y

You can use the multiple regression equation for employee salaries from the previous section to predict the annual salary of an employee with a specific amount of experience and education. For example, suppose that a randomly chosen employee has five years of experience and one year of graduate education. The predicted salary of this employee is

$$\hat{Y}_i = 76.47 + 5.32X_{1i} + 7.35X_{2i}$$
$$\hat{Y}_i = 76.47 + 5.32(5) + 7.35(1)$$
$$\hat{Y} = 110.42$$

This result shows that the predicted annual salary is $(110.42)(\$1,000) = \$110,420$.

The adjusted coefficient of determination

You can use several methods to test how well a multiple regression equation actually fits, or explains, the relationship between a dependent variable and one or more independent variables in a given data set. One of these methods is to use the *adjusted coefficient of determination* to determine how well the regression equation "fits" the sample data. The adjusted coefficient of determination is closely related to the coefficient of determination (also known as R^2) you use to test the results of a simple regression equation (shown in Chapter 15).

The adjusted coefficient of determination (also known as adjusted R^2 or ($\bar{R}^2$, pronounced "R bar squared") is a statistical measure that shows the proportion of *variation* explained by the estimated regression line.

Variation refers to the sum of the squared differences between the values of Y and the mean value of Y, expressed mathematically as

$$\sum_{i=1}^{n}\left(Y_i - \bar{Y}\right)^2$$

Adjusted R^2 always takes on a value between 0 and 1. The closer adjusted R^2 is to 1, the better the estimated regression equation fits or explains the relationship between X and Y.

The key difference between R^2 and adjusted R^2 is that R^2 increases automatically as you add new independent variables to a regression equation (even if they don't contribute any new explanatory power to the equation). Therefore, you want to use adjusted R^2 with multiple regression analysis. Adjusted R^2 increases only when you add new independent variables that *do* increase the explanatory power of the regression equation, making it a much more useful measure of how well a multiple regression equation fits the sample data than R^2.

The following equation shows the relationship between adjusted R^2 and R^2:

$$\bar{R}^2 = 1 - \left(1 - R^2\right)\left[\frac{n-1}{n-(k+1)}\right]$$

- ✔ n = the sample size
- ✔ k = the number of independent variables in the regression equation

Figure 16-2 highlights a section of the regression statistics from the spreadsheet in Figure 16-1.

Regression Statistics	
Multiple R	0.971774936
R Square	0.944346527
Adjusted R Square	0.922085137
Standard Error	5.52943278
Observations	8

Figure 16-2 shows the adjusted coefficient of determination (*Adjusted R Square*) as approximately 0.922. This is computed as follows:

$$\bar{R}^2 = 1 - \left(1 - R^2\right)\left[\frac{n-1}{n-(k+1)}\right]$$

R^2 is found on Figure 16-2; it's labeled "R Square" and equals 0.944346527. Because the sample contains eight observations, and there are two independent variables (years of experience and years of graduate education), the adjusted R^2 is computed as:

$$\bar{R}^2 = 1 - \left(1 - R^2\right)\left[\frac{n-1}{n-(k+1)}\right]$$

$$= 1 - \left(1 - 0.944346527\right)\left[\frac{8-1}{8-(2+1)}\right]$$

$$= 0.922085138$$

(This equals the value in Figure 16-2 except for a slight rounding difference.)

The range of possible values for the adjusted coefficient of determination is from 0 to 1; in mathematical terms,

$$0 \le \bar{R}^2 \le 1$$

Based on the value of adjusted R^2, the proportion of *variation* explained by the estimated regression line is approximately 0.922 or 92.2 percent.

The F-test: Testing the joint significance of the independent variables

The F-test is a special type of hypothesis test that is used to determine if the independent variables in a multiple regression equation jointly determine the value of the dependent variable. This is done by testing the hypothesis that *all slope coefficients equal 0*. If true, the regression equation doesn't explain the relationship between the dependent and the independent variables. In this case, you may use a new set of independent variables to try to explain the value of the dependent variable.

In the following sections, the steps required to carry out the F-test are explained in detail, based on the salaries example found in the section "Estimating a Multiple Regression Equation." This procedure begins with the statement of the null and alternative hypotheses, along with the choice of a level of significance. The next step is to construct the test statistic and compare it to a critical value before making a decision as to the validity of the regression equation. (Hypothesis testing is introduced in Chapter 12.)

The null and alternative hypotheses for the F-test

The first step in a hypothesis test is to specify the null hypothesis and the alternative hypothesis. A null hypothesis is a statement that is assumed to be true unless you find very strong evidence against it. An alternative hypothesis is a statement that is accepted instead of the null hypothesis if you reject the null hypothesis.

For the F-test with two independent variables, the null hypothesis is

$$H_0 : \beta_1 = \beta_2 = 0$$

This null hypothesis indicates that both slope coefficients (X_1 and X_2) equal 0. A coefficient of 0 suggests that an independent variable doesn't explain the value of the dependent variable. If you can't reject this hypothesis, then you can't use the regression equation to explain the relationship between the dependent variable (salaries) and the independent variables (years of experience and graduate education).

The alternative hypothesis is that at least one slope coefficient doesn't equal 0. In other words, at least one of the independent variables does belong in the regression equation because it explains the value of the dependent variable.

The level of significance for the F-test

The level of significance specifies the probability of a *Type I error*. This occurs when the null hypothesis is incorrectly rejected when it is actually true. A Type II error results when the null hypothesis is *not* rejected even though it is false. In many business applications, the level of significance is chosen to be 0.01, 0.05, or 0.10, and 0.05 is a common choice.

The Greek letter α ("alpha") is normally used to represent the level of significance. The choice of the level of significance depends on how important it is to avoid a Type I error compared with the importance of avoiding a Type II error. The higher the level of significance, the greater is the probability of a Type I error, and the lower is the probability of a Type II error.

It's impossible to reduce the probability of *both* a Type I and a Type II error without increasing the size of the sample used to test the null hypothesis.

The test statistic for the F-test

A test statistic is a numerical value that's used to determine if the null hypothesis should be rejected. If the test statistic has a large value (positive or negative), the likelihood that the null hypothesis will be rejected is also large.

You compute the test statistic (also known as the *F-statistic*) with this equation:

$$F = \frac{R^2 / k}{\left(1 - R^2\right) / \left[n - (k+1)\right]}$$

This test statistic is known as the F-statistic because probabilities for this statistic may be computed from the F-distribution. (The F-distribution is introduced in Chapter 13.)

In the salaries example in section "Estimating a Multiple Regression Equation," the F-statistic equals

$$
\begin{aligned}
F &= \frac{R^2 / k}{\left(1 - R^2\right) / \left[n - (k+1)\right]} \\
&= \frac{0.944346527 / 2}{\left(1 - 0.944346527\right) / \left[8 - (2+1)\right]} \\
&= 42.42
\end{aligned}
$$

The value of R^2 is taken from Figure 16-2 (it is labeled "R Square"). n equals 8 because there are eight elements in the sample. k equals 2 because there are two independent variables (years of experience and years of graduate education).

The test statistic follows the *F-distribution* with k numerator degrees of freedom and $[n - (k + 1)]$ denominator degrees of freedom. The F-distribution is characterized by two different types of degrees of freedom; these are known as *numerator* degrees of freedom and *denominator* degrees of freedom.

For the F-test, you can find probabilities for the test statistic from an F-table based on the level of significance, the number of numerator degrees of freedom, and the number of denominator degrees of freedom. (See Chapters 13 and 14 for more on the F-distribution and the F-table.)

Figure 16-3 shows a portion of Figure 16-1, highlighting the ANOVA (analysis of variance) table. Here, you see that the value of the F-statistic is 42.42082621, which is approximately equal to 42.42 (found under the *F-*stat column). Note that you can also obtain the value of the F-statistic from two values in the ANOVA table:

1. MS(Regression), which equals 1297.000933 and is found at the intersection of the row labeled "Regression" and the column labeled "MS"

2. MS(Residual), which equals 30.57462687 and is found at the intersection of the row labeled "Residual" and the column labeled "MS"

The ratio of these two values = 1297.000933 / 30.57462687 = 42.42082621, or approximately 42.42.

Figure 16-3:
The ANOVA table for the salaries example.

ANOVA

	df	SS	MS	F-stat	Significance F
Regression	2	2594.001866	1297.000933	42.42082621	0.000730686
Residual	5	152.8731343	30.57462687		
Total	7	2746.875			

R^2 is the ratio of SS(Regression) to SS(Total). Adjusted R^2 is obtained from R^2 as

$$\bar{R}^2 = 1 - \left(1 - R^2\right)\left[\frac{n-1}{n-(k+1)}\right]$$

where n = the sample size, and k = the number of independent variables in the regression equation.

The critical value for the F-test

A critical value shows the number of standard deviations away from the mean of a distribution where a specified percentage of the distribution is above the critical value, and the remainder of the distribution is below the critical value.

In general, when testing a hypothesis the test statistic is compared with one or two critical values. If the test statistic is more *extreme* than the relevant critical value, the null hypothesis is rejected. Otherwise, the null hypothesis fails to be rejected.

For the F-test, there's a single critical value, which is uniquely determined by the level of significance and the numerator and denominator degrees of freedom.

For the F-test, the numerator and denominator degrees of freedom are computed as follows:

- ✔ Numerator degrees of freedom: $k = 2$
- ✔ Denominator degrees of freedom: $[n - (k + 1)] = (8 - [2 + 1]) = 5$

You can choose the appropriate critical value from an F-table. (The F-table is introduced in Chapter 13; the values in the table are taken from the F-distribution.)

Unlike the tables used for most other probability distributions, you need one entire F-table for each level of significance. Table 16-1 shows an excerpt from the F-table for a 5 percent level of significance ($\alpha = 0.05$):

Table 16-1		**A Section of the F-Table with $\alpha = 0.05$**						
$\upsilon_2 \backslash \upsilon_1$	**2**	**3**	**4**	**5**	**6**	**7**	**8**	**9**
2	19.00	19.16	19.25	19.30	19.33	19.35	19.37	19.38
3	9.55	9.28	9.12	9.01	8.94	8.89	8.85	8.81
4	6.94	6.59	6.39	6.26	6.16	6.09	6.04	6.00
5	5.79	5.41	5.19	5.05	4.95	4.88	4.82	4.77
6	5.14	4.76	4.53	4.39	4.28	4.21	4.15	4.10
7	4.74	4.35	4.12	3.97	3.87	3.79	3.73	3.68
8	4.46	4.07	3.84	3.69	3.58	3.50	3.44	3.39
9	4.26	3.86	3.63	3.48	3.37	3.29	3.23	3.18

The top row represents the numerator degrees of freedom (υ_1); the first column represents the denominator degrees of freedom (υ_2).

In this example, you're looking for a right-tail area of 5 percent with $\upsilon_1 = 2$, and $\upsilon_2 = 5$. You find this critical value at the intersection of the column labeled *2* and the row labeled *5.* You express this critical value mathematically as

$$F_\alpha^{v1,v2} = F_{0.05}^{2,5} = 5.79$$

The decision for the F-test

If the test statistic exceeds the critical value, you reject the null hypothesis; otherwise, you don't reject it. In this case, the test statistic is approximately 42.42, and the critical value is 5.79. Therefore, you reject the hypothesis that all the slope coefficients (β_1 and β_2) are equal to zero. In other words, one (or both) of the independent variables (years of experience and years of graduate education) explains the annual salaries of the employees at this company.

Testing the null hypothesis with the p-value when testing the joint significance of the slope coefficients

As an alternative to comparing the F-statistic with a critical value, you can test the hypothesis by comparing the *p-value* (probability value) with the level of significance.

The p-value represents the probability that a test statistic will equal a specified value when the null hypothesis is true. A low p-value is evidence against a null hypothesis.

When you're using the p-value, the decision rule is this: If the p-value is less than the level of significance, you reject the null hypothesis; otherwise, you won't reject the null hypothesis.

In this example, the level of significance is 0.05 (5 percent). Figure 16-3 shows the p-value (under the *Significance F* column) as (approximately) 0.0007. Because the p-value is well below the level of significance, you reject the null hypothesis. Therefore, at least one of the slope coefficients is statistically significant at the 5 percent level.

The t-test: Determining the significance of the slope coefficients

After you use the F-test to confirm that at least one slope coefficient isn't equal to 0, you test each slope coefficient separately to determine if it belongs in the regression equation; this requires the use of a hypothesis test known as the t-test. (The test has this name because the test statistic and the critical values are taken from the Student's t-distribution. See Chapter 15 for more on this test.) The t-test lets you determine which of the slope coefficients is statistically significant or if both are statistically significant.

Null and alternative hypotheses for the t-test

With the t-test, the null hypothesis states that a slope coefficient equals 0. For example, to test the hypothesis that $\beta_1 = 0$, you would write the null hypothesis as $H_0 : \beta_1 = 0$.

There are three possible alternative hypotheses:

$H_1 : \beta_1 > 0$: This is known as a *right-tailed* test

$H_1 : \beta_1 < 0$: This is known as a *left-tailed* test

$H_1 : \beta_1 \neq 0$: This is known as a *two-tailed* test

With a right-tailed test, you are looking for evidence that the actual value of β_1 is *greater than* 0; with a left-tailed test, you are looking for evidence that the actual value of of β_1 is *less than* 0. With a two-tailed test, you are looking for evidence that the actual value of β_1 is *different from* 0. For the t-test, the two-tailed approach is usually taken.

Level of significance for the t-test

When you test hypotheses about individual regression coefficients, the level of significance (α) is often set equal to 0.05 (5 percent). Other commonly used choices include 0.001, 0.01, 0.05, and 0.10.

Test statistic for the t-test

For the t-test, the test statistic is the ratio of the estimated coefficient to the standard error of the coefficient. For example, the test statistic for determining whether $\beta_1 = 0$ is

$$t = \frac{\hat{\beta}_1}{s_{\hat{\beta}_1}}$$

This expression is known as a *t-statistic* because it follows the t-distribution. (You can compute probabilities for the t-statistic from a Student's t-table. See Chapter 11 for more discussion of the Student's t-distribution.)

You can find the values you need to construct the t-statistic from the regression statistics under the *Coefficients* and *Standard Error* columns, as shown in Figure 16-4.

Figure 16-4:
Coefficients
and
standard
errors for
the salary
example.

	Coefficients	Standard Error	t-Stat	P-value
Intercept	76.47014925	3.397844048	22.50549118	3.21898E-06
X_1 (Years of experience)	5.320895522	1.695561146	3.13813249	0.025720437
X_2 (Years of graduate education)	7.350746269	3.669054725	2.003444162	0.101492144

As you can see in Figure 16-4, for the variable X_1 (years of experience), the coefficient is (approximately) 5.32, and the standard error is (approximately) 1.70.

The ratio of these two values is

$$t = \frac{\hat{\beta}_1}{s_{\hat{\beta}_1}}$$
$$= \frac{5.32}{1.70}$$
$$= 3.13$$

Figure 16-4 also shows that for the variable X_2 (years of graduate education), or that $\beta_2 = 0$, the coefficient is (approximately) 7.35, and the standard error is (approximately) 3.67.

The ratio of these two values is

$$t = \frac{\hat{\beta}_2}{s_{\hat{\beta}_2}}$$
$$= \frac{7.35}{3.67}$$
$$= 2.00$$

Critical values for the t-test

With a multiple regression equation, you take the critical values from the Student's t-table with $n - (k + 1)$ degrees of freedom (n is the sample size and k is the number of independent variables).

The number of degrees of freedom refers to the number of *independent* elements in a sample.

When testing hypotheses about a slope coefficient, the degrees of freedom equals the sample size (n) minus k+1 (k is the number of independent variables in the regression equation). This is because the sample data is used to estimate k+1 values: These are the estimated intercept and k estimated slope coefficients. As a result, the degrees of freedom equal n–(k+1).

The critical value depends on the alternative hypothesis as follows:

- ✔ For a right-tailed test, there is a single critical value, $+t_\alpha^{n-(k+1)}$

  If the test statistic is *greater than* this value, the null hypothesis is *rejected*; otherwise, it fails to be rejected.

- ✔ For a left-tailed test, there is a single critical value, $-t_\alpha^{n-(k+1)}$

  If the test statistic is *less than* this value, the null hypothesis is *rejected*; otherwise, it fails to be rejected.

- ✔ For a two-tailed test, there are two critical values, $\pm t_{\alpha/2}^{n-(k+1)}$

  If the test statistic is *greater than* the positive critical value or *less than* the negative critical value, the null hypothesis is *rejected*; otherwise, it fails to be rejected.

When testing hypotheses about the slope coefficients in a regression equation, the appropriate number of degrees of freedom equals $n - (k + 1)$; n is the sample size and k is the number of independent variables. For the salaries example, the sample size is 8 and there are two independent variables (years of experience and years of graduate education.) Therefore, the degrees of freedom equals $n - (k + 1) = 8 - (2 + 1) = 5$.

Because this is a two-tailed test, two critical values occur:

$$\pm t_{\alpha/2}^{n-(k+1)} = \pm t_{0.025}^{5}$$

You can find these critical values in a Student's t-table, which is based on the Student's t-distribution (see Chapter 11 for details). Table 16-2 shows an excerpt:

Table 16-2	The Student's t-Distribution				
Degrees of Freedom	$t_{0.10}$	$t_{0.05}$	$t_{0.025}$	$t_{0.01}$	$t_{0.005}$
5	1.476	2.015	2.571	3.365	4.032
6	1.440	1.943	2.447	3.143	3.707
7	1.415	1.895	2.365	2.998	3.499
8	1.397	1.860	2.306	2.896	3.355
9	1.383	1.833	2.262	2.821	3.250
10	1.372	1.812	2.228	2.764	3.169

The t-distribution (also known as the Student's t-distribution) is a continuous probability distribution that has a mean of zero, is symmetrical about its mean, and has more areas in the "tails" of the distribution than the standard normal distribution. (The standard normal distribution is found in Chapter 9; the Student's t-distribution is found in Chapter 11.) The Student's t-distribution is uniquely characterized by its degrees of freedom.

You find the value of the positive critical value, $t_{0.025}^5$, at the intersection of the row labeled 5 degrees of freedom and the column labeled $t_{0.025}$. The positive critical value is 2.571. Due to the symmetry of the Student's t-distribution, the negative critical value equals the positive critical value with a negative sign: –2.571.

Decision rule for the t-test

For testing the hypothesis $H_0 : \beta_1 = 0$, you reach the appropriate decision as follows:

- ✔ If the value of the test statistic is greater than 2.571, you reject the null hypothesis $H_0 : \beta_1 = 0$ in favor of the alternative hypothesis $H_1 : \beta_1 > 0$.

- ✔ If the value of the test statistic is less than –2.571, you reject the null hypothesis $H_0 : \beta_1 = 0$ in favor of the alternative hypothesis $H_1 : \beta_1 < 0$.

- ✔ If the test statistic falls between –2.571 and 2.571, you don't reject the null hypothesis $H_0 : \beta_1 = 0$.

You follow the same process when you test the hypothesis $H_0 : \beta_2 = 0$.

For β_1, the test statistic is 3.13, which is greater than 2.571. Therefore, you reject the null hypothesis $H_0 : \beta_1 = 0$ in favor of $H_1 : \beta_1 > 0$, which indicates that β_1 is different from 0 (that is, it's statistically significant). Therefore, in the example used throughout this chapter, strong evidence shows that X_1 (years of experience) explains some of the value of Y (annual salary).

For β_2, the test statistic is 2.00, which is between –2.571 and 2.571. Therefore, you don't reject the null hypothesis $H_0 : \beta_2 = 0$. You have insufficient evidence to show that that X_2 (years of graduate education) explains the value of Y (annual salary).

Testing the null hypothesis with the p-value when testing the individual slope coefficients

As an alternative to comparing the t-statistic with critical values, you can test the hypothesis by comparing the p-value with the level of significance. The decision rule is then if the p-value is less than the level of significance, you reject the null hypothesis; otherwise, you don't reject the null hypothesis.

In the example of the employee salaries, the level of significance is 0.05 (5 percent). You can find the p-values for X_1 and X_2 by referring to Figure 16-4.

For β_1, the p-value is 0.025720432, which is less than 0.05. Therefore, you reject the null hypothesis $H_0 : \beta_1 = 0$ in favor of $H_1 : \beta_1 > 0$, which indicates that β_1 is different from 0 (that is, it's statistically significant).

For β_2, the p-value is 0.101492144, which is greater than 0.05. Therefore, you don't reject the null hypothesis $H_0 : \beta_2 = 0$. So β_2 is *not* different from 0 (that is, it's *not* statistically significant).

The results you get from using the p-value always match the results of comparing a test statistic with critical values.

Checking for Multicollinearity

One of the potential difficulties with multiple regression analysis is *multicollinearity*. Multicollinearity occurs when two or more of the independent variables are highly correlated with each other, causing the correlated variables to have large standard errors, so they appear to be statistically insignificant even if they're not. (In other words, there's a risk that independent variables are removed from the regression equation that should be included.)

Multicollinearity is unique to multiple regression because it has multiple independent variables (simple regression has only one independent variable so that multicollinearity can't occur).

A statistic known as the variance inflation factor (VIF) may be used to check for multicollinearity. As a rule of thumb, if the VIF is 10 or more, this is a sign that multicollinearity is present.

One approach to removing multicollinearity is to eliminate one of the correlated variables from the regression. Doing so lowers the p-values of the uncorrelated independent variables, which reduces the risk that they'll be considered statistically insignificant when they're not.

Chapter 17

Forecasting Techniques: Looking into the Future

Suppose you could forecast the price of Apple stock at the end of closing tomorrow. How rich could you be? What if you could foresee the future path of interest rates? How much of an advantage would you have over other investors? Trying to predict the future is an ancient art; some would suggest that the newest mathematical techniques are no more successful than tarot cards and Ouija boards.

Despite of the difficulty of forecasting the future, economists, investors, analysts, and traders do attempt to predict future values of economic variables, such as stock prices, commodity prices, interest rates, exchange rates, and so on. Many trading strategies depend on being able to use past history to correctly forecast the future. When these strategies succeed, it's an open question whether their success was due to sophisticated models or just plain dumb luck.

While forecasting is notoriously difficult, there are several classical techniques that may be useful for short-term business forecasting. These models have one thing in common — all base their predictions on past history and the assumption that history will be repeated in the future. This chapter focuses on these techniques, which include linear trend models, quadratic trend models, seasonally adjusted models, and exponential smoothing models.

Defining a Time Series

A *time series* is a sequence of random variables indexed by time. (Random variables are introduced in Chapter 7.) You express a time series as $\{y_t\}$, where y_t is the value of a random variable at time t. For example, daily closing price of IBM is a random variable because its value isn't known prior to the end of the trading day. The daily closing price of IBM stock over ten trading days can be represented as $\{y_t\} = y_1, y_2, y_3, ..., y_{10}$. y_t is the price of IBM stock at time t.

A time series may contain the following effects:

✔ **Trend effects** refers to a long-run increase or decrease in a time series. For example, gold prices taken from the past 40 years would show a very strong positive trend because prices have risen consistently over this period Trends may be due to a large number of different factors, such as population growth, technological improvement, and increasing incomes.

✔ **Seasonal effects** refer to the impact of the time of year on economic variables. For example, sales of bathing suits, surfboards, and so forth are much stronger during the warmer months. Sales of Christmas trees, turkeys, and pumpkin pies are stronger during the colder months. Many variables aren't affected by the season; for example, the price of office furniture is not likely to fluctuate due to changes in the season.

✔ **Cyclical effects** refer to the impact of the business cycle. For example, sales of expensive items, such as new homes and new cars, decline when the economy falls into recession. As another example, interest rates tend to fall during recessions and rebound during recoveries.

✔ **Irregular effects** refer to the impact of random events such as strikes, earthquakes, sudden changes in the weather, and so on.

Modeling a Time Series with Regression Analysis

A time series may be modeled in several different ways; one of these is to use regression analysis. (Simple regression analysis is covered in Chapter 15, and multiple regression analysis is covered in Chapter 16.) In this case, the value of the time series being modeled is assumed to depend only on the passage of time; for example, time is the independent variable.

The basic form of a time series regression model can be expressed as $y_t = TR_t + \varepsilon_t$.

TR_t is the trend of the time series at time t, and ε_t is an error term at time t.

To estimate a time series with regression analysis, the first step is to identify the type of trend (if any) that's present in the data. The type of trend determines the exact equation that is estimated. After this has been specified, the next step is to run a regression of the time series data using time as the independent variable. The final step is to test the validity of the results.

This section explains the different types of trends that may be encountered in time series data, such as linear trends and quadratic trends.

Classifying trends

In the following sections, I define the basic types of trends that may appear in a time series.

No trend

In the case where a time series doesn't increase or decrease over time, it may instead randomly fluctuate around a constant value. In this case, the time series has *no trend*. The trend equation is set equal to a constant, which is the intercept of a regression equation:

$$TR_t = \beta_0$$

The corresponding regression equation is $y_t = \beta_0 + \varepsilon_t$.

When no trend occurs, the values of the time series may rise or fall, but on average they tend to return to the same level (β_0; (for example, the intercept of the regression equation). Figure 17-1 shows a time series with no trend.

Notice that the values of Y are randomly rising and falling; there is no clear pattern in the data.

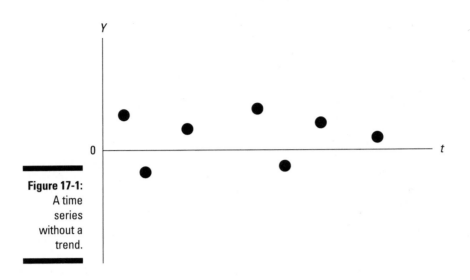

Figure 17-1:
A time
series
without a
trend.

Linear trend

With a linear trend, the values of a time series tend to rise or fall at a constant rate (β_1). The linear trend is expressed as $TR_t = \beta_0 + \beta_1 t$.

The corresponding regression equation is $y_t = \beta_0 + \beta_1 t + \varepsilon_t$.

Figure 17-2 shows a time series with a positive linear trend. With this type of trend, the independent variable y_t *increases* at a constant rate over time. (If a time series has a negative linear trend, the independent variable y_t *decreases* at a constant rate over time.)

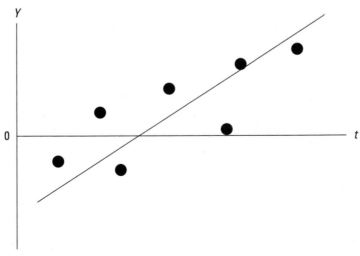

Figure 17-2:
A time
series with
a positive
linear trend.

Note that as t increases (such as time elapses), Y tends to increase on average. The trend line drawn through the values of Y has a positive slope, indicating that Y has a positive linear trend.

Quadratic trend

With a quadratic trend, the values of a time series tend to rise or fall at a rate that that is not constant; it changes over time. As a result, the trend is not a straight line. The trend is expressed as $TR_t = \beta_0 + \beta_1 t + \beta_2 t^2$.

The corresponding regression equation is $y_t = \beta_0 + \beta_1 t + \beta_2 t^2 + \varepsilon_t$.

Figure 17-3 shows a time series with a quadratic trend. In this case, the value of y_t increases at an increasing rate over time.

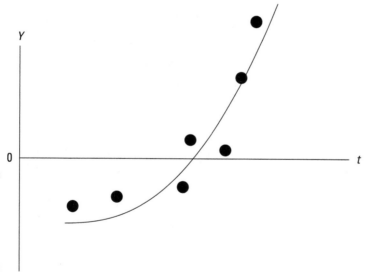

Figure 17-3: A time series with a quadratic trend.

Note that as t increases (such as time elapses), Y tends to increase at an increasing rate. The trend is curving upward; this type of curve indicates that the Y has a positive *quadratic* trend.

A quadratic equation has at least one squared term. For example, the following is a quadratic equation:

$$Y = X^2 + X + 3$$

Other possible trends

It's possible that a trend may contain terms that are raised to the third power, fourth power, or higher. This type of trend is extremely rare in business applications. Most time series of financial data have a linear trend, a quadratic trend, or no trend at all.

Estimating the trend

To estimate a time series, a trend must be estimated. You begin by creating a line chart of the time series (line charts are introduced in Chapter 2). The line chart shows how a variable changes over time; it can be used to inspect the characteristics of the data, in particular, to see whether a trend. For example, suppose you're a portfolio manager and you have reason to believe a linear trend occurs in a time series of returns to Microsoft stock. You plot the monthly prices from August 2008 to July 2013 on a graph like Figure 17-4.

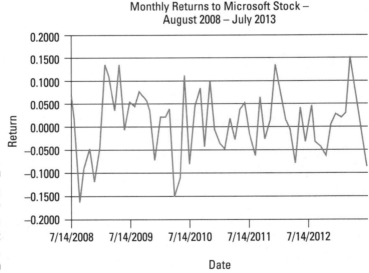

Figure 17-4:
Monthly returns to Microsoft stock.

According to Figure 17-4, no trend occurs in the data. The returns rise and fall with no particular pattern.

To formally test whether a linear trend occurs, run a time series regression with a time trend as the independent variable, which you can set up like so:

$$y_t = \beta_0 + \beta_1 t + \varepsilon_t$$

In this example, the dependent variable is the price of Microsoft stock, and the independent variable is time (measured in months).

Figure 17-5 shows the results of this regression analysis.

SUMMARY OUTPUT

Regression Statistics	
Multiple R	0.052602349
R Square	0.002767007
Adjusted R Square	−0.014426665
Standard Error	0.073283809
Observations	60

ANOVA

	df	SS	MS	F-stat	Significance F
Regression	1	0.000864286	0.000864286	0.160931714	0.689774323
Residual	58	0.311489964	0.005370517		
Total	59	0.31235425			

	Coefficients	Standard Error	t-Stat	P-value	Lower 95%	Upper 95%
Intercept	0.00140958	0.01916082	0.073565754	0.941609047	−0.036944967	0.039764128
t	0.000219156	0.000546301	0.401162952	0.689774323	−0.000874385	0.001312696

Figure 17-5: Regression of Microsoft returns against time with a linear trend.

To run this regression, the independent variable (time) is assigned numerical values as follows. You assign the first date in the sample a value 1, the second date a value of 2, and so forth. So for this example, you assign August 2008 a value of 1, September 2008 a value of 2, and so on so that the last observation in the sample, July 2013, has a value of 60.

Note that in Figure 17-5, the coefficient of time is *not* statistically significant; its p-value is approximately 0.6898. For many hypothesis tests, as a rule of thumb any p-value above 0.05 indicates that a variable is not statistically significant.

More formally, the null hypothesis $H_0 : \beta_1 = 0$ can't be rejected at the 5 percent level of significance (see Chapter 12 for details on hypothesis testing.) This means there isn't enough evidence to show there is a trend in the data.

When there's no trend, the value of $y_t = \beta_0 + \varepsilon_t$.

As another example, suppose that instead of estimating a linear trend for the returns to Microsoft stock, you estimate a linear trend for the price of Microsoft stock. Figure 17-6 shows a plot of monthly Microsoft stock prices from August 2008 to July 2013.

Figure 17-6:
Monthly
prices of
Microsoft
stock.

Figure 17-7 shows the results of running a regression of the price of Microsoft stock against time with an assumed linear trend.

The results show that the time variable is statistically significant at the 5 percent level (because the p-value for time is well below 0.05). Based on the coefficients in Figure 17-7, the estimated regression equation is $\hat{y}_t = 19.15 + 0.1975t$.

(Note that I rounded the coefficients in this equation.) This equation shows that during the sample period, the price of Microsoft stock grew by an average of \$0.1975 per month because 0.1975 is the coefficient of t, and y is measured in dollars.

SUMMARY OUTPUT

Regression Statistics	
Multiple R	0.788249636
R Square	0.621337488
Adjusted R Square	0.614808824
Standard Error	2.715991268
Observations	60

ANOVA

	df	SS	MS	F-stat	Significance F
Regression	1	702.0369613	702.0369613	95.17069461	7.7037E-14
Residual	58	427.843297	7.376608569		
Total	59	1129.880258			

	Coefficients	Standard Error	t-Stat	P-value	Lower 95%	Upper 95%
Intercept	19.14990395	0.710124377	26.99697166	1.65632E-34	17.72843558	20.57137232
t	0.19751681	0.020246616	9.755546863	7.7037E-14	0.156988806	0.238044815

Figure 17-7: Regression of Microsoft prices against time with a linear trend.

Suppose that in your role as portfolio manager you want to determine whether a quadratic trend occurs in the time series of Microsoft stock prices.

If there is a quadratic trend in a time series, the appropriate regression equation is $y_t = \beta_0 + \beta_1 t + \beta_2 t^2 + \varepsilon_t$.

There is one new term in this equation:

$$\beta_2 t^2$$

Because time is squared here, this term captures the *curvature* of the trend. If this term is statistically significant, the trend associated with this time series is said to have a *quadratic* trend.

Figure 17-8 shows the results of running this regression.

SUMMARY OUTPUT

Regression Statistics	
Multiple R	0.78837024
R Square	0.621527635
Adjusted R Square	0.608247903
Standard Error	2.7390242
Observations	60

ANOVA

	df	SS	MS	F-stat	Significance F
Regression	2	702.2518051	351.1259025	46.80272394	9.41833E-13
Residual	57	427.6284532	7.502253566		
Total	59	1129.880258			

	Coefficients	Standard Error	t-Stat	P-value	Lower 95%	Upper 95%
Intercept	19.29057072	1.097189363	17.58180618	1.0881E-24	17.09348693	21.4876545
t	0.183903898	0.082993396	2.215886931	0.030707728	0.017712491	0.350095304
t²	0.000223163	0.00131873	0.169225377	0.8662185	−0.002417548	0.002863873

Figure 17-8: Regression of Microsoft prices against time with a quadratic trend.

Figure 17-8 shows that the coefficient of time (t) is statistically significant, whereas the coefficient of time squared (t^2) is not, indicating that there is *not* a quadratic trend in the data, but there is a linear trend. Therefore, the price of Microsoft stock should be forecast with the linear trend model:

$$\hat{y}_t = 19.15 + 0.1975t$$

Forecasting a Time Series

Based on the estimated regression equation from the previous section,

$$\hat{y}_t = 19.15 + 0.1975t$$

you can use this equation to predict the future value of Microsoft stock prices. By forecasting with a time series regression model, you are using the past history of Microsoft stock to make a prediction about where the stock will be in the future.

Suppose in July 2013 you want to forecast the price of Microsoft stock for August 2013. In the section "Estimating the Trend," the dates associated with the Microsoft stock prices are assigned numerical values ranging from 1 to 60; 60 represents the most recently observed price in July 2013. Therefore, August 2013 is assigned a value of 61. To forecast the price of Microsoft stock in August 2013, 61 is substituted for t in the regression equation:

$$\hat{y}_t = 19.15 + 0.1975t$$
$$\hat{y}_t = 19.15 + 0.1975(61)$$
$$= \$31.1975$$
$$= (15.47,\ 39.17)$$

Changing with the Seasons: Seasonal Variation

Seasonal variation refers to recurring changes in a time series that are due to the season of the year. For example, the demand for oil tends to be greatest during the summer (for gasoline) and the winter (for heating). For such cases, you extend the time series regression model to include a seasonal variable (S_t):

$$y_t = TR_t + S_t + \varepsilon_t$$

You then use a scatterplot to determine whether a time series exhibits seasonal variation, and if so, what type. For example, the seasonality could be quarterly or monthly.

To see the effect of seasonality, you can use *dummy variables*.

A dummy variable is also known as an indicator variable or a binary variable. A dummy variable is used to represent the values of a *qualitative* (non-numerical) variable in a regression equation; some examples are gender, color, style, and so on.

The most important feature of a dummy variable is that it can assume only one of two values: 1 or 0. 1 is normally used to indicate a specified condition is *true*, whereas 0 means that the condition is *false*. For example, a dummy variable could represent the gender of the people who reply to a survey. In this case, 1 could represent males and 0 could represent females.

For modeling seasonal variation, you can use a dummy variable to indicate whether an observation in a time series belongs to a given season. For example, suppose you're analyzing oil demand. You want to see whether the demand for oil is related to the quarter of the year. You have reason to believe that demand peaks in the fourth and first quarters due to cold weather.

For this exercise, you define the following seasonal dummy variables:

D_1 = 1 if time period t is in the first quarter; it equals 0 otherwise.

D_2 = 1 if time period t is in the second quarter; it equals 0 otherwise.

D_3 = 1 if time period t is in the third quarter; it equals 0 otherwise.

In this case, you have only three dummy variables, not four, because including one dummy variable for each season leads to *multicollinearity* — when two or more independent variables in a regression equation are highly correlated with each other so they have large standard errors and can appear statistically insignificant even if they're not. Multicollinearity affects the reliability of the regression results, and can be avoided by not including highly correlated independent variables in the regression equation. (See Chapter 16 for more on multicollinearity.)

In this example, the coefficient of D_1 measures the impact on oil demand of the first quarter compared with the fourth quarter. In other words, the fourth quarter is used as a benchmark against which the other quarters are measured. If the coefficient of D_1 is positive, the demand for oil is *greater* in the first quarter than in the fourth quarter; if the coefficient of D_1 is negative, the demand for oil is *smaller* in the first quarter than in the fourth quarter. Similarly, the coefficient of D_2 measures the impact on oil demand of the second quarter compared with the fourth quarter, and the coefficient of D_3 measures the impact on oil demand of the third quarter compared with the fourth quarter.

The appropriate time series regression equation is

$$y_t = \beta_0 + \beta_1 t + \beta_2 D_1 + \beta_3 D_2 + \beta_4 D_3 + \varepsilon_t$$

As an example, suppose a sporting goods store sells surfboards. In this case, sales depend heavily on the specific quarter of the year. In particular, sales are strongest during the second and third quarters and are extremely weak during the first and fourth quarters.

To analyze the relationship between surfboard sales and quarters, you run a regression with, say, ten years of quarterly data. Sales are the dependent variable. The independent variables consist of a time trend and a series of three quarterly dummy variables, defined as follows:

D_1 = 1 if an observation occurs in the first quarter, otherwise 0

D_2 = 1 if an observation occurs in the second quarter, otherwise 0

D_3 = 1 if an observation occurs in the third quarter, otherwise 0

The graph in Figure 17-9 shows quarterly sales (in thousands of dollars) of the sporting goods store for 2001 to 2010. A trend line is included.

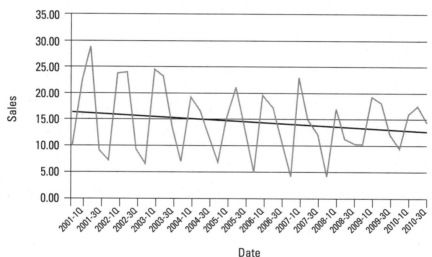

Surfboard sales ($millions per quarter)

Figure 17-9:
Quarterly sales data with seasonal variation.

Figure 17-9 shows that the trend line by itself does a poor job of explaining sales. The trend line is often extremely far from the actual sales numbers because the data are highly seasonal. Because the data are clearly affected by the seasons, it makes sense to run a regression with a trend and the seasonal dummies. Figure 17-10 shows the results.

SUMMARY OUTPUT

Regression Statistics	
Multiple R	0.883631708
R Square	0.780804995
Adjusted R Square	0.755754138
Standard Error	3.157746335
Observations	40

ANOVA

	df	SS	MS	F-stat	Significance F
Regression	4	1243.181258	310.7953145	31.1687929	4.27358E-11
Residual	35	348.997667	9.971361915		
Total	39	1592.178925			

	Coefficients	Standard Error	t-Stat	P-value	Lower 95%	Upper 95%
Intercept	13.90290102	1.382453507	10.05668614	7.31093E-12	11.09637121	16.70943083
t	−0.10708641	0.043457054	−2.46418938	0.018788462	−0.195308919	−0.018863901
D1	−4.855956296	1.418192167	−3.42404676	0.001589404	−7.73503944	−1.976873152
D2	8.246375747	1.414859161	5.828407502	1.29957E-06	5.374058965	11.11869253
D3	7.657160168	1.412855583	5.419634009	4.49853E-06	4.788910866	10.52540947

Figure 17-10: Regression of quarterly sales data with seasonal dummies and trend.

The results show that each of the independent variables has a statistically significant coefficient and, therefore, belongs in the regression equation (in other words, these variables help explain the value of sales) because the p-value is below 0.05 in each case. Here are the approximate coefficients of the variables.

Intercept	***13.9029***
Trend	−0.1071
D_1	−4.8560
D_2	8.2464
D_3	7.6572

The trend indicates that sales are decreasing by \$107.1 ($0.1071 \times \$1,000$) per month over the ten-year sample period. The coefficients of the remaining dummy variables show the value of sales compared with a trend line at the level of average fourth quarter sales. This line has an intercept of 13.9029 and a slope of −0.1071 and represents fourth quarter sales.

The coefficient of D_1 shows that sales during the first quarter are below the fourth quarter by \$4,856.00 ($4.8560 \times \$1,000$). The coefficient of D_2 shows that sales during the second quarter are above the fourth quarter by \$8,246.40 ($8.2464 \times 1,000$). The coefficient of D_3 shows that sales during the third quarter are above the fourth quarter by \$7,657.20 ($7.6572 \times \$1,000$).

Implementing Smoothing Techniques

Smoothing techniques are designed to remove random fluctuations from a time series so the trend, seasonal variation, and cyclical variation (if any) in the data are easy to identify.

Two widely used smoothing techniques are *moving averages* and *centered moving averages,* which I talk about in the next sections.

Moving averages

A *moving average* (MA) is an average of the most recent observations in a time series. For example, a five-period moving average is the average of the five most-recent values in a time series. In general, an *n-period moving average* is the average value of the n most recent observations taken from a time series.

Compute an n-period moving average with this formula:

$$\frac{y_t + y_{t+1} + y_{t+2} + \ldots + y_{t+n-1}}{n}$$

For example, the following lists the monthly prices of a stock between October 2012 and July 2013.

Month	Price
October 2012	100
November 2012	101
December 2012	103
January 2013	99
February 2013	97
March 2013	102
April 2013	101
May 2013	98
June 2013	104
July 2013	106

To construct a three-month moving average, take the average of the first three observations, in this case, October, November, and December prices:

$$\frac{(100+101+103)}{3} = 101.33$$

Then find the average of the next three observations, starting with the second observation, so you're finding the average of the second, third, and fourth observations (or November, December, and January):

$$\frac{(101+103+99)}{3} = 101.00$$

Continue the process for the entire sample. Table 17-1 shows the resulting three-month moving averages.

Table 17-1	Three-Month Moving Averages	
Month	*Price*	*3-Month Moving Average*
October 2012	100	***
November 2012	101	101.33
December 2012	103	101.00
January 2013	99	99.67
February 2013	97	99.33
March 2013	102	100.00
April 2013	101	100.33
May 2013	98	101.00
June 2013	104	102.67
July 2013	106	***

The first three-month moving average is listed next to November 2012, even though it represents the average of October2, November2, and December2. This shows that November 2012 is the "center" of the moving average.

Similarly, the three-month moving average constructed from the November2, December2, and January3 prices is shown next to December, indicating that it's the center of the average2. Plotting these moving averages and the original prices (as shown in Figure 17-11) illustrates that moving averages reduce the fluctuations in the data and shows more clearly if there is any trend in the data. (The moving averages are said to "smooth out" the data.)

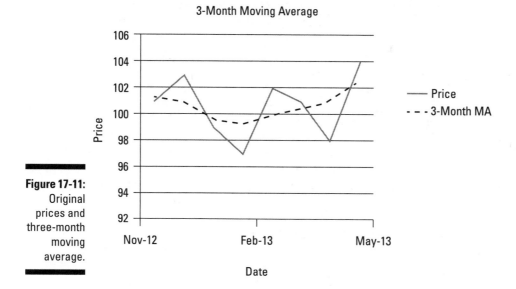

Figure 17-11:
Original
prices and
three-month
moving
average.

The number of terms used to compute a moving average is usually determined by the data. For example, 12-month moving averages are often used with monthly data.

Centered moving averages

A *centered moving average* is an average of moving averages. How's that for a definition? You use a centered moving average to remove the effect of seasonal and irregular factors from a time series, so only the trend and cyclical factors remain.

Using the stock prices from the previous example data (refer to Table 17-1), the first three-month moving average is 101.33 and the second three-month moving average is 101.

The centered moving average is then

$$\frac{(101.33 + 101)}{2} = 101.17$$

Table 17-2 shows the centered moving averages for the rest of the months.

Table 17-2		Three-Month Moving Averages and Centered Moving Averages	
Month	*Price*	*3-Month Moving Average*	*Centered Moving Average*
October 2012	100	***	***
November 2012	101	101.33	101.17
December 2012	103	101.00	100.33
January 2013	99	99.67	99.50
February 2013	97	99.33	99.67
March 2013	102	100.00	100.17
April 2013	101	100.33	100.67
May 2013	98	101.00	101.83
June 2013	104	102.67	***
July 2013	106	***	***

Figure 17-12 shows a comparison of the moving average and centered moving average. The centered moving average is smoother than the moving average.

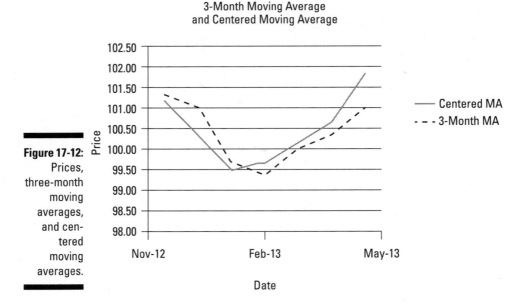

Figure 17-12: Prices, three-month moving averages, and centered moving averages.

Exploring Exponential Smoothing

The moving average and centered moving average techniques have one common feature: Both assign equal weights to all elements of a time series. For example, when you're computing a three-month moving average, you multiply each observation by a weight of one-third (or, as you may know, you can get the same results by dividing by 3 instead). If a time series consists of data that become less relevant as time elapses, it may make more sense to assign steadily declining weights to older observations. You do this with *exponential smoothing*.

With exponential smoothing, you assign weights to the members of the time series to ensure that newer observations have more importance than older observations. You implement the weighting scheme using a *smoothing constant*. This is the value that determines how much smoothing takes place; the higher the smoothing constant, the more random variation is removed from the time series, thus making the time series smoother.

To implement the exponential smoothing approach, you use the following formula:

$$E_t = \alpha y_{t-1} + (1 - \alpha)E_{t-1}$$

In this formula,

E_t = the exponentially smoothed value at time t

E_{t-1} = the exponentially smoothed value at time $t-1$ (one period in the past)

α = the smoothing constant, which assumes a value between 0 and 1; the closer the value is to 1, the more smoothing takes place

y_{t-1-} = the value of the time series at time $t-1$

As an example, look at following lists of daily gold prices between 4/15/13 and 4/24/2013:

Date	Price ($/ounce)
4/15/13	$1,481.84
4/16/13	$1,422.82
4/17/13	$1,368.21
4/18/13	$1,378.20
4/19/13	$1,381.07
4/20/13	$1,401.96
4/21/13	$1,403.53
4/22/13	$1,403.53
4/23/13	$1,421.14
4/24/13	$1,418.78

An analyst wants to apply exponential smoothing to the data in order to produce a forecast of the price of gold on 4/25/13. Suppose the analyst believes that the data needs a significant amount of smoothing in order to eliminate random daily fluctuations in gold prices and show if there is any trend in the data. He picks a high value for the smoothing constant (α); assume that he chooses 0.7 Table 17-3 shows the resulting exponentially smoothed values of the daily gold prices. (Assume that the exponentially smoothed price for 4/15/13 has already been computed from prior data to $1,493.77.)

Table 17-3	Daily Gold Prices with Exponential Smoothing	
Date	*Price ($/ounce)*	*Exponentially Smoothed Price ($\alpha = 0.7$)*
4/15/13	$1,481.84	$1493.77
4/16/13	$1,422.82	$1485.42
4/17/13	$1,368.21	$1441.60
4/18/13	$1,378.20	$1390.23
4/19/13	$1,381.07	$1381.81
4/20/13	$1,401.96	$1381.29
4/21/13	$1,403.53	$1395.76
4/22/13	$1,403.53	$1401.20
4/23/13	$1,421.14	$1402.83
4/24/13	$1,418.78	$1415.84

The exponentially smoothed price equals α times the previous day's price of gold plus $(1 - \alpha)$ times the previous day's exponentially smoothed price.

For example, on 4/16/13, the exponentially smoothed price is

$$E_t = \alpha y_{t-1} + (1 - \alpha) E_{t-1}$$
$$E_t = (0.70)(1,481.84) + (0.30)(1,493.77)$$
$$= 1,485.42$$

On 4/17/13, the exponentially smoothed price is:

$$E_t = \alpha y_{t-1} + (1 - \alpha) E_{t-1}$$
$$E_t = (0.70)(1,422.82) + (0.30)(1,485.42)$$
$$= 1,441.60$$

You compute the rest of the exponentially smoothed values the same way.

The graph in Figure 17-13 shows the relationship between actual gold prices and exponentially smoothed gold prices:

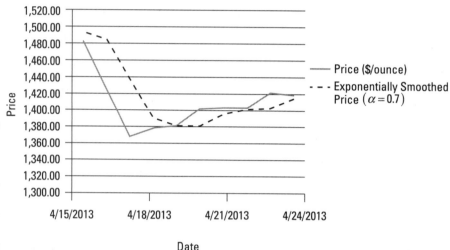

Figure 17-13:
Prices and exponentially smoothed prices for gold.

As you can see, the exponentially weighted values don't fluctuate as much as the original values. With random fluctuations removed from the data, it is easier to see the trend in the data.

Forecasting with exponential smoothing

With an exponential smoothing model, you can make a forecast for the next period with the following formula. The forecast for time $t + 1$ (one period in the future) as of time t is $E_{t+1} = \alpha y_t + (1-\alpha)E_t$.

In the gold price example from the previous section, the price on 4/24/13 is $1,418.78, while the exponentially smoothed price is $1,415.84. The forecast for 4/25/13 is, therefore

$$E_{t+1} = (0.70)(1,418.78) + (0.30)(1,415.84)$$
$$= \$1,417.90$$

Comparing the Forecasts of Different Models

Because there are several different types of models that can be used to predict the future values of a time series, it's important to be able to compare the quality of their results. Two techniques that are designed to test how well a forecasting model matches actual data are known as *mean absolute deviation (MAD)* and *mean square error (MSE)*.

- ✔ **Mean absolute deviation (MAD)** is the average absolute value of the differences between the actual values of y_t and the predicted values (for example, the absolute value of the *prediction errors*). You compute MAD with this formula:

$$MAD = \frac{\sum_{t=1}^{n} |y_t - \hat{y}_t|}{n}$$

$\hat{y}_t$ is the *predicted value* of y_t

$y_t - \hat{y}_t$ is known as the *prediction error* associated with y_t

- ✔ **Mean square error (MSE)** is the average squared prediction error. You use the following equation to compute MSE:

$$MSE = \frac{\sum_{t=1}^{n} (y_t - \hat{y}_t)^2}{n}$$

As an example, Figure 17-14 shows the prices of gold between 4/15/2013 and 4/24/2013. A time series model was used to forecast the price of gold during this period. A prediction error was computed for each date; the prediction error equals the actual price of gold minus the predicted value of gold. The absolute value of these prediction errors is computed for each date, as is the square of the prediction errors.

MAD is the average of the absolute values of the prediction errors; MSE is the average of the squared prediction errors. Figure 17-14 shows that the MAD equals 24.70, while the MSE equals 1079.44.

	DATE	PRICE	FORECAST	PREDICTION ERROR	ABSOLUTE VALUE OF PREDICTION ERROR	SQUARED PREDICTION ERROR
	4/15/2013	1,481.84	1,477.75	4.09	4.09	16.73
	4/16/2013	1,422.82	1,451.57	−28.75	28.75	826.36
	4/17/2013	1,368.21	1,371.31	−3.10	3.10	9.58
	4/18/2013	1,378.20	1,383.23	−5.03	5.03	25.28
Figure 17-14:	4/19/2013	1,381.07	1,383.54	−2.47	2.47	6.08
MAD and	4/20/2013	1,401.96	1,461.27	−59.31	59.31	3,518.21
MSE	4/21/2013	1,403.53	1,395.11	8.42	8.42	70.88
computed	4/22/2013	1,403.53	1,455.87	−52.34	52.34	2,739.84
for gold	4/23/2013	1,421.41	1,470.12	−48.73	48.71	2,372.65
price	4/24/2013	1,418.78	1,384.01	34.77	34.77	1,208.80
forecasts.				SUM	246.98	10,794.41
				AVERAGE	24.70	1,079.44

For any type of predictive model, the lower the value of the MAD or the MSE, the better the model fits the observed data. Using these measures lets you compare the results of different models (such as moving averages, exponential smoothing, and so forth) to determine which model provides the most accurate predictions for a given set of data.

One of the drawbacks of MSE is that it's more affected by extremely large prediction errors than MAD. One of the advantages of MSE is that it has more convenient mathematical properties than MAD. Because MAD is based on the absolute value, techniques for minimizing MAD are more complex than techniques for minimizing MSE.

Part V
The Part of Tens

Enjoy an additional Business Statistic Part of Tens chapter online at www.dummies.com/extras/businessstatistics.

In this part...

✔ See how statistical tests are based on the assumption of normality, and review several techniques available for testing whether a particular set of data is normally distributed.

✔ Check out several types of problems that may arise when the assumptions of regression analysis are not met; two problems that can plague simple regression analysis are *autocorrelation* and *heteroscedasticity*.

Chapter 18

Ten Common Errors That Arise in Statistical Analysis

In the *For Dummies* Part of Tens fashion, this chapter discusses ten ways people may draw incorrect conclusions from statistical tests. These erroneous conclusions can result from several sources, including incorrect assumptions, misunderstanding the meaning of a statistical test, use of inappropriate data, and measurement error.

Any one of these mistakes can lead to erroneous conclusions being drawn, no matter how sophisticated the techniques being used. Part of the art of statistics is knowing which techniques to use under different circumstances and how to correctly interpret them. The following sections discuss different types of errors that may result from the incorrect application of statistical techniques.

Designing Misleading Graphs

Graphs may give a misleading picture of a sample or population if they're not well designed. For example, if you use scales on a graph that are substantially different from the values in the data you're analyzing, you may end up with a highly distorted view of the data.

Figures 18-1 and 18-2 represent the same data with two different histograms (see Chapter 2 for an overview of histograms).

In this example, the data consist of the distribution of a bank's branches scattered throughout the four regions of the United States — North, South, East, and West.

Region	Branches
North	1,213
South	1,415
East	1,199
West	1,098

In Figure 18-1, the values on the vertical axis are separated by only 20 branches.

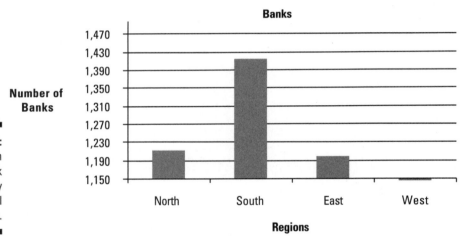

Figure 18-1:
Distribution of bank branches by geographical region.

With such closely spaced values on the vertical axis, the differences between the number of branches in each region appear to be very large. But, in fact, the difference between the largest number and the smallest number is only 317 (about 29 percent).

In Figure 18-2, the spacing of the values on the vertical axis is much wider, separated by 500 branches, making it appear that the differences between the numbers of branches are quite minimal.

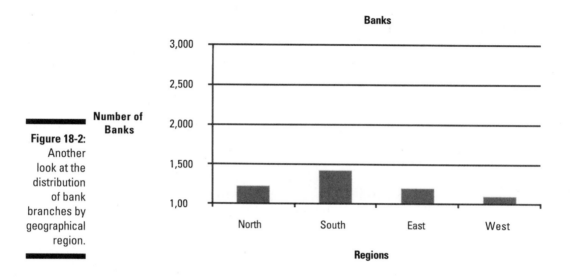

Banks

Number of Banks

Figure 18-2: Another look at the distribution of bank branches by geographical region.

North   South   East   West

Regions

These figures show how easy it is to give a distorted view of data through poor design.

Drawing the Wrong Conclusion from a Confidence Interval

When constructing a confidence interval, you can easily draw the wrong conclusion from the results. (Confidence intervals are covered in Chapter 11.) For example, suppose that a university constructs a 95 percent confidence interval for the mean GPA of its students. The sample mean is estimated to be 3.10; the 95 percent confidence interval is (2.95, 3.25).

It's tempting to conclude that the probability of the population mean being in the interval (2.95, 3.25) is 95 percent. Instead, this result indicates that for every confidence interval that's constructed from this population, in 95 cases out of 100, the confidence interval will contain the true population mean.

Misinterpreting the Results of a Hypothesis Test

One potential problem that may arise in hypothesis testing is confusing what it means when the null hypothesis isn't rejected. It's important to distinguish between accepting the null hypothesis and failing to reject the null hypothesis.

For example, suppose that a jury trial is in progress. For this hypothesis test, the following null and alternative hypotheses are used:

- Null hypothesis (H_0): The defendant is innocent.
- Alternative hypothesis (H_1): The defendant is guilty.

If the null hypothesis is rejected, the defendant is guilty. If the null hypothesis isn't rejected, the defendant isn't necessarily innocent. There's simply insufficient evidence to show that he's guilty. There's a world of difference between being "innocent" and "not guilty!"

The proper procedure in a hypothesis test is to conclude that a null hypothesis fails to be rejected unless strong contrary evidence exists against it. The conclusion should never be that the null hypothesis is accepted.

Placing Too Much Confidence in the Coefficient of Determination (R^2)

With regression analysis, researchers sometimes use the coefficient of determination to figure out whether one model "fits" the data better than another. The coefficient of determination assumes a value between 0 and 1; the closer it is to 1, presumably the better the regression model explains the relationship between X and Y. One of the drawbacks to the coefficient of determination is that it can be very close to 1 even for a model that makes no economic sense, such as a regression between two unrelated variables.

Another issue that arises with the coefficient of determination is that it automatically increases when new independent variables are added to a regression equation, even if the variables don't contribute any additional explanatory power to the regression. For this reason, the adjusted coefficient of determination is the preferred measure with multiple regression analysis because it increases only when newly added independent variables add at least some explanatory power.

Assuming Normality

Many statistical tests are based on the assumption of normality. For example, residuals are assumed to be normally distributed in regression analysis, enabling confidence intervals to be constructed for the slope coefficients.

For example, it's often assumed that the returns to stocks are normally distributed. In fact, although they're close to being normally distributed, they exhibit a property known as *fat tails,* where the actual probability of extreme outcomes (large positive returns and large negative returns) is greater than under the normal distribution. The assumption of normality causes investors to underestimate the true riskiness of their portfolios.

Several techniques are available for testing whether a particular set of data is normally distributed. For example, a Q-Q plot can be used to visually inspect data for normality. (You can read more about QQ plots at `http://en.wikipedia.org/wiki/Q-Q_plot`.)

A formal hypothesis test of normality is available; it's known as the Jarque-Bera test. (You can read more about the Jarque-Bera test at `http://en.wikipedia.org/wiki/Jarque%E2%80%93Bera_test`.)

These types of techniques should be used before jumping to any conclusions about normality.

Thinking Correlation Implies Causality

One common error in statistical analysis is to assume that if two variables are correlated, one *causes* the other. Correlation simply indicates the tendency of two variables to move in the same or opposite directions. For example, new car sales tend to rise at the same time as new home sales, but no one would suggest that new home sales *cause* new car sales. (Equivalently, no one would suggest that new car sales are *caused* by new home sales.) These variables are positively correlated because they're both directly influenced by the economy. During an expansion, both new car sales and new home sales rise; during a recession, both fall.

One particularly well-known example of the dangers of assuming that correlation implies causality comes from the 19th century British economist William Stanley Jevons. Jevons was interested in applying statistical methods to the measurement of business cycles. He noticed that the business cycle had a tendency to follow changes in sunspot activity. Sunspots went through a cycle that lasted for about 11 years, while business cycles tended to last for just under 11 years. From his studies, Jevons concluded that the sunspots were actually responsible for the business cycle. (It's not as crazy as it sounds; sunspots can lead to changes in weather patterns, which would have a huge influence on the business cycles of a primarily agriculture-based economy. In spite of this, sunspots do *not* directly cause changes in the business cycle.)

Drawing Conclusions from a Regression Equation when the Data do not Follow the Assumptions

Several types of problems may arise when the assumptions of regression analysis are not met. (Simple regression analysis is covered in Chapter 15; multiple regression analysis is covered in Chapter 16.) Two problems that can plague simple regression analysis are known as *autocorrelation* and *heteroscedasticity*.

Autocorrelation occurs when the error terms are correlated with each other (they are related to each other). It violates the assumption of independence. Two independent variables have a correlation of 0 between them. Autocorrelated error terms can cause understating the standard errors of the regression coefficients, thus increasing the risk that coefficients are incorrectly found to be statistically significant (for example, different from zero).

Heteroscedasticity occurs when the error terms don't have a constant variance. This problem can cause understating the standard errors of the regression coefficients, increasing the risk that coefficients are incorrectly found to be statistically significant (for example, different from zero).

When these problems are present, it is important to correct for them; otherwise, all results will be deceptive.

Including Correlated Variables in a Multiple Regression Equation

One potential difficulty with multiple regression analysis is *multicollinearity*. Multicollinearity occurs when two or more of the independent variables are highly correlated with each other, causing the correlated variables to have large standard errors, so they appear to be statistically insignificant even if they're not. (In other words, there's a risk that independent variables will be removed from the regression equation that should be included.)

Multicollinearity is unique to multiple regression because it has multiple independent variables (simple regression has only one independent variable so that multicollinearity cannot occur).

A statistic known as the variance inflation factor (VIF) may be used to check for multicollinearity. As a rule of thumb, if the VIF is 10 or more, it's a sign that multicollinearity is present. (You can find more information about the variance inflation factor at `http://en.wikipedia.org/wiki/Variance_inflation_factor`.) If multicollinearity is present, one of the highly correlated variables should be removed from the regression equation.

Placing Too Much Confidence in Forecasts

Many techniques are used to forecast future values of economic variables, such as stock prices, GDP growth, corporate sales, the demand for new products, and so on. Many of these techniques are highly sophisticated, which may give the false impression that they're extremely accurate. One major difficulty with forecasting techniques is that they're based on historical data that may not be repeated in the future. For example, if an economist is attempting to forecast future interest rates, his results don't capture any structural changes that occur in the economy during the forecast period, such as the selection of a new chairman of the Federal Reserve Board. In this case, future interest rates are unlikely to behave in exactly the same way that they have in the past, and the results of the forecast are inaccurate.

Two types of errors that may arise in forecasting are bias error and random error. *Bias error* occurs when a forecast is consistently greater than or less than actual values of a variable. *Random error* refers to unpredictable factors that can distort the results of a factor. These include earthquakes, strikes, sudden increases in oil prices, political turmoil, and so on.

With so much uncertainty surrounding forecasts, it would be a mistake to assume a high degree of accuracy.

Using the Wrong Distribution

In many situations, a variable is assumed to follow a specific probability distribution. For example, a computer chip manufacturer may assume that the number of defective chips produced by a specific process follows the binomial distribution. (The binomial distribution is covered in Chapter 8.) The binomial distribution is based on several assumptions, one of which is that the trials are independent of each other. Suppose that in this process, one defective chip is highly likely to be followed by another defective chip (for example, repairs to the process are needed). In this case, the trials (chips) aren't truly independent of each other. As a result, any conclusions drawn about the distribution of defective chips are likely inaccurate. The manufacturer needs to find another distribution that more accurately reflects the distribution of the chips.

Chapter 19

Ten Key Categories of Formulas for Business Statistics

In This Chapter

▶ Keeping the most important statistical concepts fresh in your memory

▶ Seeing how key statistical formulas are related

*T*his chapter provides a brief overview of many key formulas encountered in the text. This provides a handy reference guide so that you can quickly find the formulas that you need without having to search through the entire book.

Summary Measures of a Population or a Sample

Summary measures are used to describe key properties of a sample or a population. These measures can be classified as:

✔ **Measures of central tendency** identify the *center* of a data set. Three of the most widely used measures of central tendency are the mean, median, and mode.

  • The *mean* is another word for average.

  • The *median* is a value that divides a sample or a population in half: Half of the elements in the data are below the median, and half of the elements in the data are above the median.

  • The *mode* is the most frequently occurring value in a sample or a population.

- ✔ **Measures of dispersion** are used to measure how spread out, or disperse, are the values of a sample or a population. Some of the most important measures of dispersion are the variance, standard deviation, percentiles, quartiles, and the interquartile range (IQR).

  - **Variance:** The variance is calculated as the size of the average *squared* difference between the elements of a data set (a sample or a population) and the mean of the data set. The greater is the variance, the further the elements of the data set tend to be from the mean.

  - **Standard deviation:** The square root of the variance. The standard deviation is more convenient to use than the variance due to the units in which these measures are calculated. As an example, if a sample consists of dollar prices, the sample standard deviation is measured in dollars, while the sample variance is measured in dollars *squared*, which is difficult to make sense of.

  - **Percentiles:** Percentiles split a data set into 100 equal parts, each consisting of 1 percent of the values in the data set. For example, the 80th percentile represents the value in a sample or a population where 20 percent of the observations are above this value, and 80 percent are below this value.

  - **Quartiles:** Special types of percentiles, where the first quartile (Q_1) is the 25th percentile, the second quartile (Q_2) is the 50th percentile, and the third quartile (Q_3) is the 75th percentile.

  - **Interquartile range (IQR):** The difference between the third and first quartile.

- ✔ **Measures of association** provide a measure of how closely two samples or populations are related to each other. The two most important measures of association are:

  - **Covariance** is a measure of the tendency for two variables to move in the same direction or in opposite directions. If two variables increase or decrease under the same circumstances, the covariance between them is positive. If two variables move in opposite directions, the covariance between them is negative. If two variables are unrelated to each other, the covariance between them is zero (or very close to zero).

  - **Correlation** is closely related to covariance; it has more convenient properties than covariance. For example, correlation always assumes a value between -1 and 1, whereas covariance has no lower or upper limits. As a result, it is easier to tell if the relationship between two variables is very strong or very weak with correlation than with covariance.

Probability

You use probability theory to model a large number of events in business applications. Probability theory is based on *set algebra,* and the important rules are

✔ **Addition rule:** The formula for the Addition rule is:

$$P(A \cup B) = P(A) + P(B) - P(A \cap B)$$

The addition rule is designed to compute the probability of a *union* of two sets. In general, the union of sets A and B contains all the elements that are in set A, set B or both.

✔ **Multiplication rule:** The Multiplication rule has two forms:

$$P(A \cap B) = P(A \mid B) P(B)$$

$$P(A \cap B) = P(B \mid A) P(A)$$

The multiplication rule is designed to compute the probability of the *intersection* of two sets. In general, the intersection of sets A and B contains all the elements that are in *both* set A and set B.

✔ **Complement rule:** The Complement rule has two forms:

$$P(A^C) = 1 - P(A)$$

$$P(A) = 1 - P(A^C)$$

The complement rule tells you the probability of all elements that are *not* in a set. For example, suppose set A contains all the black cards in a standard deck; the complement of A (written as A^C) is a set containing all the red cards. The probability of A^C can be computed with the complement rule.

Discrete Probability Distributions

A discrete probability distribution occurs where only a finite number of different outcomes may occur. The properties of a probability distribution may be summarized by a set of *moments*. Moments are numerical values that describe key properties of a probability distribution. Some of the most important are as follows:

✔ The **expected value** is the first moment of a probability distribution. You compute it as

$$E(X) = \sum_{i=1}^{n} X_i P(X_i)$$

The expected value tells you the average value of X.

✔ The **variance** is the second moment of a probability distribution. You compute it as

$$\sigma^2 = \sum_{i=1}^{n} \left[X_i - E(X) \right]^2 P(X_i)$$

σ^2 represents the variance of X.

The variance tells you how much the different possible values of X are scattered around the expected value.

✔ The **standard deviation** isn't a separate moment; it's the square root of the variance. The formula is

$$\sigma = \sqrt{\sum_{i=1}^{n} \left[X_i - E(X) \right]^2 P(X_i)}$$

The standard deviation is preferred to the variance since the variance is measured in squared units, which are difficult to interpret.

Following are three of the most widely used discrete probability distributions in business applications:

✔ **Binomial distribution:** The binomial distribution is defined for a random process consisting of a series of trials in which only two different outcomes can occur on each trial. It enables you to determine the probability of a specified number of events occurring during a series of trials.

$$P(X = x) = \frac{n!}{x!(n-x)!} p^x (1-p)^{n-x}$$

✔ **Geometric distribution:** The geometric distribution is related to the binomial distribution; it is used to determine how many trials are needed before a specified event occurs.

$$P(X = x) = (1-p)^{x-1} p$$

✔ **Poisson distribution:** The Poisson distribution is used to determine the probability that a specified number of events will occur during an interval of time.

$$P(X = x) = e^{-\lambda} \frac{\lambda^x}{x!}$$

Continuous Probability Distributions

A continuous probability distribution is defined for an infinite number of possible values. The uniform distribution and the normal distribution are two of the most widely used continuous probability distributions in business applications.

✔ The **uniform distribution** is defined over an interval (a, b); in other words, all values between a and b. For example, the uniform distribution may be defined over the interval $(1, 10)$. This means that the distribution is defined for all values between 1 and 10. You can compute probabilities for the uniform distribution with the following equation, known as a *probability density function (pdf)*:

$$f(x) = \begin{cases} \dfrac{1}{b-a} & b \leq x \leq a \\ 0 & \text{otherwise} \end{cases}$$

✔ The **normal distribution** is by far the most important continuous probability distribution for business applications. You can get probabilities for this distribution from normal tables, specialized calculators, and spreadsheet programs. The normal distribution is defined by the following probability density function:

$$f(x) = \frac{1}{\sqrt{2\pi\sigma^2}} e^{-0.5\left(\frac{x-\mu}{\sigma}\right)^2}$$

The normal distribution is important because many business situations may be accurately modeled with the normal distribution. For example, returns to stock prices are often assumed to follow the normal distribution.

Sampling Distributions

A sampling distribution is a special type of probability distribution defined for *sample statistics*. A sample statistic is a measure that describes the properties of a sample. Three of the most important sample statistics are the sample mean ($\bar{X}$), sample variance (s^2), and sample standard deviation (s). For more details about sampling distributions, see Chapter 10.

Based on a key result in statistics known as the *central limit theorem,* the sampling distribution of the sample mean is *normal* as long as the underlying population is normal or if you choose sample sizes of at least 30 from the population. To compute a probability for the sample mean, convert it into a standard normal random variable as follows:

$$Z = \frac{\bar{X} - \mu_{\bar{x}}}{\sigma_{\bar{x}}}$$

- $\bar{X}$ is the sample mean
- $\mu_{\bar{x}}$ is the mean of the sampling distribution of $\bar{X}$
- $\sigma_{\bar{x}}$ is the standard deviation (also known as the *standard error)* of the sampling distribution of $\bar{X}$

Confidence Intervals for the Population Mean

A *confidence interval* is a range of numbers that is expected to contain the true value of the population mean with a specified probability.

The formula you use to compute a confidence interval for the population mean depends on whether you know the population standard deviation (σ).

If you know the population standard deviation, the appropriate formula is

$$\bar{X} \pm Z_{\alpha/2} \frac{\sigma}{\sqrt{n}}$$

$\bar{X}$ is the sample mean

$Z_{\alpha/2}$ is a quantile which represents the location of the right tail under the standard normal distribution with area $\alpha/2$

σ is the population standard deviation

n is the sample size

α is the level of significance

If you don't know the population standard deviation, you replace the population standard deviation with the sample standard deviation:

$$\bar{X} \pm t_{\alpha/2}^{n-1} \frac{s}{\sqrt{n}}$$

- $t_{\alpha/2}^{n-1}$ is a quantile (critical value) which represents the location of the right tail of the t-distribution with n-1 degrees of freedom with an area of $\alpha/2$
- s is the sample standard deviation

Testing Hypotheses about Population Means

Testing hypotheses about population means is a multi-step process, consisting of the null and alternative hypotheses, the level of significance, test statistic, critical value(s), and decision. (I walk you through all the steps of hypothesis testing in Chapter 12.)

You write the null hypothesis for testing the value of a single population mean as

$H_0: \mu = \mu_0$

where H_0 stands for the null hypotheses, μ is the true population mean and μ_0 is the hypothesized value of the population, or the value that you *think* is true.

The alternative hypothesis can assume one of three forms:

$H_1: \mu > \mu_0$ (known as a "right-tailed" test)

$H_1: \mu < \mu_0$ (known as a "left-tailed" test)

$H_1: \mu \neq \mu_0$ (known as a "two-tailed" test)

To test a hypothesis, you must specify a *level of significance* — the probability of rejecting the null hypothesis when it's actually true.

When you're testing hypotheses about the population mean, the test statistic and the critical value (or values) depend on the size of the sample drawn from the population and whether you know the population standard deviation.

✔ For a *small* sample (less than 30), the appropriate test statistic is

$$t = \frac{\bar{X} - \mu_0}{s / \sqrt{n}}$$

✔ $\bar{X}$ is the sample mean

✔ μ_0 is the hypothesized value of the population mean

✔ s is the sample standard deviation

✔ n is the sample size

✔ For a *large* sample (30 or more) when you know the population standard deviation (σ), the appropriate test statistic is

$$Z = \frac{\bar{X} - \mu_0}{\sigma / \sqrt{n}}$$

✔ For a *large* sample when you don't know the population standard deviation, use the sample standard deviation (s) instead:

$$Z = \frac{\bar{X} - \mu_0}{s / \sqrt{n}}$$

For small samples (the sample size is less than 30), the critical values are drawn from the t-distribution with $n - 1$ degrees of freedom. For large samples, the critical values are drawn from the standard normal distribution.

To test hypotheses about the equality of two population means, the test statistic and critical values are different, but the basic process remains unchanged. In this case, though, you write the null hypothesis as H_0: $\mu_1 = \mu_2$, where μ_1 is the mean of population 1, and μ_2 is the mean of population 2.

✔ For independent samples with equal population variances, the test statistic is

$$t = \frac{(\bar{x}_1 - \bar{x}_2) - (\mu_1 - \mu_2)_0}{\sqrt{s_p^2 \left(\frac{1}{n_1} + \frac{1}{n_2} \right)}}$$

s_p^2 is the estimated common "pooled" variance of the two populations — which you calculate with this formula:

$$s_p^2 = \frac{(n_1 - 1)s_1^2 + (n_2 - 1)s_2^2}{n_1 + n_2 - 2}$$

The critical values of independent samples with equal population variances are based on the t-distribution with $n_1 + n_2 - 2$ degrees of freedom.

✔ If the independent samples are drawn from populations that don't have the same variance, the test statistic depends on the sizes of the two samples. If at least one sample is small, the test statistic becomes

$$t = \frac{(\bar{x}_1 - \bar{x}_2) - (\mu_1 - \mu_2)_0}{\sqrt{\left(\frac{s_1^2}{n_1} + \frac{s_2^2}{n_2} \right)}}$$

Here, the critical values are also drawn from the t-distribution, but the degrees of freedom calculation is much more complex:

$$df = \frac{\left[(s_1^2 / n_1) + (s_2^2 / n_2) \right]^2}{\frac{(s_1^2 / n_1)^2}{(n_1 - 1)} + \frac{(s_2^2 / n_2)^2}{(n_2 - 1)}}$$

✔ If the independent samples are drawn from populations that don't have the same variance and both samples are large, the test statistic becomes

$$Z = \frac{(\bar{x}_1 - \bar{x}_2) - (\mu_1 - \mu_2)_0}{\sqrt{\left(\dfrac{s_1^2}{n_1} + \dfrac{s_2^2}{n_2}\right)}}$$

In this case, the critical values are drawn from the standard normal distribution.

✔ If the two samples aren't independent, they're known as *paired samples*. The test statistic is then based on the differences between the samples:

$$t = \frac{\bar{d}}{s_d / \sqrt{n}}$$

$\bar{d}$ is the average difference between paired samples, and s_d is the standard deviation of the sample differences.

In this case, the critical values are taken from the t-distribution with $n - 1$ degree of freedom.

Testing Hypotheses about Population Variances

Testing hypotheses about population variances follows the same six-step procedure as testing hypotheses about population means (see previous section and Chapter 12 for details).

For testing hypotheses about the variance of a single population, the appropriate test statistic is

$$\chi^2 = \frac{(n-1)s^2}{\sigma_0^2}$$

✔ n is the sample size)

✔ s^2 is the sample variance

✔ σ_0^2 is the hypothesized value of the population variance

The critical values are drawn from the chi-square distribution with $n - 1$ degree of freedom.

For testing hypotheses about the equality of variances of two populations, the appropriate test statistic is

$$F = \frac{s_1^2}{s_2^2}$$

s_1^2 is the variance of the sample drawn from population 1; s_2^2 is the variance of the sample drawn from population 2. The populations are assigned a number of 1 or 2 in such a way as to ensure that s_1^2 is greater than or equal to s_2^2.

The critical values are drawn from the F-distribution, which has two different types of degrees of freedom: numerator and denominator. In this case, the numerator degrees of freedom equal $n_1 - 1$, and the denominator degrees of freedom equal $n_2 - 1$.

Using Regression Analysis

You use regression analysis to estimate the relationship between a dependent variable (Y) and one or more independent variables (Xs).

- ✔ Use **simple regression analysis** to estimate the relationship between a dependent variable (Y) and one independent variable (X).

- ✔ Use **multiple regression analysis** to estimate the relationship between a dependent variable (Y) and two or more independent variables (Xs).

Several tests allow you to validate the results of a regression equation. For example, if the coefficient of an independent variable equals 0, the variable doesn't belong in the regression. A hypothesis test helps you determine whether this coefficient equals 0. In the case of multiple regression, it may make sense to test the hypothesis that the slope coefficients all equal 0; if this hypothesis can't be rejected, then the regression equation is completely invalid.

It's also important to ensure that the underlying assumptions of regression analysis aren't being violated. Three potential problems can result if the assumptions aren't true:

- ✔ **Autocorrelation** indicates that the error terms aren't independent of each other.

- ✔ **Heteroscedasticity** indicates that the error terms don't have a common variance.

- ✔ **Multicollinearity** indicates that two or more of the independent variables are highly correlated with each other. (This can only affect the results with multiple regression.)

Forecasting Techniques

There are many different forecasting techniques that can be used to predict the future values of variables, such as stock prices, gas prices, and so on. (Forecasting techniques are covered in Chapter 17.)

One widely used technique for forecasting is known as *time series regression analysis*. A time series is a set of values for a single variable collected over a period of time. For example, the daily prices of Apple stock from 2010 to 2013 would constitute a time series.

As an example, the following regression equation may be used to forecast the *trend* of a time series. (The trend shows how a time series grows over time.)

$$y_t = TR_t + \varepsilon_t$$

The trend may take several different forms, including

- No trend
- Linear trend
- Quadratic trend
- Higher-order trend

Suppose that a time series is collected for the average price of gasoline in New York State over the past ten years. If the time series does not have a trend, this would indicate that gas prices do not grow at a steady rate over time. If the time series has a linear trend, then gasoline prices grow at a constant rate over time. If the time series has a quadratic or higher-order trend, then gasoline prices grow at a rate that changes over time.

Other techniques to forecast a time series include simple moving averages, centered moving averages, and exponentially weighted moving averages. Simple and centered moving averages "smooth" out the values of a time series to produce an estimate of the trend of the series. An exponentially weighted moving average is a more sophisticated version of these techniques and is designed to place less weight on older observations to reflect their diminishing relevance.

Index

About the Author

Alan Anderson currently teaches finance, economics, statistics, and math at several different schools, including Fordham University, New York University, Manhattanville College, Purchase College, and Fairfield University. He has also spent many years in the "real world" as an economist, risk manager, and fixed income analyst. (He prefers academia!)

Alan received his PhD in economics from Fordham University, and also holds an M.S. in financial engineering from Polytechnic University.

Author's Acknowledgments

I'd like to acknowledge several people who helped get this book put together. First, thanks go to Erin Calligan-Mooney, my acquisitions editor. Thanks for giving me a chance to write this book. Thanks also go to Chrissy Guthrie and Susan Hobbs, development editors who kept me focused. Thanks to Jennette ElNaggar for the suggestions and incredible copyedit. And thanks to Jeff Rummel for providing a creative and sound technical review and to Barry Schoenfeld for helping make my writing clear and concise. You guys were a great team . . . thank you all.

Publisher's Acknowledgments

Acquisitions Editor: Erin Calligan-Mooney

Project Editor: Chrissy Guthrie
  Susan Hobbs

Copy Editor: Jennette ElNaggar

Technical Editors: Jeff Rummel

Art Coordinator: Alicia B. South

Project Coordinator: Kristie Rees

Cover Image: ©iStockphoto.com/
  Hocus Focus Studio

Apple & Mac

iPad For Dummies,
5th Edition
978-1-118-49823-1

iPhone 5 For Dummies,
6th Edition
978-1-118-35201-4

MacBook For Dummies,
4th Edition
978-1-118-20920-2

OS X Mountain Lion
For Dummies
978-1-118-39418-2

Blogging & Social Media

Facebook For Dummies,
4th Edition
978-1-118-09562-1

Mom Blogging
For Dummies
978-1-118-03843-7

Pinterest For Dummies
978-1-118-32800-2

WordPress For Dummies,
5th Edition
978-1-118-38318-6

Business

Commodities For Dummies,
2nd Edition
978-1-118-01687-9

Investing For Dummies,
6th Edition
978-0-470-90545-6

Personal Finance

Personal Finance
For Dummies,
7th Edition
978-1-118-11785-9

QuickBooks 2013
For Dummies
978-1-118-35641-8

Small Business Marketing Kit
For Dummies,
3rd Edition
978-1-118-31183-7

Careers

Job Interviews
For Dummies,
4th Edition
978-1-118-11290-8

Job Searching with
Social Media
For Dummies
978-0-470-93072-4

Personal Branding
For Dummies
978-1-118-11792-7

Resumes For Dummies,
6th Edition
978-0-470-87361-8

Success as a Mediator
For Dummies
978-1-118-07862-4

Diet & Nutrition

Belly Fat Diet For Dummies
978-1-118-34585-6

Eating Clean For Dummies
978-1-118-00013-7

Nutrition For Dummies,
5th Edition
978-0-470-93231-5

Digital Photography

Digital Photography
For Dummies,
7th Edition
978-1-118-09203-3

Digital SLR Cameras &
Photography For Dummies,
4th Edition
978-1-118-14489-3

Photoshop Elements 11
For Dummies
978-1-118-40821-6

Gardening

Herb Gardening
For Dummies,
2nd Edition
978-0-470-61778-6

Vegetable Gardening
For Dummies,
2nd Edition
978-0-470-49870-5

Health

Anti-Inflammation Diet
For Dummies
978-1-118-02381-5

Diabetes For Dummies,
3rd Edition
978-0-470-27086-8

Living Paleo For Dummies
978-1-118-29405-5

Hobbies

Beekeeping
For Dummies
978-0-470-43065-1

eBay For Dummies,
7th Edition
978-1-118-09806-6

Raising Chickens
For Dummies
978-0-470-46544-8

Wine For Dummies,
5th Edition
978-1-118-28872-6

Writing Young Adult Fiction
For Dummies
978-0-470-94954-2

Language &
Foreign Language

500 Spanish Verbs
For Dummies
978-1-118-02382-2

English Grammar
For Dummies,
2nd Edition
978-0-470-54664-2

French All-in One
For Dummies
978-1-118-22815-9

German Essentials
For Dummies
978-1-118-18422-6

Italian For Dummies
2nd Edition
978-1-118-00465-4

Available in print and e-book formats.

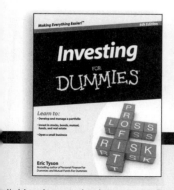
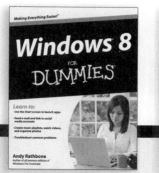

Math & Science

Algebra I For Dummies,
2nd Edition
978-0-470-55964-2

Anatomy and Physiology
For Dummies,
2nd Edition
978-0-470-92326-9

Astronomy For Dummies,
3rd Edition
978-1-118-37697-3

Biology For Dummies,
2nd Edition
978-0-470-59875-7

Chemistry For Dummies,
2nd Edition
978-1-1180-0730-3

Pre-Algebra Essentials
For Dummies
978-0-470-61838-7

Microsoft Office

Excel 2013 For Dummies
978-1-118-51012-4

Office 2013 All-in-One
For Dummies
978-1-118-51636-2

PowerPoint 2013
For Dummies
978-1-118-50253-2

Word 2013 For Dummies
978-1-118-49123-2

Music

Blues Harmonica
For Dummies
978-1-118-25269-7

Guitar For Dummies,
3rd Edition
978-1-118-11554-1

iPod & iTunes
For Dummies,
10th Edition
978-1-118-50864-0

Programming

Android Application
Development For
Dummies, 2nd Edition
978-1-118-38710-8

iOS 6 Application
Development For Dummies
978-1-118-50880-0

Java For Dummies,
5th Edition
978-0-470-37173-2

Religion & Inspiration

The Bible For Dummies
978-0-7645-5296-0

Buddhism For Dummies,
2nd Edition
978-1-118-02379-2

Catholicism For Dummies,
2nd Edition
978-1-118-07778-8

Self-Help & Relationships

Bipolar Disorder
For Dummies,
2nd Edition
978-1-118-33882-7

Meditation For Dummies,
3rd Edition
978-1-118-29144-3

Seniors

Computers For Seniors
For Dummies,
3rd Edition
978-1-118-11553-4

iPad For Seniors
For Dummies,
5th Edition
978-1-118-49708-1

Social Security
For Dummies
978-1-118-20573-0

Smartphones & Tablets

Android Phones
For Dummies
978-1-118-16952-0

Kindle Fire HD
For Dummies
978-1-118-42223-6

NOOK HD For Dummies,
Portable Edition
978-1-118-39498-4

Surface For Dummies
978-1-118-49634-3

Test Prep

ACT For Dummies,
5th Edition
978-1-118-01259-8

ASVAB For Dummies,
3rd Edition
978-0-470-63760-9

GRE For Dummies,
7th Edition
978-0-470-88921-3

Officer Candidate Tests,
For Dummies
978-0-470-59876-4

Physician's Assistant Exam
For Dummies
978-1-118-11556-5

Series 7 Exam
For Dummies
978-0-470-09932-2

Windows 8

Windows 8 For Dummies
978-1-118-13461-0

Windows 8 For Dummies,
Book + DVD Bundle
978-1-118-27167-4

Windows 8 All-in-One
For Dummies
978-1-118-11920-4

Available in print and e-book formats.